The
Emotionally
Healthy
Church

Updated and Expanded Edition

Reading these accounts was like having a long conversation with a trusted friend. Pete and Geri Scazzero are finding and sharing what we are all longing for—wholeness at the center of our rushed and ragged lives—so that when we are ministering to others we are not dying inside.

Carl George
Director, Consulting for Growth, Diamond Bar, California

Captivating! Absolutely must reading not only for pastors and church leaders, but for anyone wanting to grow in faith, maturity, and marriage. It's candid, honest, eye-opening, and challenging. Pastor Scazzero has broken important new ground in our understanding of the vital relationship between emotional maturity and spiritual integrity. His easy-to-read format shows how unresolved emotional brokenness can destroy ministry and people.

Craig Ellison, Ph.D.
Director of Alliance Graduate School of Counseling
Author of *From Stress to Well-Being*

This book unmasks a "super-spirituality" in many churches that cannot deal honestly with the depth of our spiritual and emotional brokenness. Pete Scazzero shows us how the gospel frees us to admit our brokenness and then gives us many practical ways to move forward. I recommend this book for pastors and church leaders.

Tim Keller, Senior Pastor
Redeemer Presbyterian Church, New York City

"The whole gospel for the whole person" — great theology, but in practice little more than a slogan in many churches. Pete Scazzero's savvy and much-needed book on the emotional health of the church takes this core truth to a new level. You'll find yourself here, as well as many of the people you have bumped into or collided with in this wonderful and mysterious thing the Bible calls "the body of Christ."

Ben Patterson
Author, *Waiting: Finding Hope When God Seems Silent*

I was moved by this story and its application points that intersected with my life. I appreciate the great openness that Pete Scazzero brings to the table. Only a veteran of many battles can tell a story like this. Scazzero opens his heart with boldness and shares practical life lessons that any leader will grow from.

Steve Sjogren, Launching Pastor
Vineyard Community Church, Cincinnati, Ohio

The Emotionally Healthy Church

Updated and Expanded Edition

A STRATEGY *for*
DISCIPLESHIP
that ACTUALLY
CHANGES LIVES

Peter L. Scazzero

with WARREN BIRD

ZONDERVAN.com/
AUTHORTRACKER
follow your favorite authors

ZONDERVAN

The Emotionally Healthy Church
Copyright © 2003, 2010 by Peter L. Scazzero

This title is also available as a Zondervan ebook. Visit www.zondervan.com/ebooks.

Requests for information should be addressed to:

Zondervan, *Grand Rapids, Michigan 49530*

Library of Congress Cataloging-in-Publication Data

Scazzero, Peter L., 1956
        The emotionally healthy church : a strategy for discipleship that actually changes
lives / Peter L. Scazzero; with Warren Bird. — Expanded ed.
                p. cm.
        Includes bibliographical references.
        ISBN 978-0-310-29335-4 (hardcover, jacketed)
            1. Emotional maturity — Religious aspects — Christianity.   2. Discipling
(Christianity)   I. Bird, Warren.   II. Title.
        BV4597.3. S32   2009
        253 — dc22   2009032590

All Scripture quotations, unless otherwise indicated, are taken from the Holy Bible, *Today's New International Version*™, *TNIV*®. Copyright © 2001, 2005 by Biblica, Inc.™ Used by permission of Zondervan. All rights reserved worldwide.

Any Internet addresses (websites, blogs, etc.) and telephone numbers in this book are offered as a resource. They are not intended in any way to be or imply an endorsement by Zondervan, nor does Zondervan vouch for the content of these sites and numbers for the life of this book.

Cover design: Tobias' Outerwear for Books

Interior design: Tracey Walker

Printed in the United States of America

12 13 14 15 16 17 18 /DCI/ 25 24 23 22 21 20 19 18 17 16 15 14 13 12 11 10 9

CONTENTS

Part 1
Discipleship's Missing Link

Part 2
Biblical Basis for a New Paradigm
of Discipleship

Part 3
Seven Principles of an Emotionally Healthy Church

Part 4
Where Do We Go from Here?

FOREWORD

Late one cold winter evening our phone rang. A young pastor I had known and admired for some years was unexpectedly calling. His voice was tense as he poured out the story of the crisis he was facing both in his marriage and his ministry. I listened, gave some words of encouragement and counsel, and prayed with him.

Before we hung up I said to him, "I do not believe this is the end of your ministry. In spite of the pain you are going through, it may be the best thing that could happen to you at this point." Sometimes when we seem to be at the end, our real work is just beginning!

That young pastor was Peter Scazzero, and that crisis was a "grace disguised." For out of it has come for Pete a stronger sense of his calling and identity, a deeper love in marriage, a healthier and more vital congregation, a fuller understanding of discipleship, and this fine and helpful book.

I hope *The Emotionally Healthy Church* will be widely read and taken to heart by many Christian pastors and leaders. I believe Peter Scazzero is on target when he writes that "the overall health of any church or ministry depends primarily on the emotional and spiritual health of its leadership."

We know healthy churches need healthy leaders. What is fresh is Scazzero's insistence that this must include emotional health. Leaders have long been urged to maintain their spiritual vitality, physical exercise, and intellectual growth. But less emphasis has been placed on emotional well-being.

Emotions were discounted in much of the evangelical teaching I heard growing up. We were taught about "facts, faith, and feelings" — in that order. Faith was to be based on the facts of the Christian message (an essential emphasis, to be sure), but we should not rely on feelings because they were unreliable, secondary, and untrustworthy. Certainly there is truth here. Feelings do go up and down—mine certainly do! But while our emotions may be changeable, they are not unimportant!

The Bible does not overlook the emotional quotient of our humanity. Its characters—Joseph's brothers in their sibling rivalry, Moses in his anger, Paul in his tearful longing for a visit from Timothy, his son in the faith—were real people with real emotions. Our Lord himself had a powerful emotional life as a man who could weep in sorrow, be strong in anger, and yet experience the fullness of joy.

Part of our reluctance to deal honestly and openly with our emotions has been an inadequate view of the incarnation. We affirm that our Lord Jesus was God in the flesh, while deep down we assume that Jesus' human nature was not really real but a kind of masquerade.

The Bible also helps us to understand ourselves, and that is what Peter Scazzero has learned and shares with us, both out of the pain he and his wife, Geri, have experienced, and through his rereading of Scripture.

As I read *The Emotionally Healthy Church*, I could identify with so much of the material. I have lived similar experiences and times of emotional testing. So have most of the young pastors and Christian leaders with whom I have spiritual mentoring conversations. Peter Scazzero's story of growing through pain into personal and congregational health through the Spirit of Christ holds hope for all of us!

Leighton Ford, President
Leighton Ford Ministries
Charlotte, North Carolina

Preface to Expanded Edition

After several years of living out the principles of *The Emotionally Healthy Church* within the local church I pastor, I wrote them in the first edition of this book. My intention was to speak particularly to pastors, elders, deacons, and ministry and small group leaders. Little did I know that the book's message would spread beyond church leaders to countless others struggling with the integration of emotional health and biblical spirituality. Even more of a surprise was the centrality of this issue not only for the church in North America, but around the world.

During the seven years since the first edition, my understanding of the six principles that make up emotionally healthy churches has grown deeper, sharper, and broader. I have grown theologically as I have encountered new personal and leadership applications of the material. As a result, each chapter has been edited, expanded, and updated.

Moreover, this journey has led me to add a seventh, indispensable principle: lead with integrity. The pace of my life slowed down considerably when I began integrating emotional health with my discipleship. It takes time—lots of it—to feel, to grieve, to listen, to reflect, to be mindful of what is going on around and in us. This radically shifted my priorities at home and in my work. Emotional health also created a hunger within Geri and me for a deeper communion with God. This in turn led to an exploration of contemplative spiritual practices, culminating in a four-month sabbatical in 2003–2004. Our aim was to study the riches of the contemplative tradition and its applications for a missional church like ours. This immersion into such spiritual disciplines as silence and solitude transformed us, and eventually, our church. Insights from these experiences are sprinkled throughout the book.

While the contemplative tradition helped me considerably in my efforts to lead with integrity, I had yet to apply emotional health to my leadership. That turned out to be a challenging, complex task. I describe this unfolding in the new chapter 11, "Slow Down to Lead with Integrity."

One final note: Resist the temptation to breeze through these pages. This is not a book meant to be read quickly in one or two sittings. This is not simply the latest fascinating idea to incorporate in your God-talk with colleagues or parishioners. I invite you to wrestle deeply with these truths as you consider how they apply to both your inner life and leadership. You could spend a lifetime plumbing the depths of each—from limits, to brokenness, to grieving, to learning to love well. Please read slowly, prayerfully, and thoughtfully. As you do, ask the question, "How is God coming to me through this?" Consider making personal applications in a journal or in the back of the book, noting the page number for future reference.

Be sure to grasp the central thesis: *Emotional health and spiritual maturity are inseparable. It is not possible to be spiritually mature while remaining emotionally immature*. When you understand this, you will walk through a door in your spiritual journey. Few ever return to a tip-of-the-iceberg discipleship that overemphasizes activity but does not deeply transform from the inside out. By God's grace, you will never be the same. And you will embark on an exciting journey toward a beautiful life that will touch everyone around you—in your family, church, workplace, and neighborhood.

Part 1

Discipleship's Missing Link

INTRODUCTION

A few years ago my wife, our family of four daughters, and I were invited to participate in a Christian family camp in Colorado for a one-week vacation. We expected it to be the trip of a lifetime.

We landed at Denver International Airport and began the three-hour drive into the mountains. While driving, I grew very tired, thinking perhaps the plane trip and a lack of caffeine may have contributed to my sleepiness. I asked my wife, Geri, to drive, but she was terrified by the narrowness of the mountainous roads.

At one point, however, I momentarily blacked out and swerved out of our lane. I pulled over. Now that we were out of the mountains, Geri took over the driving. We attributed my momentary lapse to fatigue.

When we arrived at the camp, about nine thousand feet above sea level, we checked in and prepared for a wonderful week in the Rocky Mountains. The view was breathtaking, the mountains an awesome reflection of God's glory. The schedule for the week included age-appropriate activities for each of our children, who ranged in ages at the time from six to fifteen, and also for us as adults.

I couldn't sleep the first night. Maybe it was the new pillow. I prayed that it was not the flu. I participated in the day's activities and fought off the aches and pains. The second night was a repeat of the first, only now I developed a cough that wouldn't quit. Yes, I had the flu — no question about it.

Geri, the girls, and I prayed for God to heal me so I could enjoy this opportunity of a lifetime. God didn't seem moved.

A doctor from the Midwest happened to be attending the camp week with his family. I approached him on the breakfast line and informed him that I had some flulike symptoms with a cough. Would he mind prescribing something so I could get some sleep at night? "No problem," he responded. "I'll get you the strongest cough medicine available and an antibiotic."

By the third and fourth days, however, I worsened. At this point Geri wasn't speaking to me. She assumed I had overworked prior to vacation and had worn my body down. Her visions of us enjoying this dream vacation as a couple or family were gone. She was disappointed, to say the least. I coughed all night, so she moved into the other room with our two older girls. By day five, we exchanged looks, but few words.

She was sad and angry. I felt guilty. History seemed to be repeating itself with my getting sick on vacations and holidays.

What was so odd for me was that I appeared to be worsening every day. On day five I could barely walk to dinner and had begun spitting up some red phlegm. "It must be the red cough medicine," I told myself. I was unable to eat and had just about finished the bottle of medicine. The cough only grew more relentless. It was clearly in my chest.

By our sixth and final night, I still had not slept. I began to grow afraid. It was becoming difficult to get out of bed. It took me thirty minutes to move from the bed to the bathroom.

It was obvious I was in trouble. I needed to get to a doctor.

The next morning I informed Geri I needed help. I was getting worse.

The kids were having the best vacation of their lives. It was a long way from the streets of New York. So I endured through lunch and tried to say good-bye as best I could to everyone and we got in the car to visit a doctor. He was from Texas and up in the Colorado mountains to serve a nearby youth camp.

He checked my symptoms, listened to my chest, and suggested that I had pneumonia. His nurse then hooked my finger up to a machine to check my oxygen level and could see I was having trouble breathing.

Maybe I was having a heart attack. Who knew?

At this point they grew alarmed and instructed me to get to a hospital to check out my pneumonia.

The nearest hospital was almost two hours away. Geri drove. I felt my life ebbing away, and I began drifting in and out of consciousness.

We drove through countless small towns. No hospitals. Where were the hospitals? I missed New York City!

Wrong Counsel Almost Ruined My Life

Finally we arrived at our destination, where a friend of a friend was lending us his townhouse. We dropped off the kids. One of his neighbors saw me lying in the back of our minivan. Geri described my symptoms. The woman excitedly told her, "Get him to the medical clinic down the hill right away. He has HAPE."

We didn't know what she was talking about, but Geri came back to the car looking compassionate. That helped.

The nurse in the medical clinic took one look at me and rushed me past the people in the waiting room. They hooked me up to an oxygen machine that measured oxygen levels and found my breathing at less than 44 percent capacity.

Immediately another doctor rushed in and put me on another machine to give me oxygen. She then informed me that I would have been in a coma within a few hours and dead by the next morning. I was choking to death. X-rays revealed my lungs had filled with water.

I had High Altitude Pulmonary Edema (HAPE), a severe form of altitude sickness, popularized by the movie *Vertical Limit*. It is relatively uncommon for people to get HAPE between 8,000 and 14,000 feet.

The medical personnel considered flying me down to a lower altitude immediately, but I responded well to the oxygen. Within twenty minutes I was asleep for the first time in almost a week.

I spent the next week connected to an oxygen tank. It took almost three weeks for my lungs to clear up and for me to be able to walk without becoming short of breath.

Many doctors, including some in Colorado, are unfamiliar with HAPE. How could they be? Colorado has the highest altitudes in the continental United States.

The first two doctors I saw misdiagnosed me. In all fairness, I had diagnosed myself the first time, and the doctor simply agreed. But I almost died.

These other doctors were not equipped to be counseling sick patients in the mountains of Colorado. Their wrong counsel almost ended my earthly life. In the same way, I realized, we pastors and leaders often give faulty counsel to spiritually sick people who fill our churches. Our training has been inadequate to address the deep needs underneath the surface of people's lives.

Along the way in my journey of growing as a Christian, I received teaching and training that did a lot of good. Unfortunately, the solutions were mostly temporary. The prescriptions failed to root out the sinful patterns and habits in my life.

Our Wrong Counsel Keeps People Spiritually Immature

> Unfortunately, many people remained sick and some even "died" under my leadership.

I have to admit that, like those doctors, I have misdiagnosed people who have come to me for help. When someone had relational problems or emotional issues, I applied every spiritual remedy I knew. Unfortunately, many people remained sick and some even "died" under my leadership.

For example:

- A couple comes to me after the husband has admitted to a one-year affair with a family friend that occurred five years earlier in their marriage. I am grateful for the conviction of the Holy Spirit in his life. I pray for them and recommend a marriage book I know with a good chapter on forgiveness for the wife. I exhort them both to pursue God wholeheartedly. I pray and hope for the best.
- A gifted musician joins our church to use his gifts for God. He is charismatic and experienced. The congregation loves him. He asks many of us to pray for his wife, that God will put her heart in the right place. We do so. I pray and hope for the best. We later learn that this is not a minor friction. The conflict was building up for years, she had moved out and resettled five hundred miles away, and he is undeniably part of the problem.
- Armstrong is a friend and leader in the church. He serves whenever there is a need. The only problem is that he is temperamental, unpredictable, and moody. We tiptoe around him. I pray and hope for the best.
- Larry is forty years old, single, and unemployed again. He has a résumé four pages long. He rarely stays at a job or in a relationship with the opposite sex for more than a few months. We pray for him, encourage him to affirm his identity in Christ, and ask God to open new doors for him. I pray and hope for the best.

Today, I no longer simply pray and hope for the best. Each of the above scenarios required a level of discipleship that went beyond a skin-deep, superficial, quick fix. They each later submitted to a scalpel by taking a serious, prayerful look at the deeper issues I will outline in this book. First, however, I as a leader had to undergo a revolution in the way I understood and approached discipleship.

Imbalanced Spirituality

The sad truth is that too little difference exists, in terms of emotional and relational maturity, between God's people inside the church and those outside who claim no relationship to Jesus Christ. Even more alarming, when you go beyond the praise and worship of our large meetings and conventions and into the homes and small group meetings of God's people, you often find a valley littered by broken and failed relationships.

Do any of the following people remind you of someone in your church?

1. The board member who never says "I was wrong" or "Sorry."
2. The children's church leader who constantly criticizes others.
3. The high-control small group leader who cannot tolerate different points of view.
4. The middle-aged father of two toddlers who is secretly addicted to pornography.
5. The thirty-five-year-old husband busily serving in the church, unaware of his wife's loneliness at home.
6. The worship leader who interprets any suggestion as a personal attack and personal rejection.
7. The Sunday school teacher struggling with feeling of bitterness and resentment toward the pastor but afraid to say anything.
8. The exemplary "servant" who tirelessly volunteers in four different ministries but rarely takes any personal time to take care of himself or herself.
9. Two intercessors who use prayer meetings to escape from the painful reality of their marriage.
10. The people in your small group who are never transparent about their struggles or difficulties.

They may present themselves as spiritually mature, but something is terribly imbalanced about their spirituality. The sad reality is that too many people in our churches are fixated at a stage of spiritual immaturity that current models of discipleship have not addressed.

Many are supposedly "spiritually mature" but remain infants, children, or teenagers emotionally. They demonstrate little ability to process anger, sadness, or hurt. They whine, complain, distance themselves, blame, and use sarcasm — like little children when they don't get their way. Highly defensive to criticism or differences of opinion, they expect to be taken care of and often treat people as objects to meet their needs.

> The sad reality is that too many people in our churches are fixated at a stage of spiritual immaturity that current models of discipleship have not addressed.

Why?

The answer is what this book is about. The roots of the problem lie in a faulty spirituality, stemming from a faulty biblical theology (chs. 3 and 4). Many Christians have received helpful training in certain essential areas of discipleship, such as prayer, Bible study, worship, discovery of their spiritual gifts, or learning how to explain the gospel to someone else. Yet Jesus' followers also need training and skills in how to look beneath the surface of the iceberg in their lives (ch. 5), to break the power of how their past influences the present (ch. 6), to live in brokenness and vulnerability (ch. 7), to know their limits (ch. 8), to embrace their loss and grief (ch. 9), to make incarnation their model for loving well (ch. 10), and to slow down in order to lead with integrity (ch. 11). Loving God and others well is both the climax and point of the entire book.

Despite all the emphasis today on spiritual formation, church leaders rarely address what spiritual maturity looks like as it relates to emotional health. For this reason, our churches are filled with people who remain emotionally unaware and socially immature. Sadly, I can think of a number of non-Christian people who are more loving, balanced, and civil than many church members I know (including myself!).

The link between emotional health and spiritual maturity is a large, unexplored area of discipleship. We desperately need, I believe, to reexamine the whole of Scripture — and the life of Jesus in particular — in order to grasp the dynamics of this link.

While I do believe in the important place of professionally trained Christian counselors to bring expertise to the church, I believe the church of Jesus Christ is to be the primary vehicle for our growth in spiritual and emotional maturity. Sadly, for too long we have delegated "emotional" issues to the therapist's office and taken responsibility only for "spiritual" problems in the church. The two are inseparably linked and critical to a fully biblical discipleship.

> The link between emotional health and spiritual maturity is a large, unexplored area of discipleship.

I believe wholeheartedly that the Lord Jesus and his church are the hope of the world. My commitment is to Scripture as the Word of God, the authority under which we as God's church are to live. I have been teaching it for my entire adult life. I remain committed to the indispensability of Scripture, prayer, fellowship, worship, faithfulness in using our spiritual gifts, small groups and community life, stewardship of our resources, and the centrality of the gospel to all of life. But unless we integrate emotional maturity as a focus in our discipleship, we are in danger of missing God's point completely — love.

I write as a pastor, not a therapist or professional counselor. I am the senior pastor of a large, multiethnic, international church with people from over sixty-five different countries in the congregation. Thus, I am writing out of a profound love for the church of Jesus Christ. I am also keenly aware that "the center of gravity in the Christian world has shifted inexorably southward, to Africa, Asia, and Latin America. Already today, the largest Christian communities on the planet are to be found in Africa and Latin America."[1] My prayer is that this book will contribute to the development of spiritual fathers and mothers of the faith for these churches and others around the world.

Embracing the truth about the emotional parts of myself unleashed nothing short of a revolution in my understanding of God, Scripture, the nature of Christian maturity, and the role of the church. I can no longer deny the truth that emotional and spiritual maturity are inseparable.

God's mercy has enabled me to survive and tell this story. If you would like God to transform both you and your church, I invite you to read on.

Chapter 1

As Go the Leaders,
So Goes the Church

The overall health of any church or ministry depends primarily on the emotional and spiritual health of its leadership. In fact, the key to successful spiritual leadership has much more to do with the leader's internal life than with the leader's expertise, gifts, or experience.

It took me a long time to realize that yet another leadership seminar or more information was not the key to "successful" church leadership. In fact, my journey toward leading an emotionally and spiritually healthy church was not triggered in a seminar or book. Instead, it was brought to a head with a very painful conversation at home.

My Wife Couldn't Take It Anymore

"Pete, I'm leaving the church," my wife Geri had muttered quietly. I sat still, too stunned to respond.

"I can't take any more of this stress — the constant crises," she continued.

Geri had been more than patient. I had brought home constant pressure and tension from church, year after year. Now the woman I had promised to love just as Christ loved the church was exhausted.

We had experienced eight unrelenting years of stress.

"I'm not doing it anymore," she concluded. "This church is no longer life for me. It is death."

When a church member says, "I'm leaving the church," most pastors don't feel very good. But when your wife of nine years says it, your world is turned upside down.

> "This church is no longer life for me. It is death."

We were in the bedroom. I remember the day well.

"Pete, I love you, but I'm leaving the church," she summarized very calmly. "I no longer respect your leadership."

I was visibly shaken and didn't know what to say or do. I felt shamed, alone, and angry.

I tried raising my voice to intimidate her: "That is out of the question," I bellowed. "All right, so I've made a few mistakes."

But she calmly continued, "It's not that simple. You don't have the guts to lead—to confront the people who need to be confronted. You don't lead. You're too afraid that people will leave the church. You're too afraid of what they'll think about you."

I was outraged.

"I'm getting to it!" I yelled defensively. "I'm working on it." (For the last two years, I really had been trying, but somehow still wasn't up to it.)

"Good for you, but I can't wait any more," she replied.

There was a long pause of silence. Then she uttered the words that changed the power balance in our marriage permanently: "Pete, I quit."

It is said that the most powerful person in the world is one who has nothing to lose. Geri no longer had anything to lose. She was dying on the inside, and I hadn't listened to or responded to her calls for help.

She softly continued, "I love you, Pete. But the truth is, I would be happier separated than married. At least then you would have to take the kids on weekends. Then maybe you'd even listen!"

"How could you say such a thing?" I complained. "Don't even think about it."

She was calm and resolute in her decision. I was enraged. A good Christian wife, married to a Christian (and a pastor I may add), does not do this. I understood at that moment why a husband could fly into a rage and kill the wife he loves.

She had asserted herself. She was forcing me to listen.

I wanted to die. This was going to require me to change![1]

The Beginnings of This Mess

How did we get to this point?

Eight years previously, my wife and I had a vision to begin planting a church among the working classes in Queens, New York City, that would develop leaders to plant other churches both in New York City and around the world.

Perhaps it is more accurate to say that I had a vision and Geri followed. Wasn't that the biblical way large decisions were supposed to be made in a marriage?

Now, four children later, she was battle weary and wanted a life and a marriage. By this time I agreed. The problem was my sense of responsibility to build the church, and to do so for other people. I had little energy left over to parent our children or to enjoy Geri. I had even less energy to enjoy a "life," whatever that was! Even when I was physically present, such as at a soccer game for one of our daughters, my mind was usually focused on something related to the church.

I remember wondering, *Am I supposed to be living so miserably and so pressured in order that other people can experience joy in God?* It sure felt that way.

Weeks had turned into months. Months into years. The years had become almost a decade, and the crisis was now in full bloom. The sober reality was that I had made little time during those nine years for the joys of parenting and marriage. I was too preoccupied with the incessant demands of pastoring a church. (How well I now know that I will never get those years back.)

Jesus does call us to die to ourselves. "Whoever wants to be my disciple must deny themselves and take up their cross and follow me" (Mark 8:34). The problem was that we had died to the wrong things. We mistakenly thought that dying to ourselves for the sake of the gospel meant dying to self-care, to feelings of sadness, to anger, to grief, to doubt, to struggles, to our healthy dreams and desires, and to passions we had enjoyed before our marriage.

> Jesus does call us to die to ourselves. The problem was that we had died to the wrong things.

Geri has always loved the outdoors and nature. She values her large, extended family. She loves the field of recreation, creating opportunities for people to have fun. There was rarely time for those pleasures.

Workaholics for God

We were very busy for God. Our lives were filled with serving, doing, and trying to love other people. It felt at times that we weren't supposed to do some of the things that would give me energy and joy, so that others could have these feelings. In actuality, we had died to something God never intended to be killed (as I will explain later).

I remember sitting at the dinner table with my brother-in-law as he talked about his joy in being a referee and coach for girls' basketball teams.

"Must be nice," I mumbled to myself. "Too bad I can't have that kind of freedom."

I had a profound experience of God's grace in Jesus Christ when I became a Christian at age nineteen. His love filled me with passion to serve him. Over time, however, this passion became a burden. The incessant demands of the church planting in New York City, in addition to my neglect of the emotional dimensions of spirituality, slowly turned my joy into "duty." My life became out of balance, and I slowly bought into the lie that the more I suffered for Christ, the more he would love me. I began to feel guilty about taking too much time off and enjoying places like the beach.

My spiritual foundation was finally being revealed for what it was: wood, hay, and stubble (1 Cor. 3:10–15). I had limped along for so many years that the limp now seemed normal.

Geri's courageous step on that cold January evening saved me. God intervened dramatically through Geri's words, "I quit."

It was probably the most loving, courageous act of service she has ever done for me. It forced me to seek professional help to resolve my "vocational" crisis. Unconsciously, I hoped the counselor would straighten Geri out so I could get on with my life and the church.

Little did I know what was ahead!

> I had limped along for so many years that the limp now seemed normal.

God forced me to take a long, painful look at the truth — the truth about myself, our marriage, our lives, the church. Jesus said, "You will know the truth, and the truth will set you free" (John 8:32). It was demoralizing to admit, finally, that the intensity of my engagement in spiritual disciplines had not worked spiritual maturity into my life.

Why? I ignored the emotional components of discipleship in my life.

Life before This Crisis of Intimacy

I grew up in a New Jersey suburb, in an Italian American family, only one mile from the skyscrapers of Manhattan.

I went away to college in 1974, got involved in a Bible study on campus and became a follower of Jesus Christ during my sophomore year. That experience launched me into a spiritual journey that would include, over the next six years, the Catholic charismatic movement; a bilingual Spanish-English, inner-city, mainline Protestant church; an African-American church; Pentecostalism; and evangelicalism.

After teaching high school English for one year, I joined the staff of InterVarsity Christian Fellowship, an interdenominational ministry that facilitates Christian groups on university and college campuses. I worked for three years at Rutgers University and other New Jersey colleges. Then I went off to graduate studies at Princeton Theological Seminary and Gordon-Conwell Theological Seminary.

During those college years I met and became good friends with the young woman who would later become my wife. In 1984 Geri and I were married, and we entered a whirlwind — not even realizing at first that the winds were anything but normal. At the five-month mark of married life, I graduated from seminary, and the next day we moved to Costa Rica. For one year we studied Spanish in preparation to return to New York City. Geri returned to her parents eight months pregnant. I returned from Costa Rica two nights before our first baby was born.

One month later the three of us moved to Queens, New York City. I spent a year serving as an assistant pastor in an all-Spanish immigrant church and teaching in a Spanish seminary. The experiences gave us opportunities to perfect our Spanish and discern God's will for our future. That year also initiated us into the world of two million illegal immigrants from around the globe, who fill large cities like New York. We became friends with people who had fled death squads in El

Salvador, drug cartels in Columbia, civil war in Nicaragua, and implacable poverty in Mexico and the Dominican Republic.

The Start of the Dream?

Then, in September 1987, we started New Life Fellowship Church in a working-class, multiethnic, primarily immigrant section of Queens. (Of the two-and-a-half million residents of Queens, more than two-thirds are foreign-born.) The immediate Corona-Elmhurst neighborhood of our current church meeting site includes people from 123 nations. *National Geographic* calls "Elmhurst 11373 the most ethnically diverse zip code in the United States."[2] Roger Sanjek picked the Corona-Elmhurst section of Queens, New York, for his study called *The Future of Us All*, calling it "perhaps the most ethnically mixed community in the world" and noting its rapid change from 1960 at 98 percent white, 1970 at 67 percent, 1980 at 34 percent, and 1990 to 18 percent white.[3]

Our first worship service began with 45 people. God moved powerfully in those early years. After little more than a year we had grown to 160 people. By the end of the third year, I began a Spanish congregation. By the end of the sixth year, there were 400 in the English congregation plus another 250 in our first Spanish congregation. Large numbers of these people had become Christians through New Life.

My parachurch days with InterVarsity Christian Fellowship taught me practical ministry skills, such as how to lead a Bible study, how to share the gospel, and how to answer questions non-Christians commonly ask. My seminary education gave me the intellectual tools I needed—Greek, Hebrew, church history, systematic theology, hermeneutics, and more.

Unfortunately, neither background prepared me for planting a church in Queens. I was immediately thrust into a crash course to understand what Paul meant when he said that the gospel comes "not with wise and persuasive words, but with a demonstration of the Spirit's power" (1 Cor. 2:4).

During those early years of New Life, God taught us a great deal about prayer and fasting, healing the sick, the reality of demons, spiritual warfare, the gifts of the Holy Spirit, and hearing God's voice. Whatever I learned, I taught the congregation.

People were becoming Christians, with hundreds beginning a personal relationship with Jesus Christ. The poor were being served in new, creative ways. We were developing leaders, multiplying small groups, feeding the homeless, and planting new churches. But all was not well beneath the surface, especially on a leadership level.

We always seemed to have too much to do in too little time. While the church was an exciting place to be, it was not a joy to be in leadership — especially for my wife, Geri, and me. There was a high turnover of staff and leaders, all of which we ultimately attributed to spiritual warfare in the intensity of New York City. Perhaps this was the natural growing pains and fallout of any large corporation or business. But we weren't a business. We were a church family.

However, Geri and I did know that something was missing. Our hearts were shrinking. Church leadership felt like a heavy burden. We were gaining the whole world by doing a great work for God while at the same time losing our souls (cf. Mark 8:35).

> We were gaining the whole world by doing a great work for God while at the same time losing our souls.

Something was deeply wrong. I secretly dreamed of retirement, and I was only in my midthirties. Despite ongoing spiritual checkups — no immorality, no unforgiveness, no coveting, and so on — I could not pinpoint the source of my lack of joy. The foundation of my own personal character and development could not sustain the church we were building. It was a shaky foundation, waiting to collapse.

A Crawl toward a Crisis

During this time, Geri felt like a single parent with all the responsibilities she carried alone for our four small children. She was tired of high-pressure urban living. She was weary of the stress that I seemed to bring home weekly from church.

She wanted more of a marriage. She wanted more of a family. She wanted a life.

The bottom began to fall out when, in 1993–94, our Spanish congregation experienced a split, and relationships disintegrated that I had thought were rock solid. God was beginning to get my attention and seemed to be pushing me deeper and deeper into a pit at each turn. I approached the bottom of the pit, kicking and screaming,

I thought I was tasting hell. It turned out I was.

Little did I know the bottom was still two years away.

The event God used to get me into the pit initially was in the form of a betrayal by one of the assistant pastors of the Spanish-language congregation. For months I had heard rumors that he was dissatisfied and wanted to leave New Life Fellowship to start a new church, taking most of the people with him.

"That's impossible," I'd say to myself. "He is like a brother to me." After all, we had known each other for ten years.

When I asked him about the rumors, he would categorically deny them: "Pedro, nunca" ("Never, Pete").

I will never forget my shock the day I went to the afternoon Spanish service and two hundred people were missing. Only fifty people were there. Everyone else had gone with him to start another congregation.

Over the next several weeks, what seemed like a tidal wave swept over the remaining members of that congregation. Phone calls exhorted them to leave the house of Saul (me) and go over to the house of David (the new thing God was doing). People I had led to Christ, discipled, and pastored for years were gone. I would never see many of them again.

When we talked in private over two years later, this assistant pastor said, "You made promises to disciple me, but your words meant nothing. You did not deserve to lead these people."

When the split occurred, I did not defend myself. I tried to follow Jesus' model and be like a lamb going to the slaughter (Isa. 53:7). "Just take it, Pete; Jesus would," I repeatedly said to myself.

In reality, I felt as if I had let myself be raped.

I accepted all blame for the destruction. While I felt deeply betrayed, much of the failure was mine. This associate pastor had a legitimate gripe: I was overextended. I was pastoring two growing churches, one in English and one in Spanish, and I was too busy getting the "job" done and putting out fires. I lacked the flexibility and hours to fulfill my promise to give him time, friendship, or training.

Even so, I had a love for him like a brother. With the psalmist, I experienced the reality of someone "with whom I once enjoyed sweet fellowship at the house of God" (Ps. 55:14), only later to discover that "my companion attacks his friends; he violates his covenant" (Ps. 55:20). I did not believe such a betrayal was possible in the church.

Perhaps, more importantly, I was mesmerized by his gifts and abilities. The Spanish congregation admired his dynamic leadership qualities. Did it really matter that he was not broken and contrite of heart

(Ps. 51:16–17)? Did it really matter whether his character was lacking in some areas?

Yes.

The main problem was that I lacked both the courage and maturity to confront him.

The sad truth is that my "godly, lamblike response" had little to do with imitating Jesus and much more to do with unresolved issues and emotional baggage I was carrying from my past.

> My "godly, lamblike response" had little to do with imitating Jesus and much more to do with unresolved issues and emotional baggage I was carrying from my past.

My taste of hell went deeper than the congregational split. Suddenly, I found myself living a double life. The outward Pete sought to encourage the discouraged people who remained at New Life. "Isn't it amazing how God uses our sins to expand his kingdom? Now we have two churches instead of one," I proclaimed. "Now more people can come into a personal relationship with Jesus. If any of you want to go over to that new church, may God's blessings be upon you."

I lied.

I was going to be like Jesus (at least the Jesus I had imagined him to be), even if it killed me. It did — in my inward self.

My hell was that inside I was deeply wounded and angry. These feelings gave way to hate. My heart did not hold any forgiveness. I was full of rage, and I couldn't get rid of it.

When I was alone in my car, just the thought of what had happened would trigger a burst of anger, a knot in my stomach. Within seconds, curse words would follow, flying almost involuntarily from my mouth: "You are a @#&%" and "You are full of $*#%."

My First Call for Help

I finally acknowledged my desperation both at church and at home. "Becoming a pastor was the worst decision I've ever made," I told God in prayer.

I desperately searched for help. At last, a good pastor friend referred me to a Christian counselor. Geri and I went. It was March 1994.

I felt totally humiliated. Everything in me wanted to run. I felt like a child walking into the principal's office. "Counseling is for messed-up people," I complained to God (stating something I no longer agree with). "Not me. I'm not screwed up!"

After our initial two-day meeting, the counselor made three observations: (1) I was consumed with the church; (2) Geri was depressed and lonely; and (3) our marriage lacked intimacy.

We weren't sure what marital intimacy was, so I bought Geri a book on marriage. She could figure it out. I returned to work at the church.

Pausing and reflecting on the state of my soul were both frightening and liberating. At the time I thought all my problems stemmed from the stress and complexity of New York City. I blamed Queens, my profession, our four small children, Geri, spiritual warfare, other leaders, a lack of prayer covering, even our car (it had been broken into seven times in three months). Each time I was certain I had identified the root issue.

I hadn't.

The root issues were inside me. But I couldn't — or wouldn't — admit that yet.

The next two years were marked by a slow descent into an abyss. It felt like an infinite black hole was threatening to swallow me. I cried out to God for help, to change me. It seemed as if God closed heaven to my cry rather than answered it.

> The root issues were inside me. But I couldn't — or wouldn't — admit that yet.

Things went from bad to worse.

I continued preaching weekly and serving as the senior pastor. But my confidence to lead effectively had been thoroughly shaken by the split in the Spanish congregation. I hired additional staff and asked them to lead, which they did. Hadn't I failed miserably? Feeling they surely could do better, I let them begin rebuilding the church.

Soon the church no longer felt like the church with the original vision we had when we planted it. Meanwhile, I struggled to be honest with how I presented the situation to others. I had a terrible habit of embellishing or editing the truth lest people get upset. (God calls that lying; I renamed it good vision-casting.) I struggled to be honest with myself about my feelings, listening especially to the feelings that did not fit into my Christian grid, such as anger, bitterness, and sadness.

I also struggled to be honest with other people. Progress was slow and hard. I wrestled with whether I was departing from the faith. The questions I was raising and the feelings I was experiencing were considered off-limits in most of the Christian circles in which I had lived the previous twenty years.

Wasn't I supposed to be more than a conqueror in Jesus Christ (Rom. 8:37)? Why does there seem to be so much pathology covered over by a veneer of spirituality? How is it that so many people who have been Christians a long time are so judgmental and critical?

I was absolutely sure God was leading me on a new path. But where was everyone else? I struggled back and forth.

"How is it going, Pete?" a good friend would ask.

"Oh, everything is going just great. I sense God is breaking up the hard ground and planting new seeds for the future," I would reply optimistically.

The only problem: Those words were only a very small portion of the truth.

The thought of people angry at me caused me to shrink back to wait for another day. I feared that if I told different leaders in the church how I honestly perceived them—as proud, unteachable, and at times untruthful—they would leave. After the Spanish division more than a year and a half earlier, that thought was too painful to bear. I preferred to be quiet and hope the church problems would disappear all by themselves.

They did not.

I attended leadership conferences to learn about spiritual warfare and how to reach an entire city for God. I attended "refreshing meetings" at other churches. If there was a way to soak in more of God, I wanted to find it. I attended an out-of-state prophetic conference, where I received a number of encouraging personal prophecies. I intensified early-morning prayer meetings at New Life. I rebuked demons that were out to destroy my life. I studied the history of revivals. I sought counsel from numerous, nationally known church leaders.

One of my journal entries during this time sums up where I was:

> Lord, I can see the Promised Land on the other side of the Red
> Sea—wholeness, a joyful marriage and family, joy in serving

you, walking in the role you have for me in leadership—but I have no idea how to open the Red Sea to get there. Do you, God? If you do, could you please open it?

Geri Quits the Church

I felt I was making progress personally. Perhaps it wasn't visible externally yet, but something was happening. At least I thought so. For Geri, however, things were as they had been throughout our marriage—miserable.

In the second week of January 1996, Geri told me she was quitting the church.

I finally hit rock bottom. I notified our elders of my dilemma. They agreed to a one-week intensive retreat for us with some professional help to see if Geri and I could sort this out.

On February 13, 1996, we went away to a Christian counseling center. Our hope was to step out of our crisis and get some objectivity about the church. I hoped for a quick end to our pain.

We spent the next five full days with two counselors. This little, short-term "Christian community" was safe enough for us to give ourselves permission to speak our hidden feelings to one another.

What we did not anticipate was an authentic spiritual experience with God. For me, it began in the strangest way. Geri and I had talked late into the night. At about 2:00 a.m., she woke me, stood up on the bed, and, with a few choice words, let me have it. For the first time she told the brutal truth about how she felt about me, our marriage, and the church.

We Discover a Missing Bridge

Somehow Geri's explosion, while painful, was a liberating experience for both of us. Why? She had stripped off the heavy spiritual veneer of "being good" that kept her from looking directly at the truth about our marriage and lives.

I listened. She listened.

We looked at our parents' lives and marriages. I looked at New Life Fellowship honestly. The church clearly reflected my family of origin in significant ways.

Neither of us had ever sensed a "permission to feel" like this before.

The sad reality we discovered was that Jesus had penetrated only superficially into the depth of our persons — even though we had been Christians for almost twenty years.

> Jesus had penetrated only superficially into the depth of our persons — even though we had been Christians for almost twenty years.

Our experience that initially felt like death proved to be the beginning of a journey and the discovery of a relationship that would change my life, my marriage, my family, and ultimately the church. For the first time, I discovered the lingering power of the families we were born into. We left them when we got married, but somehow they were still shaping our lives.

Paul teaches that once a person comes to faith in Christ, "the old things [have] passed away; behold, new things have come" (2 Cor. 5:17 NASB). I never imagined that influential sin patterns, passed on from generation to generation in my family, were still operative. Since I believed the power of Christ could break any curse, I glossed over the idea that I was still being shaped by a home I had left long ago.

Examining my heart revealed a mixed set of drives. Part of my passion was for God's glory. Other parts were driven by a complex set of motives that I did not have the tools or the time to sort out. We began to look beneath the surface of our lives into entirely new arenas.

In my prayers, I told God that I was sorry. I had been sincere about giving my all to serve God and his kingdom. Who would have ever dreamed that my commitments would result in such disappointments? With all my background in prayer and the Bible, it was quite a shock to realize that whole emotional layers of my life existed that God had not yet touched. These became the seeds of the seven principles of emotionally healthy churches found in chapters 5 through 11.

A New Set of Eyes?

After this breakthrough, it seemed as if God had given me a new set of eyes to read Scripture. Truths that I only understood intellectually soon became part of my experience with God.

I saw Jesus able to express his emotion with unashamed, unembarrassed freedom:

- He shed tears (Luke 19:41).
- He was filled with joy (Luke 10:21).
- He grieved (Mark 14:34).
- He was angry (Mark 3:5).
- Sadness came over him (Matt. 26:37).
- He felt compassion (Luke 7:13).
- He felt sorrow (John 11:35).
- He showed astonishment and wonder (Mark 6:6; Luke 7:9).
- He felt distress (Mark 3:5; Luke 12:50).

Jesus was anything but an emotionally frozen Messiah.

At the same time, I observed how Jesus was able to separate himself from the expectations of the crowds, his family, and his disciples. His relationship with his Father freed him from the pressures of those around him. He was not afraid to live out his own unique life and mission, regardless of other people's agenda for his life.

Along with my life partner, Geri, I sensed we had a long road ahead, both as two separate individuals and as a married couple. The goal was not to change the church but to change us — or rather, to allow God to change us. Yet we immediately realized we were in unexplored territory, on a journey that was taking us beyond the Christian training we had received during the previous twenty years. We were taking a ride that only God could control. We were being led far from our safe shore of understanding God and relating to others. The rigid, tight box into which we had unwittingly placed God had been split open.

> The goal was not to change the church but to change us — or rather, to allow God to change us.

A part of us couldn't wait to see what God would do next. But another part of us was frightened. God clearly wanted us to open up to his Spirit the depths of our interior that we were only now discovering. This looked as if it was going to be very bloody — like a death.

Our understanding of the inseparability of emotional health and spiritual maturity would be a process, much like our daily relationship with God. Individuals may have a critical moment of receiving Jesus as their personal Lord and Savior, but there is, for almost everyone, a period of many months or many years beforehand in which God is working in them.

In the same way, it took repeated encounters over two years for God to claw away my limited view of him and the Christian life.

For example, God was clearly speaking to me through the gift of depression, an unhappy spouse, and a life that would periodically spin out of control. My only response to these painful realities was: "God, please remove them as quickly as possible so I can go on with your work!"

The only problem was I was not open to God speaking or moving in my life in those ways. My paradigm included God speaking through Scripture, prayer (an inner voice), sermons, a prophetic word, and sometimes, circumstances—but surely not this!

The Unexpected Beneficiary—New Life Fellowship

What God did in our lives spilled out into the church immediately, beginning with our staff team, then our elder board, and eventually the rest of our leadership. For the first time, I understood what it meant to minister out of who you are, not what you do. My discovery was contagious. We went from being "human doings" to "human beings." The result has been a rippling effect, very slowly, through the entire church. Beginning with the staff and elders, interns, ministry and small group leaders, the congregation at large—directly and indirectly—we have intentionally integrated the principles outlined in this book throughout the church.[4] (See chart.)

> For the first time, I understood what it meant to minister out of who you are, not what you do.

Juan and Marta

The day before I started a three-month sabbatical away from the church, Geri and I sat down at our kitchen table to meet with Juan and Marta, who had come to Christ under our ministry. They were at the time pastoring one of the Spanish-language congregations at New Life.

In their early years of leadership, Juan and Marta were vivacious, excited Christians. Juan had become a Christian at New Life. Now,

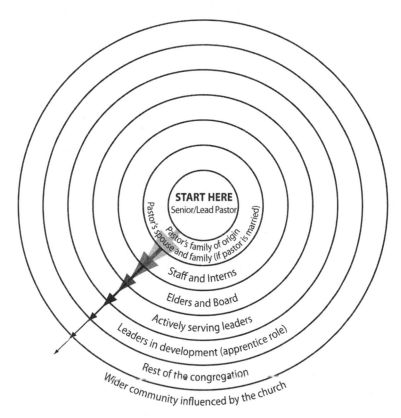

START HERE
Senior/Lead Pastor

Pastor's family of origin

Pastor's spouse and family (if pastor is married)

Staff and Interns

Elders and Board

Actively serving leaders

Leaders in development (apprentice role)

Rest of the congregation

Wider community influenced by the church

Concentric Circles of Applying Emotional Health

seven years later, they were exhausted and feeling guilty about neglecting their two children. They were overwhelmed with all that was in front of them — problems, crises, demands, and the enormous needs from a large congregation of immigrants.

After listening to them for three hours, I felt ashamed. Juan and Marta were the products of our ministry — and they were just like their teachers!

Would this legacy of frantic, joyless, imbalanced leadership forever be the kind of fruit Christian ministry produces? I admitted later to Geri that a part of me was sad to have led them to Christ and to being pastors. What a hard life of mostly needless suffering they now endured.

Geri and I asked their forgiveness.

Paul

Paul fasted and prayed regularly. Working as a computer technician in Manhattan, he used his vacations to attend conferences on prayer and prophetic ministry around the country. Soon he began fasting and praying with increasing regularity. During small group meetings, he could be found reading his Bible to receive personal words from God for the group. He frequently gave personal words of prophecy anywhere and to anyone—whether they wanted them or not.

Somebody needed to say something to him. But surely not me! What could I do? I struggled to fast through a meal, let alone for lengthy periods!

The truth, however, was that Paul was unteachable and condescending to the rest of us who were not as "spiritual" as he was. Part of becoming emotionally mature for me was to model loving confrontation, telling him what it was like to be with him and give him honest feedback as his pastor. I lovingly told him the truth about his critical spirit and pride that flowed out of his "surpassing revelations." At least I tried.

He soon felt God move him to another church.

As Go the Leaders...

According to some scholars, the four presidents prior to Abraham Lincoln were "compromise leaders," unwilling to confront the difficult issue of slavery between the North and the South. Abraham Lincoln, by contrast, was a mature leader with a solid sense of who he was. He knew what he believed and valued—regardless of the consequences—when he entered the White House. The strength and maturity of his character and convictions in many ways forced the nation to confront the reality of the abomination of slavery. The Civil War followed.

> The starting point for change in any nation, church, or ministry has always been the leader: As go the leaders, so goes the church.

The starting point for change in any nation, church, or ministry has always been the leader: As go the leaders, so goes the church.

But it is not enough for the leader to change.

God wants to set others free as well — whether this is their first year as a Christian or their fiftieth, whether they are single or married, and whatever their church role may be (new member, leader, or pastor). When you do the hard work of becoming an emotionally and spiritually mature disciple of Jesus Christ, the impact will be felt all around you.

The next chapters lay out a fresh paradigm for what it means to be a follower of Jesus in ways that your story becomes more of Jesus' plan for your life.

CHAPTER 2

SOMETHING IS DESPERATELY WRONG

Something is desperately wrong with most churches today. We have many people who are passionate for God and his work, yet who remain disconnected from their own emotions or those around them. The combination is deadly, both for the church and the leader's personal life.

Our pastoral staff team was in a coffee shop near the movie theater. We were shaken up. There wasn't much to say. We had just seen *The Apostle*. Each of us had an uneasy feeling that the movie had brilliantly placed a searchlight into our own flawed Christian pasts. Equally important, it visually portrayed the painful implications of a narrow, inadequate Christian discipleship.

Around the time of the movie's release, God had been showing the implications of splitting off emotional health from our spirituality. *The Apostle* addressed the issue head on. The wounds of our own past were still raw.

The Apostle, released in 1997, is a powerful movie about a Christian leader—the Reverend Eulis "Sonny" Dewey, played by Robert Duvall. Set in the 1980s in rural Texas, the movie opens with Sonny and his mother driving down a highway as they happen upon a multicar accident.

Slipping past the state troopers, Sonny approaches one of the smashed cars to find a bloodied, semiconscious young man in the driver's seat with his girlfriend lying dead beside him. Sonny, passionate for Jesus, whispers in the man's ear that if he will invite Jesus into his heart right then and there, God will forgive his sins, and he will be able to go to heaven. The state trooper attempts to drag Sonny away from the car wreck, but the preacher pushes him away with his arm as he finishes the work of leading this dying young man to Christ. He returns to his car and reports to his mother about the good work God has just done.

Sonny spends most of his time on the road leading revivals. Spiritual passion permeates his life. He loves his children—his "beauties"—he calls them. Meanwhile, his beautiful but long-suffering wife, Jessie, grows tired of both his adulteries and her being alone. She asks for a divorce.

It turns out she also is having an affair with the youth pastor at church. She and the youth pastor, using church bylaws, soon wrest control of Sonny's congregation away from him.

In a moment of jealous rage, Sonny gets drunk and attacks the youth pastor with a baseball bat while the youth pastor is coaching his son's game. Eventually the youth pastor dies.

Meanwhile, Sonny leaves town, destroying his old identity and setting off to find a new life. He stops his car in the middle of an intersection, gets down on his knees in the roadway, and asks, "Which way, God? Which way?"

He soon resurfaces in a small community in Louisiana. After sincerely seeking God through prayer and fasting, he perceives a new calling and direction from God, bearing the name and title of "The Apostle E. F." With mesmerizing sincerity, he baptizes himself in a nearby lake as a way of commemorating this new beginning.

With the help of a respected local African-American pastor, he begins a new church. He works multiple jobs in order to pay for rehabbing a dilapidated and closed church facility. He starts a radio ministry, fixes up a used bus, and begins picking up people to attend church—both African American and Anglo American.

His relationship with God is infectious. The church prospers. People come to faith in Christ. He feeds the hungry. The community is impacted. The small, racially mixed congregation loves his zeal and preaching.

Underneath his impressive faith, however, ugly gaps remain and erupt in his spiritual formation. While starting the new church he meets Toosie, a woman who works in the radio station. She draws his romantic affections. Sonny also gets into a fistfight with a troublemaker who questions his integrity.

Eventually the authorities catch up with the tragic mistake in Sonny's past. The police arrest him, and he is sent to jail. But even in prison we see Sonny enthusiastically leading a chain gang in Christian song so that they too might know the powerful Lord Jesus, who changes lives.

Sonny has a temper. He is a womanizer. He misuses alcohol. He kills a man in a moment of passion. At the same time, observers cannot deny the evidence that Sonny is a true believer in Jesus Christ. He preaches the new birth and is committed to the power of the Holy Spirit in order to live a supernatural life.

> He is a zealous, committed Christian whom we admire, and yet ... he is an imposter.

Sonny, like most of us, is a complex individual. He is a zealous, committed Christian whom we admire, and yet he is also terribly inconsistent. Most painful, perhaps, is his lack of awareness of the harm that will come from appearing to be more than he really is. In some ways he is an imposter. He easily compartmentalizes his faith and spirituality from the totality of his humanity. Most of us in Christian leadership and in the church can relate to more about him than we like to admit.

The gaps in Sonny's Christian life undermine his message and leadership. I wish this were only Hollywood. It is not.

Unfortunately, too many similar examples abound in real life.

Bob Pierce and World Vision

In 1950 Bob Pierce founded what has become World Vision (www.worldvision.org), the world's largest Christian relief and development agency. Today that organization serves more than one hundred million people a year in nearly one hundred countries. Passionate for Jesus and for a world without hunger or disease, Bob Pierce began humbly, helping children orphaned by the Korean War. Every outreach he touched grew in size and scope. With unstoppable vision and energy he dreamed the impossible and then did everything imaginable to make it happen.

Books and magazine cover stories were written about him. His friends said, "He is a man restless to win souls"; "I have never met a person with greater compassion"; and "He is a true Christian Samaritan who literally laid down his life for the needy 'little' people of the world."

Bob often prayed, "Let my heart be broken by the things that break the heart of God." That zeal drove him to the ends of the earth, marked by a seemingly inexhaustible passion to meet spiritual and human needs wherever he saw them.

Unfortunately, his approach had disastrous consequences for his family. As one family friend stated politely, Bob's wife, Lorraine, "knew deprivation of a different kind than those to whom her husband was ministering."

The stark reality is that he all but abandoned his own family. He consistently put opportunities for expanded ministry and greater impact ahead of his wife and children. For example, when one of his daughters phoned him on an overseas trip to say she needed him to come home, he declined, not understanding her desperate need. His wife, who was with him, pleaded with him to return with her. Instead, he chose to fly on to Vietnam.

When Mrs. Pierce arrived home, she was shocked to discover their daughter recovering from an attempt to take her life. "I just needed to feel Daddy's arms around me," she explained, adding, "I knew he wouldn't come." Alerted to their daughter's emotional battle, the Pierces tried to get her help, but their belated efforts failed. Two years later, she took her life.

Bob's relationship with his wife also deteriorated over time. At one point, years passed when they did not even speak. His relationships with his two remaining children were equally strained. Although God gave the family a night of reconciliation before his death, Bob Pierce lived many of the last years of his life alienated from everyone in his immediate family.

Years of eighteen-hour days, unsanitary food, and constant jet lag gradually depleted Bob's emotional reserves and made him susceptible to all kinds of physical difficulties. One biographer wrote, "The temper that he had battled all his life to control got the upper hand more and more often, and the mind that had once operated with computer-like accuracy began short-circuiting occasionally, causing a growing erraticism in his behavior."

Bob's oft-cited request, "Just let me burn out for God," was sadly being fulfilled.

Bob's relationship with the board of World Vision also had an unhappy, tension-filled ending. In 1963 the World Vision board overruled him for the first time, voting to cancel his weekly radio broadcasts, citing financial factors. Later that year the board put him on medical leave; he was overseas as usual and chose to stay there for his recuperation—apart from his family. He eventually got better, but the tensions at World Vision did not.[1]

In 1967, at a highly charged board meeting, Bob Pierce resigned. The legal documents of agreement were brought the next day, and Bob signed away his life's work.

> Are stories like these of broken relationships and occasional reconciliation the exception, limited only to unusually gifted people? Sadly, they are not.

Bob Pierce died of leukemia in 1978. Within weeks, his daughter Marilee Pierce Dunker began writing a book, *Man of Vision, Woman of Prayer*,[2] telling of both the miracles overseas and the "dark side" of their painful home life.

Are stories like these of broken relationships and occasional reconciliation the exception, limited only to unusually gifted people? Sadly, they are not. I could tell dozens of stories from the people in our church and literally thousands from around the country. You probably could too.

Roger and His Gifts Alone

If there is such a thing as a "poster child of the church," then Roger was it. His father, father-in-law, and twelve other family members are in the clergy. Roger attended both a Christian college and seminary twice, once as a child when his father attended school and eighteen years later as he attended the very same schools.

"In a sense the cards were stacked," Roger says today. "All I knew from birth were the church and ministry. I had a deep passion for them, but as I would discover later, they didn't necessarily translate into a passion for Christ—and certainly not an intimacy with him."

Early in his ministry Roger knew something was wrong. Not only was he unfulfilled in a small traditional parish setting, but he was also experiencing depression again, as he had both in college and in seminary. A denominationally funded career-assessment session advised him to leave the ministry because of a weak sense of self, the absence of emotional boundaries, and the presence of a strong entrepreneurial spirit that did not fit well in the established church. He ignored their counsel. Instead he took a traditional, theologically broad church in Queens where he felt called to be a change agent.

It was tough from the start. Roger began to implement changes in the worship, add new programs, and reset the board's priorities in order to grow the church. Several members received Christ at a Billy Graham Crusade, and new converts joined the church. Soon, Roger and his wife were receiving nasty letters and were the subject of controversy and gossip around the church.

Church attendance doubled. Giving dramatically increased. The budget tripled. And the pastor crashed.

"I didn't know it at the time, but I was running on all gifts and no grace," admits Roger. "I was blinded to my own emptiness and emotional abyss." After every monthly church board meeting, he would cry and physically tremble.

After five years Roger felt he was at the breaking point. He even took the summer off—without pay—in total desperation, but to no avail. "It was a wasted summer. I didn't seek out the Lord. I didn't seek out any help. I didn't even know where to turn," he says today.

Things continued to decline for Roger. Attendance grew, and many people now stood behind him, but finances were tight and relations with the church board became worse. "Every criticism and every misunderstanding came as if it were a fatal blow to me personally," he says.

Roger's problem finally exhausted him. The pressures led him to announce his resignation with no foreseeable income, no severance package, no transition, no counseling, and no emotional strength left. He felt like a failure, a disgrace.

What went wrong? Roger was emotionally immature. His family's frequent moves taught him how to meet people but not how to connect with them. Whenever he would seek for a deeper level of discipleship, he felt turned away—with only a few exceptions—and was told, "Your life should be together by now." So he allowed the secret chamber of his heart to grow larger, darker, and well secured from everyone, eventually including his wife.

"I learned to stuff my problems deeper," he admits. "I was not emotionally healthy. For me church was always a place where I felt I had to be guarded about the deepest, darkest things about myself. It was never a safe place."

In sad reality, neither his life, nor the churches he served, nor even his relationships at home were healthy. Roger will return one day, I believe, to significant pastoral leadership, but for now he's doing the right thing by inviting God to put his house in order—personally, at home, and in close relationships to others.

Faulty Models from Home to Church

I remember my early days as an InterVarsity staff worker on a university campus and later as I traveled around the country speaking at church-growth conferences, stunned by the inner lives of many leaders and pastors of our churches. All too common were denial, pride, defensiveness, frenetic schedules, workaholism, covetousness for higher-impact churches (which is idolatry; see Col. 3:5), and a trail of lonely spouses. It felt like too much to bear. In the early days, I believed it was simply an aberration, a rare occurrence. Over time, however, I realized it was the norm.

I determined that I would be different. The only problem is that I didn't know how!

The emotional stability of North American homes is at an all-time low. In the United States at the time of this writing, about half of all marriages end in divorce.[3] What is perhaps most shocking is that the divorce rate in several states traditionally known as the Bible Belt is among the highest in the country.[4] George Barna has documented that the divorce rate for people who describe themselves as Christians is even higher than for the public as a whole.[5]

Even among Christian leaders the collapse of the home is shockingly high. More surprising is how commonly it occurs for a Christian leader to be caught in an affair, with a prostitute, with a pornographic addiction, or in an equally destructive out-of-control situation. Too many go on as if nothing has happened.

To get a clue about what may be broken in situations like this, consider the example of someone who decided to talk honestly about his inner world. In January 2002, the man widely regarded as the father of Christian marriage ministries—Ray Mossholder, of Marriage Plus Ministries—filed for divorce from his wife of forty-two years and announced plans to remarry. This widely respected Christian leader, whose ministry is credited with saving more than eleven thousand couples from divorce, had been heard by millions on his radio and TV broadcasts.

He announced the news of his marriage breakup in a letter to supporters, referring to "the story of the shoemaker who was so busy that his own wife had to go without shoes." He added: "I have been that shoemaker. I make no excuse for it."

Nevertheless, neither his wife nor children could stop him from announcing plans to marry another woman as soon as the divorce was final. He insisted that he was not turning away from God; he was merely leaving his believing wife of forty-two years.

The saddest statement of all was something else he included in this letter to his donors. He acknowledged being "often hypocritical when I talked about how great [our marriage] was. What I taught was truth; however, it seemed that we were never able to apply it in our own marriage."[6]

Why? I believe statements like Mossholder's and examples like *The Apostle*, Bob Pierce, and Roger from New Life Fellowship all stem from a faulty paradigm (or model) of Christian discipleship.

The "Loving" Small Group That Crashed

When we began New Life Fellowship in September 1987, we were committed to developing small groups as an integral part of our discipleship and community-building strategy. We invested much energy in training leaders in skills such as how to lead a Bible study, facilitate worship, build community, reach out to their neighbors, and pray effectively, as well as how to delegate and understand the seasons of a small group. We developed resource manuals for "small group leaders" and for "coaches" (supervisors) of these groups. As I look back now, they were all "above the surface" kinds of skills. They failed to equip people in foundational emotionally healthy skills such as speaking clearly, directly, honestly, and respectfully; listening without making assumptions; and resolving conflicts maturely. The following story demonstrates the limits and gaps of our approach.

In the early 1990s, Bob and Carol, a couple with a strong gift of hospitality, were leading one of our small groups. Their small group flourished, with an average of fifteen people attending each Friday night. The participants worshiped. They prayed for one another. They studied Scripture. They spent time together outside the group meetings. They enjoyed a meal together each week. "In the beginning," remarks Bob, "I would have described it as a very loving group."

Cracks began to surface when Millie, a group member, informed two other women one evening about a "suspected" affair going on between two people in another New Life small group. They were legitimately concerned and anxious. They wanted to help. These women then told their husbands, who eventually informed Bob. He was astonished that this rumor was circulating at the same time of their group's study on James 3 and the power of the tongue for either good or evil.

Bob spoke to Millie and the others, assuming the gossip would then stop. In reality it was simply swept under the rug, with no one ever speaking directly and honestly about the alleged moral indiscretion.

The crack widened and the bottom fell out when Millie informed Bob that another member of the group was convinced that Bob's wife was having an affair. This small group member had confided in Millie, hoping she could speak to Bob.

By this time a number of growing conflicts developed between group members. Conflict spreads like cancer when untreated. This group's cancer was spreading rapidly and mortally.

Bob, appalled by the accusations and how they were handled so unbiblically, was shaken to the core. It not only revealed the lack of maturity in the group but cracks in his own marriage and life that needed to be addressed. Bob realized, for example, that he had been overextended in helping other people after work and had become emotionally unavailable to his own family. It would take almost two years to heal their marriage.

"I thought I was building people up in the Word of God," lamented Bob. "I finally realized I had built nothing. People would ask forgiveness and then disappear. We would talk about the Bible, but we didn't know how to live what we learned."

> "I thought I was building people up in the Word of God," lamented Bob. "I finally realized I had built nothing."

Within a short three months, this "loving" group was decimated by all the unresolved hurt. The people scattered. Millie and her husband left the church and soon moved out of state.

Bob and Carol, disillusioned, also left the church. It would take four years for them to return and begin to trust Christians again. As Bob later reflected on what had happened, he said, "We didn't know what we were doing."

He was right. They, along with the rest of us in senior leadership, did not have the emotional/spiritual maturity or training to go beneath the surface in such a way as to help this small group.

Identifying the Emotional Components of Spiritual Maturity

Despite our significant investment in small group leadership training, we did not understand the central role of emotional health in spiritual maturity to living in Christian community. Our discipleship model failed to acknowledge emotional growth — the progression from emotional infancy or adolescence into emotional adulthood. We did not know that resolving conflict, for example, was not simply about applying a few simple steps such as those laid out in Matthew 18:15–18. It was only later that we realized the need to apply a number of other biblical truths to skillfully and maturely resolve conflicts. This includes an awareness of how one's family historically resolved conflict; one's dominant conflict style (for example, avoidance, attacking, distraction, shutting down); a healthy awareness of one's brokenness; and the ability to enter into other people's perspective in a Christlike way.

At the time, the only thing we knew for sure was that something was wrong with our small group leadership development and our approach to building healthy communities. Yet as I said in the opening of chapter 1, as go the leaders, so goes the church. We cannot grow an emotionally healthy church if we ourselves are not addressing issues deep beneath the surface of our lives.

> Resolving conflict is not simply about applying a few simple steps such as those laid out in Matthew 18:15–18.

Let's move now to Part 2 and explore the scriptural basis for a new, desperately needed paradigm of discipleship.

Part 2

Biblical Basis for a New Paradigm of Discipleship

CHAPTER 3

DISCIPLESHIP'S NEXT FRONTIER — EMOTIONAL HEALTH

With one breath, God made us human. Yet, somehow, today we slice out the emotional portion of who we are, deeming it suspect, irrelevant, or of secondary importance. Contemporary discipleship models often esteem the spiritual more than the physical, emotional, social, and intellectual components of who we are. Nowhere, however, does a good biblical theology support such a division.

The Copernican Revolution Needed Today

For at least 1,400 years it was universally accepted and "mathematically proven" that the earth was the center of the universe. Had not Ptolemy, the great ancient Greek astronomer, demonstrated it? Everyone accepted as fact that the sun and universe revolve around the earth. Then Copernicus, a Polish scientist in the 1500s, challenged that assumption, followed later by Galileo. They saw the problems and inconsistencies with this longstanding view of the world and presented a radically new paradigm. In their analysis, the earth was simply one of the many planets orbiting the sun in a vast universe. Galileo went even further, saying that even the sun is only a small player in an uncountable number of galaxies.

This new paradigm shook the foundations of how society and church viewed themselves. It was deeply unsettling to admit that people were only a small speck in a vast galaxy. For such a sacrilegious way of looking at the universe and its implications for people's faith, Galileo was summoned to Rome, found to be "vehemently suspected of heresy," and eventually condemned to house arrest for life. He was also forbidden to publish. (He got off rather lightly by the standards of his time!)

The change from Ptolemy's world picture to that of Copernicus came as a result of evidence that the old way of looking at things was no longer adequate. The more Galileo studied the movement of stars and planets in light of Ptolemy's system, the more it became clear that it was not true. From that point on, everyone began to look at the universe with a new set of glasses. All kinds of prior information and data could now be considered and analyzed in new ways. A shift like this to a new model or paradigm can be thought of as a kind of conversion.

I am using the term *paradigm* purposefully. It was popularized by Thomas Kuhn in his book *The Structure of Scientific Revolutions.*[1] He defines a paradigm as a way of seeing and thinking about reality. It is the lens, the filter through which we interpret the data and information of our lives. To Kuhn, revolutions in scientific thought can only come about when people are able to break out of an old pattern of seeing and thinking to something new.

Today we still use the phrase *Copernican revolution* to describe a whole new way of looking at life, one that shakes the foundations of how we feel, think, or see something. I believe the thesis of this book — that emotional health and spiritual health are inseparable — will amount to a Copernican revolution for many in the Christian community.[2] It is not possible for a Christian to be spiritually mature while remaining emotionally immature.

> It is not possible for a Christian to be spiritually mature while remaining emotionally immature.

For some reason, however, the vast majority of Christians today live as if the two concepts have no intersection. Our standards of what it means to be "spiritual" totally bypass many glaring inconsistencies. We have learned to accept that:

- You can be a dynamic, gifted speaker for God in public and be an unloving spouse and parent at home.
- You can function as a church board member or pastor and be unteachable, insecure, and defensive.

- You can memorize entire books of the New Testament and still be unaware of your depression and anger, even displacing it on other people.
- You can fast and pray a half-day a week for years as a spiritual discipline and constantly be critical of others, justifying it as discernment.
- You can lead hundreds of people in a Christian ministry while driven by a deep personal need to compensate for a nagging sense of failure.
- You can pray for deliverance from the demonic realm when in reality you are simply avoiding conflict, repeating an unhealthy pattern of behavior traced back to the home in which you grew up.
- You can be outwardly cooperative at church but unconsciously try to undercut or defeat your supervisor by coming habitually late, constantly forgetting meetings, withdrawing and becoming apathetic, or ignoring the real issue behind why you are hurt and angry.

Plato in the Church

Where did we get the idea that spiritual maturity can be achieved apart from an integration of the emotional aspects of who we are? Where did the subtle bias come from that values the spiritual over the physical, emotional, social, and intellectual components of who we are?

The answer is complex but can be summarized simply as the influence of a Greek philosopher named Plato, who lived several centuries before Christ. His influence through a variety of persons in church history (such as Augustine) continues to impact us today.

The unspoken message in many of our churches is: "The body is bad. The spirit is good." Somehow, a subtle message has filtered into our churches

> A subtle message has filtered into our churches that to be human, to be emotional, is somehow sinful — or at least less than spiritual.

that to be human, to be emotional, is somehow sinful — or at least less than spiritual. This comes far more from Platonism and Gnosticism than from Holy Scripture.[3]

Most people, when asked what it means to be formed in the image of God (Gen. 1:26–27; 5:1; 9:6; Ps. 8:5; Rom. 8:29; 1 Cor. 11:7; 15:49; Eph. 4:24; Col. 1:15; 3:11; 1 John 3:2), focus only on the spiritual. We think of modeling our lives after Jesus in areas such as prayer, reading the Word, serving others, tithing, and worship.

The only problem is that we are more than spiritual beings. God made us whole people, in his image (see Gen. 1:27). That includes physical, spiritual, emotional, intellectual, and social dimensions. Consider the following illustration:

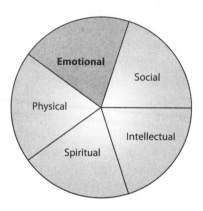

Denying any aspect of what it means to be a fully human person made in the image of God carries with it catastrophic, long-term consequences — in our relationship with God, with others, and with ourselves. Unhealthy developments are inevitable when we fail to understand ourselves as whole people, made in the image of our Creator God. For some reason, however, we exalt the spiritual over the other critical aspects that make us human. We ignore:

- The physical: "Who has time to exercise or to eat right or to get enough rest? Our body will perish anyway."
- The social: "Don't worry about those friendships. Kingdom work is what really counts. You'll have time to be with friends in heaven."
- The intellectual: "Be wary of developing your mind or studying too much. You'll end up with no heart for God."

- The emotional: "It seems that when you get in touch with your feelings, you become more confused and not closer to God. Be wary of psychologizing the gospel!"

Over time, this unbiblical paradigm led to an attitude that regarded feelings and emotions as being opposed to the Spirit (especially anger, which became one of the seven deadly sins, despite the "be angry and sin not" and "be slow to anger" teachings of Scripture). In the minds of many today, the repression of feelings and emotions has been elevated to the status of Spirit or virtue. Denying anger, ignoring pain, skipping over depression, running from loneliness, avoiding confusing doubts, and turning off our sexuality has become a way of working out our spiritual lives.

In *The Cry of the Soul*, Dan Allender and Tremper Longman III describe why it is so important to listen to, and deal with, our emotions:

> Over time, this unbiblical paradigm led to an attitude that regarded feelings and emotions as being opposed to the Spirit.

> Ignoring our emotions is turning our back on reality; listening to our emotions ushers us into reality. And reality is where we meet God ... *Emotions are the language of the soul.* They are the cry that gives the heart a voice ... However, we often turn a deaf ear — through emotional denial, distortion, or disengagement. We strain out anything disturbing in order to gain tenuous control of our inner world. We are frightened and ashamed of what leaks into our consciousness. *In neglecting our intense emotions, we are false to ourselves and lose a wonderful opportunity to know God.* We forget that change comes through brutal honesty and vulnerability before God.[4] (emphasis added)

Jesus — Both God and Human

Throughout my Christian journey, I continually affirmed the God named Jesus. The problem was that I rarely considered the human named Jesus — or my own humanity, for that matter. My journal entries and written prayers confirmed that the Jesus I worshiped and followed for the first seventeen years of my Christian life was not very human. Nor was I.

One of the early church heresies was Docetism, the belief that Christ had not really become human because of the insurmountable difference between the divine and human world. Some, therefore, thought that Jesus only seemed to be human but actually never gave up his divine nature or essence.[5] While I did not intellectually believe such an unbiblical notion, my life in God did not back up what I professed. I ignored my human limits and ran myself ragged to do more and more for God. I regarded negative feelings such as anger or depression as anti-God and avoided them. I fell into the trap of living as if spending all day in prayer and the Word was more spiritual than cleaning the house, doing laundry, or taking care of the kids.

At the Council of Chalcedon in AD 451, church leaders declared that Jesus was fully God and fully human — a widespread, historical interpretation of Scripture that I also affirm. The Council affirmed that God visited our planet as the Word became flesh and lived among us (John 1:14). They defined the relationship of Christ's two natures as related but without confusion and division.[6]

The Jesus I worshiped, by contrast, was very much God and much less a man. I never understood, for example, the account of Jesus in the garden of Gethsemane. Here we see a fully human Jesus — emotionally depressed, mentally confused, and spiritually overwhelmed. He is being pushed to the edge of his human limits. We see him falling to the ground "and being in anguish, he prayed more earnestly, and his sweat was like drops of blood falling to the ground" (Luke 22:44). I had never considered Jesus to be under this kind of emotional stress. It is no wonder some people reject this fleshly, human, struggling, not always one-hundred-percent-sure-of-the-will-of-God Jesus.[7]

> What concerns me is the many Christian leaders I meet who are emotionally numb.

What concerns me is the many Christian leaders I meet who are emotionally numb. They are not aware of anything that could be called feelings or emotions. When you ask them how they feel, they may use the term "I feel" but in actuality they report only a statement of fact or a statement of what they think. Their emotions are in a deep freeze. Their body language, tone of voice, and facial expressions indicate that emotions are present, but they are not aware enough even to identify them. Even for those of us who are the "touchy-feely" types, we are often unaware of the depths behind our emotions.

Our Exterior and Interior World

I was an imposter and didn't know it. Like most people in Christian leadership, I worked hard at being a committed and loving Christian. I labored at serving people, forgiving people, humbling myself, and being joyful. The problem was that I was miserable much of the time and unable to admit this to anyone, including myself.

I couldn't bring myself to believe it. My inner world was not in sync with my exterior behavior. The Bible has a word for this gap, a term that Jesus repeatedly used toward religious leaders: *hypocrisy* (see Matt. 23). It literally means "playacting."[8] What is particularly frightening is that this "playacting" is often taught and expected in our churches. The result is that huge numbers of people are totally unaware of the dichotomy between their exterior and interior worlds.

By exterior world, I am referring to the people to whom we relate and the things going on around us. Our interior world is that which is going on inside us. This interior represents what we feel, value, honor, esteem, love, hate, fear, and believe in.

To truly love God with all our heart, soul, mind, and strength requires that we know not only God but also our interior — the nature of our own heart, soul, and mind. Understanding that world of feelings, thoughts, desires, and hopes with all its richness and complexity is hard work. It also takes time — lots of it.

My great dilemma for years was that I was too busy building a bigger church and looking for ways to have a greater impact. Who had time for this kind of morbid introspection? Wouldn't reflection time slow down the work of God? What good for God and others could come out of tapping into my unconscious or unidentified wishes, fears, and hopes?

It is painful to take our first deep, long look inside of our hearts. Jeremiah 17:9 affirms: "The heart is more deceitful than all else and is desperately sick; who can understand it?" (NASB). The reason for this goes back to the fall of Adam and Eve in the garden of Eden. Since then, we have been divided from God, separated from one another, and split internally within ourselves. Shame, loneliness, hiding, self-protection, lying, and other emotional pain mark Adam and Eve in Genesis 3. These responses also characterize every one of us who has lived ever since.

> It takes work, energy, inconvenience, time, courage, solitude, and a solid understanding of the grace of God in the gospel to grow in Christlikeness.

For this reason, it takes work, energy, inconvenience, time, courage, solitude, and a solid understanding of the grace of God in the gospel to grow in Christlikeness. This further contributes, I believe, to why the frontier of emotional health has largely been ignored in most discipleship, spiritual formation, and mentoring models in our churches and seminaries. For this we are paying the heavy price of stunted growth and shallow disciples in our churches.

A Second "Conversion"

I had originally thought that my conversion to Jesus Christ as Savior and Lord was my total surrender. Little did I know that it was only the beginning.

I had been a Christian for seventeen years when I discovered the link between spiritual and emotional health. I felt like a baby beginning to crawl all over again. I was using muscles I didn't know I had and exploring internal territory that had, hitherto, remained untouched.

I had ignored the emotional component in my seeking after God. The spiritual-discipleship approaches of the churches and ministries that had shaped my faith had no language, theology, or training to help me in this area. It didn't matter how many books I read or seminars I attended in the other areas — physical, social, intellectual, spiritual. It didn't matter how many years passed, whether seventeen or another fifty. I would remain an emotional infant until the emotional component of God's image in me was exposed and transformed through Jesus Christ. The spiritual foundation on which I had built my life (and had taught others) was cracked. There was no hiding it from those closest to me.

My failure to pay attention to God and to what was going on inside me caused me to miss many gifts. God lovingly came and spoke to me through my pain, inviting me to change, but I just wasn't listening.

I never expected God to meet me through such feelings as sadness, depression, and anger.

When I finally discovered the link between emotional and spiritual health, a Copernican revolution began for me — and it was frightening. I felt as if I were betraying the forefathers who had shaped me spiritually. The ship had left the shore, and I did not know where it was going. But there was no going back.

This revolutionary paradigm — that emotional health and spiritual maturity are inseparable — was a new frontier for my own personal development and for New Life Fellowship Church. It affected every area of church life, from sermons to leadership meetings to classes to mentoring to board meetings to Sunday worship. Those things too often considered small and imperfect slowly began to take center stage over the big and the spectacular. The fruit was breathtaking.

I rediscovered, on an entirely new level, the love and grace of God. My spiritual life with Jesus blossomed. Geri and I began investing in our marriage as the first priority of our discipleship. We soon overflowed with a newfound taste of joy and delight in our relationship. We tasted God's glory and committed ourselves to lead the church out of the quality of our marriage. The last fifteen years have been a dream come true. Our four daughters, along with all of New Life, naturally benefited from a father and senior leader who was walking more authentically and honestly. And finally, the joy of leading and serving Christ returned. I learned that Jesus' yoke is easy and his burden is light — even for pastors and leaders! There really is another way to do leadership in the church.

> This revolutionary paradigm — that emotional health and spiritual maturity are inseparable — was a new frontier for my own personal development and for New Life Fellowship Church.

Do all Christians have the courage to allow the power of the gospel to penetrate the emotional component of our persons, to expose untouched areas of our iceberg? Do I? Do you? Turn the page and see where you stand personally on the biblical qualities that indicate whether you are an emotional infant, child, adolescent, or adult.

Chapter 4

Inventory of Spiritual/ Emotional Maturity

The previous chapter outlined a biblical basis for a new paradigm of discipleship, one that includes emotional maturity. The following diagnostic is a simple tool to help you determine your level of spiritual/ emotional maturity.

Take a few minutes to reflect on this simple inventory to get a sense of where you are as a disciple of Jesus Christ, both as an individual and at church. It will help you get a sense of whether your discipleship has touched the emotional components of your life and, if so, how much. It will challenge you to consider whether you are an emotional infant, child, adolescent, or adult. Each stage of emotional maturity is described at the end of the chapter.

> Take a moment to pray that God will guide your responses and to remember that you can afford to be honest because he loves you dearly without condition.

It's natural to feel uneasy or uncomfortable about some of the questions. Try to be as vulnerable and open as possible. Remember that the inventory will reveal nothing about you that is news to God. Take a moment to pray that God will guide your responses and to remember that you can afford to be honest because he loves you dearly without condition.

Because of space limitations, I have kept Part A to a minimum. I suspect most readers will be far more familiar with the concepts indicated in Part A than in Part B.

Emotional/Spiritual Health Inventory

Please answer these questions as honestly as possible.
Use the scoring method as indicated.

Not very true *Sometimes true* *Mostly true* *Very true*

PART A: General Formation and Discipleship

1. I feel confident of my adoption as God's son/daughter and rarely, if ever, question his acceptance of me.   1 2 3 4

2. I love to worship God by myself as well as with others.   1 2 3 4

3. I spend regular quality time in the Word of God and in prayer.   1 2 3 4

4. I sense the unique ways God has gifted me individually and am actively using my spiritual gifts for his service.   1 2 3 4

5. I am a vital participant in a community with other believers.   1 2 3 4

6. It is clear that my money, gifts, time, and abilities are completely at God's disposal and not my own.   1 2 3 4

7. I consistently integrate my faith in the marketplace and the world.   1 2 3 4

TOTAL _____

PART B: Emotional Components of Discipleship

Principle 1: Look beneath the Surface

1. It's easy for me to identify what I am feeling inside (Luke 19:41 – 44; John 11:33 – 35).   1 2 3 4

2. I am willing to explore previously unknown or unacceptable parts of myself, allowing Christ to transform me more fully (Rom. 7:21 – 25; Col. 3:5 – 17).   1 2 3 4

3. I enjoy being alone in quiet reflection with God and myself (Mark 1:35; Luke 6:12).   1 2 3 4

4. I can share freely about my emotions, sexuality, joy, and pain (Ps. 22; Prov. 5:18 – 19; Luke 10:21).   1 2 3 4

5. I am able to experience and deal with anger in a way that leads to growth in others and myself (Eph. 4:25 – 32).   1 2 3 4

6. I am honest with myself (and a few significant others) about the feelings, beliefs, doubts, pains, and hurts beneath the surface of my life (Ps. 73; 88; Jer. 20:7 – 18).   1 2 3 4

TOTAL _____

	Not very true	Sometimes true	Mostly true	Very true

Principle 2: Break the Power of the Past

7. I resolve conflict in a clear, direct, and respectful way, not what I might have learned growing up in my family, such as painful putdowns, avoidance, escalating tensions, or going to a third party rather than to the person directly (Matt. 18:15 – 18).

    1 2 3 4

8. I am intentional at working through the impact of significant "earthquake" events that shaped my present, such as the death of a family member, an unexpected pregnancy, divorce, addiction, or major financial disaster (Gen. 50:20; Ps. 51).

    1 2 3 4

9. I am able to thank God for all my past life experiences, seeing how he has used them to uniquely shape me into who I am (Gen. 50:20; Rom. 8:28 – 30).

    1 2 3 4

10. I can see how certain "generational sins" have been passed down to me through my family history, including character flaws, lies, secrets, ways of coping with pain, and unhealthy tendencies in relating to others (Ex. 20:5; cf. Gen. 20:2; 26:7; 27:19; 37:1 – 33).

    1 2 3 4

11. I don't need approval from others to feel good about myself (Prov. 29:25; Gal. 1:10).

    1 2 3 4

12. I take responsibility and ownership for my past life rather than blame others (John 5:5 – 7).

    1 2 3 4

TOTAL _____

Principle 3: Live in Brokenness and Vulnerability

13. I often admit when I'm wrong, readily asking forgiveness from others (Matt. 5:23 – 24).

    1 2 3 4

14. I am able to speak freely about my weaknesses, failures, and mistakes (2 Cor. 12:7 – 12).

    1 2 3 4

15. Others would easily describe me as approachable, gentle, open, and transparent (Gal. 5:22 – 23; 1 Cor. 13:1 – 6).

    1 2 3 4

16. Those close to me would say that I am not easily offended or hurt (Matt. 5:39 – 42, 1 Cor. 13:5).

    1 2 3 4

17. I am consistently open to hearing and applying constructive criticism and feedback that others might have for me (Prov. 10:17; 17:10; 25:12).

    1 2 3 4

18. I am rarely judgmental or critical of others (Matt. 7:1 – 5).

    1 2 3 4

19. Others would say that I am slow to speak, quick to listen, and good at seeing things from their perspective (James 1:19 – 20).

    1 2 3 4

TOTAL _____

	Not very true	Sometimes true	Mostly true	Very true

Principle 4: Receive the Gift of Limits

20. I've never been accused of "trying to do it all" or of biting off more than I could chew (Matt. 4:1–11).   1 2 3 4

21. I am regularly able to say "no" to requests and opportunities rather than risk overextending myself (Mark 6:30–32).   1 2 3 4

22. I recognize the different situations where my unique, God-given personality can be either a help or hindrance in responding appropriately (Ps. 139; Rom. 12:3; 1 Peter 4:10).   1 2 3 4

23. It's easy for me to distinguish the difference between when to help carry someone else's burden (Gal 6:2) and when to let it go so they can carry their own burden (Gal. 6:5).   1 2 3 4

24. I have a good sense of my emotional, relational, physical, and spiritual capacities, intentionally pulling back to rest and fill my "gas tank" again (Mark 1:21–39).   1 2 3 4

25. Those close to me would say that I am good at balancing family, rest, work, and play in a biblical way (Ex. 20:8).   1 2 3 4

TOTAL ____

Principle 5: Embrace Grieving and Loss

26. I openly admit my losses and disappointments (Ps. 3; 5).   1 2 3 4

27. When I go through a disappointment or a loss, I reflect on how I'm feeling rather than pretend that nothing is wrong (2 Sam. 1:4, 17–27; Ps. 51:1–17).   1 2 3 4

28. I take time to grieve my losses as David (Ps. 69) and Jesus did (Matt. 26:39; John 11:35; 12:27).   1 2 3 4

29. People who are in great pain and sorrow tend to seek me out because it's clear to them that I am in touch with the losses and sorrows in my own life (2 Cor 1:3–7).   1 2 3 4

30. I am able to cry and experience depression or sadness, explore the reasons behind it, and allow God to work in me through it (Ps. 42; Matt. 26:36–46).   1 2 3 4

TOTAL ____

Principle 6: Make Incarnation Your Model for Loving Well

31. I am regularly able to enter into other people's world and feelings, connecting deeply with them and taking time to imagine what it feels like to live in their shoes (John 1:1–14; 2 Cor. 8:9; Phil. 2:3–5).   1 2 3 4

	Not very true	Sometimes true	Mostly true	Very true
32. People close to me would describe me as a responsive listener (Prov. 10:19; 29:11; James 1:19).	1	2	3	4
33. When I confront someone who has hurt or wronged me, I speak more in the first person ("I" and "me") about how I am feeling rather than speak in blaming tones ("you" or "they") about what was done (Prov. 25:11; Eph. 4:29 – 32).	1	2	3	4
34. I have little interest in judging other people or quickly giving opinions about them (Matt. 7:1 – 5).	1	2	3	4
35. People would describe me as someone who makes "loving well" my number one aim (John 13:34 – 35; 1 Cor. 13).	1	2	3	4

TOTAL ____

Principle 7: Slow Down to Lead with Integrity

	Not very true	Sometimes true	Mostly true	Very true
36. I spend sufficient time alone *with* God to sustain my work *for* God.	1	2	3	4
37. I regularly take a 24-hour period each week for Sabbath-keeping — to stop, to rest, to delight, and to contemplate God.	1	2	3	4
38. Those closest to me would say that my marriage and children take priority over church ministry and others.	1	2	3	4
39. I am not afraid to ask difficult, uncomfortable questions, to myself or to others, when needed.	1	2	3	4
40. I do not divide my leadership into sacred/secular categories. I treat the executive/planning functions of leadership as meaningful as prayer and preparing sermons.	1	2	3	4

TOTAL ____

Inventory Results

For each group of questions on pages 61 – 64:

- Add your answers to get the total for that group. Write your totals on the top portion of page 66, as the sample on the next page illustrates.
- Next, plot your answers and connect the dots to create a graph on the middle portion of page 66, again following the sample on page 65.
- Finally, see pages 66–67 for interpretations of your level of emotional health in each area. What patterns do you discern?

SAMPLE

	Questions	Total

Part A

General Formation and Discipleship   1 – 7   <u>24</u>/28

Part B

Principle 1 – **Look beneath the Surface**   1 – 6   <u>20</u>/24

Principle 2 – **Break the Power of the Past**   7 – 12   <u>11</u>/24

Principle 3 – **Live in Brokenness and Vulnerability**   13 – 19   <u>12</u>/28

Principle 4 – **Receive the Gift of Limits**   20 – 25   <u>14</u>/24

Principle 5 – **Embrace Grieving and Loss**   26 – 30   <u>16</u>/20

Principle 6 – **Make Incarnation Your Model for Loving Well**   31 – 35   <u>14</u>/20

Principle 7 – **Slow Down to Lead with Integrity**   36 – 40   <u>15</u>/20

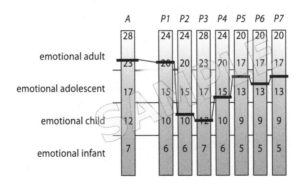

	Questions	Total
Part A		
General Formation and Discipleship	1 – 7	___/28

Part B

	Questions	Total
*Principle 1 – **Look beneath the Surface***	1 – 6	___/24
*Principle 2 – **Break the Power of the Past***	7 – 12	___/24
*Principle 3 – **Live in Brokenness and Vulnerability***	13 – 19	___/28
*Principle 4 – **Receive the Gift of Limits***	20 – 25	___/24
*Principle 5 – **Embrace Grieving and Loss***	26 – 30	___/20
*Principle 6 – **Make Incarnation Your Model for Loving Well***	31 – 35	___/20
*Principle 7 – **Slow Down to Lead with Integrity***	36 – 40	___/20

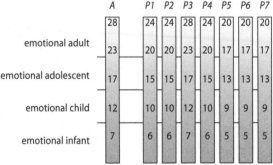

	A	P1	P2	P3	P4	P5	P6	P7
emotional adult	28 23	24 20	24 20	28 23	24 20	20 17	20 17	20 17
emotional adolescent	17	15	15	17	15	13	13	13
emotional child	12	10	10	12	10	9	9	9
emotional infant	7	6	6	7	6	5	5	5

Interpretation Guide: Levels of Emotional Maturity[1]

Emotional infant. I look for other people to take care of me emotionally and spiritually. I often have difficulty in describing and experiencing my feelings in healthy ways and rarely enter the emotional world of others. I am consistently driven by a need for instant gratification, often using others as objects to meet my needs. People sometimes perceive me as inconsiderate and insensitive. I am uncomfortable with silence or being alone. When trials, hardships, or difficulties come, I want to quit God and the Christian life. I sometimes experience God at church and when I am with other Christians, but rarely when I am at work or home.

Emotional child. When life is going my way, I am content. However, as soon as disappointment or stress enter the picture, I quickly unravel inside. I often take things personally, interpreting disagreements or criticism as a personal offense. When I don't get my way, I often complain, throw an emotional tantrum, withdraw, manipulate, drag my feet, become sarcastic, or take revenge. I often end up living off the spirituality of other people because I am so overloaded and distracted. My prayer life is primarily talking to God, telling him what to do and how to fix my problems. Prayer is a duty, not a delight.

Emotional adolescent. I don't like it when others question me. I often make quick judgments and interpretations of people's behavior. I withhold forgiveness to those who sin against me, avoiding or cutting them off when they do something to hurt me. I subconsciously keep records on the love I give out. I have trouble really listening to another person's pain, disappointments, or needs without becoming preoccupied with myself. I sometimes find myself too busy to spend adequate time nourishing my spiritual life. I attend church and serve others but enjoy few delights in Christ. My Christian life is still primarily about doing, not being with him. Prayer continues to be mostly me talking with little silence, solitude, or listening to God.

Emotional adult. I respect and love others without having to change them or becoming judgmental. I value people for who they are, not for what they can give me or how they behave. I take responsibility for my own thoughts, feelings, goals, and actions. I can state my own beliefs and values to those who disagree with me — without becoming adversarial. I am able to accurately self-assess my limits, strengths, and weaknesses. I am deeply convinced that I am absolutely loved by Christ and, as a result, do not look to others to tell me I'm okay. I am able to integrate *doing* for God and *being* with him (Mary and Martha). My Christian life has moved beyond simply serving Christ to loving him and enjoying communion with him.

Part 3

Seven Principles of an Emotionally Healthy Church

CHAPTER 5

PRINCIPLE 1:
LOOK BENEATH THE SURFACE

I n emotionally healthy churches, people take a deep, hard look inside their hearts, asking, "What is going on that Jesus Christ is trying to change?" They understand that a person's life is like an iceberg, with the vast majority of who we are lying deep beneath the surface. They invite God to bring to their awareness and to transform those beneath-the-surface layers that hinder them from becoming more like Jesus Christ.

Looking Everywhere but Inside

In *The Poisonwood Bible*, a gripping novel by Barbara Kingsolver,[1] Nathan Price is determined and zealous to bring the Word of God to the Belgian Congo. The year is 1959, and the African country is in political turmoil. Threats of war do not scare Nathan. During his three-month stint in World War II, he had lost many buddies on the famous Bataan Death March. He had returned from war determined to save more souls than had perished on Bataan Peninsula. His command of and commitment to Scripture is unambiguous and uncompromising.

Despite his wife's reservations about the hardships of such an undertaking, Nathan takes her and their four children into Africa to settle in a small village. *The Poisonwood Bible* unfolds the tragic story of the Price family over the next thirty years through the alternating points of view of Orleanna Price and their four children. All end up being victims of Nathan's failure to take a long, hard look inside himself.

What is most striking in reading this novel is the preacher's lack of awareness—with himself, with his wife, with each of his four children, and with the Congolese people themselves. He never takes the time to listen, for example, to the native people's fears of baptizing their children in the river because it is crocodile infested. Nor does it ever occur to him that in the native language, where meaning hangs on intonation, that a certain term means "glorious, precious, and dear" when spoken properly but "poisonwood tree" when spoken with his American accent. At the end of each sermon he shouts, "Jesus is poisonwood!" a mispronunciation of "Jesus is glorious!" As his daughter Adah says at the novel's end, "I am born of a man who believed he could tell nothing but the truth, while he set down for all time the Poisonwood Bible."

Going beyond the harsh living conditions and the incendiary political situation, the real story traces this family's survival of their father's Christianity (and bad theology) that keeps him from being an effective lover of people. He is a machine. He is on autopilot for God. He is zealous to win souls and to do God's work.

Orleanna had been trained to submit obediently to her husband and is powerless to ease the pain of their new life in the Congo. She is unable to protect her children from the consequences of his behavior. Eventually, the youngest dies because Nathan is unwilling to evacuate her, regardless of the pleas of his family and other missionaries. By the end of the book, Nathan's marriage tragically disintegrates while he continues to carry on God's work. That was their pattern all along as Orleanna laments early in their marriage:

> Nathan habitually overlooked me. If I complained about our life, he would chew his dinner while looking tactfully away, as one might ignore a child who has deliberately broken her dolls and then whines that she has nothing to play with. *To save my sanity, I learned to pad around hardship in soft slippers and try to remark on its good points.*[2] (emphasis added)

Nathan is an extreme case, and the author of this novel has been accused of taking cheap shots at the church.[3] The problem is that I relate to Nathan. In fact, many of us in Christian leadership can relate more than we might like to admit to his failure to take a deep, hard look inside. His lack of inner depth reveals itself over time, especially as his children grow up and his wife finally leaves him. Tragically, he will not look inside even when his external world falls apart.

Beneath the Surface of the Iceberg

The real horror is how easy it is to remain in a comfortable, distorted illusion about our lives. Something may not be true, but we become so used to it that it feels right. Others who live and work closely with us can usually pick up some of our inconsistencies and defensive maneuvers. Few, however, have the courage and skill to point them out in a mature, loving way.

For the first fifteen years of my life as a Christian (and the previous nineteen apart from Jesus), I rarely took time to look deeply into (as the psalmist alternately calls it) my interior, my heart, my depths, or my soul. Yes, I spent an average of two to three hours a day with God in prayer, Scripture reading, listening to God's voice, confessing my sins, and journaling. Regularly, I spent a day in prayer and fasting at a Jesuit retreat center near my house—and I still do.

Even so, I can confidently say that I was not taking a deep, hard look inside. I wanted to preach powerful, anointed messages. My focus was upward and outward—growing our church, reaching people for Christ, raising up leaders, buying a building. But an authentic relationship with Christ also takes us into the depths—the shadows, the strongholds and the darkness deep within our own souls that must be purged. Surrendering to this inward and downward journey is difficult and painful.

> For the first fifteen years of my life as a Christian, I rarely took time to look deeply into (as the psalmist alternately calls it) my interior, my heart, my depths, or my soul.

After one of our small groups ended badly a number of years ago, Geri and I took one of the group leaders out for coffee. Our goal was to provide loving feedback about his unhelpful behavior during our meetings. It was an important mentoring moment. After Geri shared a few specifics, I became uncomfortable and oversensitive to his feelings. Perhaps he was feeling bad. So I began to lie, telling him how great it was to have him in our group. Geri looked at me incredulously. We had an interesting conversation later that evening! A few days later I apologized to the leader for not loving and respecting him enough to be truthful. Interestingly, he appreciated it.

Humans, Like Icebergs, Have Many Deep Layers below the Surface.

How could something like this happen? Wasn't I giving God an opportunity to examine my heart?

My great concern with the call to a "deep, hard look inside" is that most people believe they are already doing so. I did for years. The sad reality, however, was that I had not allowed Jesus to transform the deep layers underneath the surface. My life was like an iceberg, with many weightier portions hidden under the surface of the waterline. Even though they were beneath the surface, they dominated my visible life.

As the photo above illustrates, only about 10 percent of an iceberg is visible at the surface. That is the part of our lives of which we are consciously aware. Note, however, that the *Titanic* sank because it collided with a section of the submerged 90 percent of an iceberg. Most leaders shipwreck or live inconsistent lives because of forces and motivations beneath the surface of their lives, which they have never even considered.

Solomon said it well, "Above all else, guard your heart, for everything you do flows from it" (Prov. 4:23). It can be frightening to trust

God's grace and love in order to look deeply inside. Most of us do not know how. I know I didn't.

The late Dag Hammarskjöld, once the secretary general of the United Nations, suggested that we have become adept at exploring outer space, but we have not developed similar skills in exploring our own personal inner spaces. He wrote, "The longest journey of any person is the journey inward."[4] Most of us feel much more equipped to manipulate objects, control situations, and "do" things than to take that very long journey inward.

> It can be frightening to trust God's grace and love in order to look deeply inside.

Painful Honesty

What I am talking about requires unmasked, painful honesty. Truth, Jesus said, will set us free (John 8:32). Honesty requires fully looking at the whole truth. I call it "unmasked" because, like Adam and Eve in the garden of Eden, we would rather hide from truth and protect ourselves than come out exposed, naked to God. This has been a problem of sin since the beginning of time (Gen. 3:1 – 19). It is "painful" because, while the truth ultimately liberates us and brings us closer to God, initially it is something we would rather avoid.

One of the struggles in C. S. Lewis's Chronicles of Narnia, *Voyage of the Dawn Treader*, pictures what it feels like to follow God in taking a deep, hard look inside. Eustace, a young boy, becomes a big, ugly dragon as a consequence of being selfish, stubborn, and unbelieving. Now he wants to change and go back to being a little boy, but he can't do it himself. Eventually the great lion Aslan (representing Jesus) appears to him and leads him to a beautiful well to bathe. But since he is a dragon, he can't enter the well.

Aslan tells him to undress. Eustace remembers that he can cast off his skin like a snake. He takes off a layer by himself, dropping it to the ground, feeling better. Then as he moves to the pool, he realizes there is yet another hard, rough, scaly layer still on him. Frustrated, in pain, and longing to get into that beautiful bath, he asks himself, "How many skins do I have to take off?"

After three layers, he gives up, realizing he cannot do it. Aslan then says, "You will have to let me undress you." To which Eustace replies:

> *I was afraid of his claws, I can tell you, but I was pretty nearly desperate now. So I just lay flat down on my back and let him do it.* The very first tear he made was so deep that *I thought it had gone right into my heart.* And when he began pulling the skin off, it hurt worse than anything I've ever felt ... Well, he peeled the beastly stuff right off — just as I thought I'd done it myself the other three times, only they hadn't hurt — and there it was lying on the grass: only ever so much thicker, and darker, and more knobbly looking than the others had been. And there was I as smooth and soft ... Then he caught hold of me ... and threw me into the water. It smarted like anything but only for a moment. After that it became perfectly delicious and as soon as I started swimming and splashing I found that all the pain had gone from my arm. And then I saw why. I'd turned into a boy again ... *After a bit the lion took me out and dressed me ... with his paws ... in these new clothes I'm wearing.*[5] (emphasis added)

C. S. Lewis describes it well: To go in this radically new direction feels as if God's claws are going so deeply into us that they are cutting into our very heart.

Pain — The Stimulus to Go beneath the Surface

God often uses pain to get us to change. My experience working with people as a pastor over the last twenty-two years has convinced me that unless there is sufficient discomfort and anguish, most will not do the hard work to take a deep, honest look inside. This seems especially to apply to men and women in midlife. It has rightly been said, "We change our behavior when the pain of staying the same becomes greater than the pain of changing."[6]

Through pain, we often develop a hunger for change. We say: "I must have it. Something must break through in my life. I cannot continue 'playing church.'" On the one hand, I have seen young people training to be leaders respond brilliantly and experience significant changes in their lives when exposed to a discipleship model that integrates emotional and spiritual maturity. They are not in a crisis nor in extreme pain, yet they mature and grow. On the other hand, it seems to take a crisis or extreme distress to get others of us, who have been in the church a long time, to change.

There seems to be a direct correlation between the intensity level of distress in people and the level of intensity they will bring to taking an honest look beneath the surface of their lives. I know many people who have begun this new journey in their Christian life, but only after their spouse refused to go along with the present way of doing life, or after they find themselves in the grips of an addiction or moral failure. Others will only do the hard work to begin looking inside when there is little other choice, as in my case. Sometimes a church division or crisis will drive a congregation's leadership to corporately look inside their hearts in a newer, deeper way.

> I have seen young people training to be leaders respond brilliantly and experience significant changes in their lives when exposed to a discipleship model that integrates emotional and spiritual maturity.

In short, if I am willing to go deep beneath the iceberg of my present self, I have to be willing to suffer the discomfort and pain that is part of pioneering new parts of myself—the good, the bad, and the ugly. People in emotionally healthy churches do these regular heart checkups as they hit walls in their journey with Christ.

Two years ago I found myself stuck, once again, at New Life. As a result, I had to look beneath the surface of my life. It was a painful process.

I began to see how much of my life was driven by external validation, that other people would tell me I was okay. Volunteers and staff didn't move toward me after difficult conversations about their performance. They distanced themselves from me.

I sometimes avoided meetings I knew would be hard. I preferred to not ask difficult questions or to speak up when something was clearly wrong.

I discovered that the skills to lead in this next phase were not hard to learn. The real difficulty was making the time, thinking carefully "before the Lord," summoning the courage to have difficult conversations, and following through all the way.

What exactly does it look like to go beneath the surface for yourself and with others? There are four primary components:

1. Awareness of what you are feeling and doing
2. Asking the "why" (motivation) question
3. Linking the gospel and emotional health
4. Getting rid of our "glittering images"

1. Developing an Awareness of What I Am Feeling and Doing

Jesus had a full sense of what he was about. On the evening before his arrest, he took the role of a slave and began washing the twelve disciples' feet, even Judas's. The apostle John notes, "Jesus knew that the Father had put all things under his power, and that he had come from God and was returning to God" (John 13:3). He was deeply aware of who he was and what he was doing. This enabled him to break from the expectations of his family, friends, disciples, and the wider religious culture and to follow God's unique plan for his life. In the same way, a deep awareness of what we are feeling and doing gives us the courage to begin doing life differently (and hopefully more in line with God's will) and developing new, healthier relational patterns.

> Scripture portrays Jesus as one who had intense, raw, emotional experiences and was able to express his emotions in unashamed, unembarrassed freedom to others.

Scripture portrays Jesus as one who had intense, raw, emotional experiences and was able to express his emotions in unashamed, unembarrassed freedom to others. He did not repress or project his feelings onto others. Instead, we read of Jesus responsibly experiencing the full range of human emotion throughout his earthly ministry. In today's language, he would be considered *emotionally intelligent*, a term popularized by Daniel Goleman.[7]

- He was greatly disturbed in spirit and deeply moved (John 11:33).
- He wept at the gravesite of Lazarus and over the city of Jerusalem (John 11:33–36; Luke 19:41).
- He was angry with his disciples (Mark 10:14).

- He was furious at the crass commercialism in the temple (John 2:13–17).
- He showed astonishment (Matt. 8:10).
- He had an emotional longing to be with the twelve apostles (Luke 22:15).
- He had compassion for widows, lepers, and blind men (Matt. 20:34; Mark 1:41; Luke 7:13).[8]

Jesus lived that way with himself but also with others. Readers can observe countless incidents in the Gospels of Jesus' discerning what was below the surface of people's actions and then acting accordingly. For example, after cleansing the temple early in his ministry, Jesus did not entrust himself to those believing in him for his miracles (John 2:23–25) because he knew what was in the iceberg of their hearts. We consistently see Jesus seeking to take people, especially his small community of twelve, below the surface in order to transform them from the inside out.

For some of us, a simple but helpful exercise to begin the process of paying attention to our emotions is to listen to our physical body's reactions in situations — a knot in the stomach, a tension headache, teeth grinding, hands or arms clenched, palms becoming sweaty, neck tightening, foot tapping, or insomnia. Ask yourself, "What might my body be telling me about my feelings right now?" For others of us, becoming aware of our physical bodies is a big step in the right direction. Take time to pause in silence before the Lord to listen to him each day. You may be very surprised on what he reveals from your iceberg.

Bill's Hollow Ministry

Many church leaders function on autopilot, too busy to take the time to contemplate what is really going on inside and outside of their lives. Most Christians, I am afraid, are self-conscious but not self-aware. We are more worried about what other people think of us than about wrestling with our feelings and motivations.

Bill became a Christian through a campus ministry in college and then graduated from a leading conservative seminary. Returning to New York City, his hometown, he took up a job as a computer consultant to "tent-make"

> Most Christians, I am afraid, are self-conscious but not self-aware.

so that he could bring his teaching and administrative gifts to bear in the church. By this time he was married with four small children.

The problem with Bill, however, was that with all his gifts and abilities, his ministry was hollow. Something was missing. He taught the Bible and led a small group, but he did not share himself.

When he was initially asked about the importance of being aware of his feelings, he reacted strongly, "You can't depend on your emotions. You can't let your emotions run you!"

One day Bill's world collapsed when his wife told him she wasn't sure she loved him anymore and that she was unhappy in the marriage. "All of a sudden, I felt like my life was one big open wound," he says.

Both he and his wife, Ashley, had experienced a lot of pain growing up, especially from the kids in the neighborhood. "I was very lonely during my childhood," says Bill. "Whenever I came outside to join the kids in the neighborhood games, they'd run away. I wanted friendship, but all I got was rejection." As a result he developed a hard, exterior shell, allowing few people to really know the "real" Bill.

"I didn't share what was going on inside of me with anyone else, including my wife," Bill admits. The pain in his marriage finally forced him to reconsider what might be below the surface in his life and why he was so flat emotionally.

In time, Bill came to grips with the reality that he had built brick walls to divide himself from the pain and turmoil of the outside world. "I performed like a well-oiled engine that was encircled by concrete," he says. "I was like an emotional black hole, with emotional signals getting lost in my highly rational thinking."

What has been most impressive for me in watching Bill is how his ministry with others has broadened and deepened along with the inner work he has been doing on his own iceberg below the surface.

His teaching and leadership in the small group over the next couple of years stunned the members of his group. Bill became transparent and open, sharing his weaknesses and struggles to walk out the Scriptures at home, at work, and in the church. Instead of fixing other people's problems, he now related to them on a peer level as another broken human being. Much of his judgmentalism dissolved.

The metamorphosis was so significant that one married man in his forties from his small group recently said to me, "I figure if God can change a guy like Bill and make him the kind of humble, godly man he is today, it's okay for me to give it a try too."

Awareness versus Self-Absorbed Introspection

Some of us feel that it's greedy and selfish to pay attention to what we are feeling and doing. In my early years as a Christian, I heard few, if any, discussions about the awareness of feelings as one key to discipleship. There are many other important issues related to maturing in Christ, but an honest examination of our emotions and feelings is central. This inward look is not to encourage a self-absorbed introspection that feeds narcissism. The ultimate purpose is to allow the gospel to transform all of you—both above and below the iceberg. The end result will be that you and I will be better lovers of God and other people.

Without doing the work of becoming aware of your feelings and actions, along with their impact on others, it is scarcely possible to enter deeply into the life experiences of other people. How can you enter someone else's world when you have not entered your own?

When I read the story of Job's ranting before God, Jeremiah's anguish about God's word burning "in [his] heart like a fire" (Jer. 20:9), Moses' struggles in the wilderness, or David's anguish of feeling abandoned by God, I observe leaders of God in the brutal, painful honesty of wrestling with emotions, feelings, and the realities going on around them. That's why their life stories speak to us so powerfully.

> How can you enter someone else's world when you have not entered your own?

2. Asking the "Why?" or "What's Going On?" Question

In meeting the Samaritan woman at the well (John 4), Jesus consistently confronted her with the "why" question. He went below the surface of her actions to wrestle with bigger life-related questions: Why are you at the well in the middle of the day? Because you are ashamed? Why are you running from husband to husband? What void are you trying to fill?

She attempted to sidetrack the conversation, keeping it above the surface. So she asked Jesus about the best place to worship (John 4:20). Jesus, instead, called her to examine her life beneath the surface of the iceberg and consider her immoral lifestyle as an indication of her insatiable thirst for love.

Jesus also pointed others to "why" questions. He once corrected the Pharisees and teachers of the law, who were passionate about external behavior issues but were not doing the difficult work on their insides. "Again Jesus called the crowd to him and said, 'Listen to me, everyone, and understand this. Nothing outside you can defile you by going into you. Rather, it is what comes out of you that defiles you'" (Mark 7:14 – 15). Jesus tried to reorient the people to the "why's" of their behavior, to their motivations, and to their hearts (7:21).

Once I begin to be aware of what I am doing, how I am feeling, and how it is impacting others, I need to ask myself the difficult "why" questions. For example:

- Why am I always in a hurry? Why am I so impatient?
- Why am I so anxious?
- Why am I overly concerned that others tell me I'm okay as a leader or teacher?
- Why am I so devastated that Malita told me after church on Sunday that she didn't get anything out of my sermon?
- Why do I dread this meeting today at 2:00 p.m.? Why am I so flooded with fear?
- Why am I over-concerned that I succeed in my ministry?
- Why do I avoid confronting difficult people at church?
- Why do I have a need to immediately return all phone calls and emails? Or why do I avoid returning certain phone calls, emails, or text messages?

Wrestling with these types of probing questions about the depths of our hearts is, to say the least, an uncomfortable experience!

In the past I spent hours with God, beseeching him to bless my agenda and help me achieve my goals. However, now I spend much more time with God, praying for his will to be done, not my own. And I rest in his love, wrestling with the "why" questions in an open, receptive way before him.

It takes courage to ask myself: What am I really feeling in this situation? What might be going on here? King Saul was unaware of what was going on inside of him. His "doing" for God did not flow from his "being" with God. We see him repeatedly blind to his jealousy, fear, hatred, and anger. Unlike David, we don't observe him cultivating his relationship with God. Eventually, his life choices destroy him (see 1 Sam. 17 – 31).

Blaise Pascal wrote: "All men's miseries derive from not being able to sit in a quiet room alone."[9] This involves taking my feelings and thoughts about why I am feeling this way and bringing them honestly to God. I ask, "What does this represent? What might you, God, be saying to me? What do I learn about myself in this? About life? About other people?"

3. Linking the Gospel and Emotional Health

Once we begin looking beneath the surface of our lives (and that of others), we encounter an abyss of ugliness that can be frightening. As one wise Puritan said, "If God ever allowed us to see more than 1 percent of our sin, we would fall down dead!"

Going beneath the surface of our lives can feel as if we are walking on a tightrope fifty feet above ground without a safety net below. The gospel is like the safety net. It alone gives us the foundation to take the risk of stepping out onto the tightrope in order to explore our inner depths.

The gospel says you are more sinful and flawed than you ever dared believe, yet you are more accepted and loved than you ever dared hope because Jesus lived and died in your place. A great exchange takes place when we put our trust and faith in Jesus Christ. "God made him who had no sin to be sin for us, so that in him we might become the righteousness of God" (2 Cor. 5:21).

Our church holds regular Leadership Community Meetings for small group leaders, ministry leaders, and their apprentices. We spent two years together studying and integrating the gospel and emotional health. We studied Galatians and Romans in depth, followed by a segment on personal formation (e.g., limits, family mapping, boundaries, etc.) and a segment on skill development. Out of those years have sprung a number of other venues where we relate the gospel to emotional health, such as small groups and classes.

Let me share the stories of two people in their own words to illustrate how the gospel intersects with looking beneath the surface.

John

I love the gospel. Before I really understood it, although I had been a Christian over ten years, I hid from my wretchedness, my defenses, my broken parts, even the abuse I suffered as a young boy. In fact, I was always in hiding — hiding my anger, jealousy, arrogance, conditional love, selfishness, brokenness, mistakes, weaknesses, and inadequacies. These things were unacceptable in the Christian circles I knew, especially among leaders. I didn't think I would be liked or allowed to lead if I was not strong and together. Who would then listen to me? I had to prove myself capable, strong, perfect, and confident.

In the past, when I had a hard time loving others, I would begin to despair. "I'm a Christian and I'm not able to do the very essence of Christianity," I'd lament. Then I realized I was depending on my self-righteousness to recommend myself to God's favor. I unconsciously had what people call the daisy mentality — "He loves me, he loves me not, he loves me, he loves me not" — based on how well I was doing in my spiritual life.

> I am perfectly loved and accepted by God because of Christ's life, death, and resurrection for me ... I can come out of hiding!

Through a study of Galatians, I received a fresh and powerful grasp of the gospel of Jesus Christ. I don't have to prove myself to anyone — which is how I was unconsciously living my life. I am perfectly loved and accepted by God because of Christ's life, death, and resurrection for me. I love knowing that I have nothing left to prove because I am valued, loved, and accepted by Jesus Christ. I can actually be free to be me. I can come out of hiding!

I am free to fail, to share my weaknesses and needs with others, to admit I too have struggles, to admit "I was wrong, please forgive me," to recognize that I don't have all the answers, and to relax, not thinking I have to take care of everyone else.

Susan

In the years I have been at New Life, I have been helped to embrace the truth of the gospel and to be freed by it. One lovely image that affected me as a woman is of Christ's righteousness being like a glorious wedding dress that makes me utterly gorgeous to God. As I meditated on the truth that because of Christ's sacrifice I really am "holy in his sight, without blemish and free from accusation" (Col. 1:22), the truth of the gospel began to touch me on an emotional level.

I remember coming across a passage in Isaiah 62:5 that says, "As a bridegroom rejoices over his bride, so will your God rejoice over you." My first thought was, "Can this really be true? Does God really love me this passionately?" Then I remembered that because of Christ's death, I have become his beloved. The crucifixion is the foundation on which I can base my whole life. I am utterly loved to the core of my being. My God adores me in a personal, emotional sense.

The knowledge that I stand before God as his beloved, because of Christ, has freed me to explore some of the disturbing and dark aspects of who I am. I can face the truth that I have a problem with control, for example. I can reflect about it honestly, pray about it, and talk to others about it freely. I know that my control issues and all my other sin patterns don't surprise God or threaten my standing with him. He calls me his beloved because of Christ's flawlessness, not mine. Because Christ's righteousness is the foundation of my self-concept, I no longer have to "keep up appearances" with myself, God, or anyone else.

> The knowledge that I stand before God as his beloved, because of Christ, has freed me to explore some of the disturbing and dark aspects of who I am.

God's Free Grace

In his preface to his commentary on Galatians, Martin Luther said that the gospel can never be taught, urged, and repeated enough. A Christian's righteousness, he wrote, is utterly separate from anything we do. "For we do nothing for it, and we give nothing for it—we only receive and allow another to work—that is, God."[10]

God has given us the gospel to create a safe environment to look beneath the surface. I don't have to prove that I'm lovable or valuable. I don't have to be right all the time. I can be vulnerable and be myself even if others don't accept me. I can even take risks and fail. Why? Because God sees the 90 percent of the iceberg hidden below the surface, and he utterly, totally loves me in Christ.

We have a saying we often use at New Life Fellowship: "You can be yourself because there is nothing left to prove." The determining factor in our relationship with God is not our past or present record or performance. It is Jesus' past record that has been credited to my account as a gift.

A revelation of God's free grace gives us the courage to face the painful truth about ourselves. As we step out onto the tightrope of discovering the unpleasant things about ourselves, we have a safety net below—the gospel of Jesus Christ.

The Upcoming Wedding—A Symptom of Spiritual Immaturity

Jill and Joshua had attended New Life for only a few months. As medical students, they eloped, but then made plans to be formally married a few months later back in Joshua's home state. His mother and father wanted a big reception and so invested a lot of energy in securing a catering hall, picking the menu, deciding on the colors of the flowers and decorations, and setting up table-seating arrangements. Then the catering hall sent Jill and Joshua a bill for ten thousand dollars, half the cost for the evening reception.

Jill approached my wife and me, struggling with the situation. "We thought they were paying for the reception. It was their idea. We never really talked about who would pay for it, though. My future mother-in-law chose all the colors for the tables and decorations. I really like red, but she chose pink," she complained with a smile. "She already thinks I'm strong-willed. In fact, part of the problem is that she is Chinese, and I am Indonesian. Pray for me. Pray for her."

The problem, however, was that this situation required a spirituality that integrates emotional maturity. Prayer is important, but there were many other issues for Jill. Up to this point, she was looking only at the visible 10 percent of the iceberg. What would it mean to mentor her through a process that looks beneath the surface?

Geri and I sat down with Jill and challenged her about the lack of honesty around the wedding. She was not being authentic, and her honesty needed to be worked out in three general areas:

First, Jill needed to be honest with herself. What was really going on inside of her? What did she really feel, want, desire? It was deep below the surface, and part of our time with them focused on helping her recognize it.

Second, we invited her to be honest with her fiancée, Joshua. She hadn't spoken honestly with him either. What did she really want and feel? And what were his feelings and desires? We took time to teach them some basic speaking and listening skills to facilitate this process.

Third, we asked questions and explored with them why it is they eloped without their parents' blessing or knowledge. Was the elopement only a symptom of larger issues beneath the surface? Our goal was to help them walk in their parents' shoes. We wanted to serve as an objective third party to help them understand what a legitimate boundary was, and was not, when it came to their parents' involvement.

It was also important to review scriptural teaching about the nature of marriage and what it means to honor our parents, love well, and build a healthy marriage.

We encouraged them to really listen to Joshua's parents, inviting them to share *their* feelings, and disappointments, about the elopement. Imagine Jill and Joshua mature enough, broken enough to not get defensive as they listen to his parents' dreams for the wedding.

They moved out of New York City shortly after these conversations so our time with them was cut short. But given the time, we would have sketched a family genogram with each of them to help them understand how their past family situations have impacted the present (to be introduced in the next chapter). We did recommend resources such as *Boundaries* by Henry Cloud and John Townsend.[11]

There is no other way for Jill to love her mother-in-law, her husband, and herself well unless she allows God into the depth of her person and wrestles with the complexities of the situation. This is the messy, wonderful way God conforms us to the image of his Son (Gal. 4:19).

In fact, a church committed to emotional health is a messy place. "Skeletons" come out of the closet, and we face problems and tensions honestly and directly rather than ignoring them, hoping or pretending they will somehow go away.

4. Getting Rid of the "Glittering Image"

Susan Howatch's novel *Glittering Images* traces the spiritual journey of Charles Ashworth, an ordained PhD priest in the Church of England. He is a widower in his late thirties, loyal to the church, upstanding, respected, and well loved by those in authority over him. He is also a friend with the Archbishop of Canterbury, who has asked that he go to the parish of Bishop Jardine of Starbridge to investigate a possibility of moral failure or scandal in Jardine's life.

What Charles discovers about the charismatic, fifty-eight-year-old Jardine and Jardine's relationship both with his sickly wife and with his wife's beautiful assistant, Lyle Christie, raises serious suspicions. It turns out that Jardine is living a double life and has convinced himself that his double life is God's will. Because his wife is sickly and has no desire for sex, he has married Lyle Christie. He has done this with his wife's full blessing. The bishop and Lyle have lived secretly as husband and wife for five years before Charles Ashworth shows up.

The complexity and the stress of the situation push Charles over the edge, and he ends up hopelessly drunk at the front door of a powerfully discerning spiritual director named Father Darrow.

During his times with Father Darrow, Charles slowly begins to dig beneath the surface of the public person he presents to everyone, the "glittering image" that is always proper and polished. He begins to become aware and acknowledge the negative feelings he has denied and the inconsistencies in his behavior with people. For example, he attempted to kiss the beautiful assistant, Lyle, within twenty-four hours of meeting her. He lies in the name of God to get God's work done. He secretly drinks too much to numb his pain.

When he is asked by Darrow to be brutally honest and to go beneath the iceberg in his life, he replies that he can't. Others, such as his father, have "got a colossal hold over me," he explains.

"Who's 'me'?" says Darrow.

"My true self ... the glittering image."

"Ah yes," says Darrow, "and of course that's the only Charles Ashworth that the world's allowed to see, but you're out of the world now, aren't you, and I'm different from everyone else because I know there are two of you. I'm becoming interested in this other self of yours, the self nobody meets. I'd like to help him come out from behind the glittering image and set down this appalling burden which has been tormenting him for so long."

"He can't come out."

"Why not?"

"You wouldn't like him or approve of him."[12]

Charles Ashworth finally acknowledges and confronts the stranglehold the glittering image has over his life. He begins to realize the enormous amount of time and energy he has devoted to win everyone's liking and approval. With the help of a mature spiritual counselor, he begins to excavate the roots of why and how he created that false person living in a "glittering image."

A critical process in becoming free involves looking at the story of his life with some objectivity and how it has contributed to the person he is today. He also benefits significantly by having a trusted friend to do it with him.

That influence of previous experiences leads us to our next chapter, the second principle of an emotionally healthy church: breaking the negative power of their past on their present.

CHAPTER 6

PRINCIPLE 2:
BREAK THE POWER OF THE PAST

In emotionally healthy churches, people understand how their past affects their present ability to love Christ and others. They've realized from Scripture and life that an intricate, complex relationship exists between the kind of person they are today and their past. Numerous external forces may shape us, but the family we have grown up in is the primary and, except in rare instances, the most powerful system that will shape and influence who we are.

Standing Naked before an Icy Wind

I can remember reading *Glittering Images* (see previous chapter) as if it were yesterday. A good friend had recommended the book after I shared with him what I was struggling with. I was beginning for the first time to wonder about whether my past with my family had impacted the person I am today.

After Charles Ashworth finds himself under the spiritual direction of Father Darrow, he confronts, for the first time, his relationship with his own father and the dynamics of his family growing up.

Charles had spent his whole life seeking approval and praise from his father. He was sent to the best schools, given the finest opportunities in middle-class England at the time, and repeatedly warned to live a "good straight decent life." Morality, duty, efficiency, and uprightness were stressed.

When a major family argument occurs between Charles and his father, the father physically strikes his wife across her face. Later, Charles offers to take his mother away, but she is horrified. She then verbalizes an unspoken family commandment that has ruled their family. "What would everyone think?" she asks. "We've got to keep up appearances. Nobody must ever know."

Then she cries again but finally says, "We're really very happy—he's just a little difficult now and then."

By this point Charles has his doctorate in theology, is a professor, and serves as assistant to the Archbishop of Canterbury. He is rising up the ladder in the Church of England of the 1930s. But he is utterly oblivious to the ways the maladaptive patterns of his past are preventing him from living a free life today in Christ.

Charles both hates and loves his father. He despises himself for not loving his dad. He is conflicted, even desperate, for acceptance and love. After finally opening up this area of his life, he describes the experience as "standing naked before an icy wind."

When I finished reading the novel, I began to journal about significant events in my own childhood that may have affected me today. I reflected on my relationship with my mom and dad, my brothers and sister. I wondered, for the first time with any seriousness, whether there might be any emotional baggage or unfinished business from my past affecting my leadership or marriage today.

I was "standing naked before an icy wind." Everything in me wanted to escape this new path of dying with Jesus.

Up to this point my theology dictated I was a new creation in Christ. The old had passed away (2 Cor. 5:17). Christ had transformed my life in so many ways when I became a Christian at age nineteen. As Paul explains in Romans, Galatians, and Ephesians, the moment I became a Christian, God declared me pardoned, legally set free from the penalty of my sins. I was adopted with all the rights of an heir and given the Holy Spirit to enable me to live out that wonderful adoption.

> I wondered, for the first time with any seriousness, whether there might be any emotional baggage or unfinished business from my past affecting my leadership or marriage today.

Yes, my childhood had its ups and downs. Didn't everyone's? I certainly wasn't in the business of blaming my parents for all my problems in life. If we came from a family where we felt loved, a home that was reasonably stable and whole, it generally takes much longer to be willing to identify ways of behaving and relating that do not belong in the family of God.

My attitude was, "I'm in the family of God. The Scriptures are my authority, and now the path of my life is guided by a commitment to the lordship of Jesus and the advancement of his kingdom work on earth. I am doing so many things differently from my nuclear and extended family. For example, I don't hold grudges against people. I do dishes. I 'help' with the kids. I actively follow Jesus. I work with people from a variety of cultures."

This list is actually superficial. I was blind to how much my family in which I grew up dominated my daily life, especially my leading of the spiritual family called New Life Fellowship.

The truth, however, was that I was resistant to go back over my story and reflect on how my past might be negatively affecting my ability to love people.

I hear often, "Pete, perhaps my family was not perfect, but it sure was a lot more together than most others." That is not the issue. Every family has been damaged.

Like everyone in the human race, I too descended from the family tree of Adam and Eve. Their intent after they disobeyed God was to shield and defend themselves from God and each other. This aim of protecting ourselves from God and others manifests in different ways—controlling, fixing, fear, withdrawing, ignoring, denying, pacifying, or loneliness, anxiety, frustration, resentment, blaming, and more.

Geri and I and Our Marriage

I will never forget the first time Geri and I did a very simple genogram, examining our marriage in light of our parents. A genogram is a way of drawing a family tree that looks at information about family members and their relationships over two to three generations.[1] Each of us described our father, our mother, and a few general characteristics of their relationship. How did they resolve conflict? Express anger? Understand gender roles? Parent their children? What issues of emotional intensity deeply affected them, such as a childhood death of a parent or the extended medical needs of a sibling?

Geri and I sat back on our chairs and looked at each other, saying with our facial expression something we could not deny after almost ten years of marriage. There were positive contributions into our lives from our parents' marriages, but we were surprised by the unhealthy patterns we had also unconsciously picked up. Wherever Christ was in our lives, he had not transformed, at least in any substantial way, the way we related as a married couple.

We realized the life-transforming power of Jesus had not touched large areas of our lives — areas this book is calling "emotional health." Because we did not have the ability to integrate and apply Scripture to so many areas of life beyond a surface level, it became readily apparent why people whom we were mentoring at church were not breaking through in many areas of their lives either. All the Bible studies, the prayer and fasting, or the small group meetings would not change that. I felt like an emperor without any clothes.

> Christ had not transformed, at least in any substantial way, the way we related as a married couple.

Yes, it was true. Because of the model I had set, New Life Fellowship was one mile wide but only one inch deep. My resistance to look at my own past and wrestle with its implications for the present had deeply impacted the entire church family. Few people were looking at issues beneath the surface. Even fewer were looking at their past to see how it impacted their present. Looking back, I am embarrassed at how I could have deluded myself that an immature leader (me) with an immature marriage (us) could possibly grow a mature congregation.

King David and His Family

The Ten Commandments contain a provocative statement by God: "For I, the LORD your God, am a jealous God, punishing the children for the sin of the parents to the third and fourth generation of those who hate me, but showing love to a thousand generations of those who love me and keep my commandments" (Ex. 20:5–6). Fortunately, the positive legacies of our family last a thousand generations! Yet God

Solomon "heart not fully devoted"
—sexual addiction

Rehoboam "heart evil before God"
—sexual sin

Uriah

other wives / concubines

Bathsheba

300 concubines

700 wives

Solomon

60 concubines

18 wives

Rehoboam

Eglah

Abital

Haggith

Maacah

Tamar

Absalom

Absalom "hated Amnon"
—adultery
—murder
—sexual sin

Ahinoam

Amnon

Abigail

Amnon "David's firstborn"
—sexual sin

Michal

David "man after God's heart"
—adultery
—murder
—sexual sin

David

Jesse

Division

Southern Kingdom

Northern Kingdom

LEGEND

□ = male

○ = female

David, Solomon, and Generational Sin

says clearly that the sins of those who go before us are passed on to our children, our grandchildren, our great-grandchildren, and even our great-great-grandchildren. Assuming each of my children marries and has children and that continues on, and that each of them lives to eighty years of age, the influence of my choices today will continue until at least AD 2318! That's four generations.

If you examine the genogram on page 94, you cannot help but notice that at least three themes surface from generation to generation. The first relates to having a heart for God. David's father, Jesse, was clearly a believer, although we don't know much about him (1 Sam. 16). David is referred to as "a man after God's own heart." He stands out as one of the towering spiritual figures in Scripture, writing magnificent psalms and music for God's people to use in worship for generations. However, around the age of forty or fifty, he compromises his relationship with God, committing adultery with the beautiful Bathsheba and murdering her husband. Rather than immediately repenting, he chooses a path of cover-up, lies, and abuse of power. This decision reverberates through his family and the nation of Israel for generations. His character appears slowly to erode, probably over a number of years, leading finally to a monumental collapse of judgment.

His son Solomon does build a temple for God, but his heart is described as not fully devoted to God. He mixes worship of the God of Israel with the gods of the nations around him. By the third generation this decline in spirituality reaches the bottom. Solomon's son Rehoboam ignores the God of Israel and engages in idolatry and detestable practices of other nations.

A second theme of sexual sin is also prominent in the genogram. Like the pagan kings of the ancient Near East, David collects wives. He also commits adultery with Bathsheba. His oldest son, Amnon, rapes his half sister Tamar and disgraces her forever. This is followed by his son Solomon, who carries further the sexual sins of his father, accumulating seven hundred wives and three hundred concubines. In turn, Solomon's son Rehoboam has eighteen wives and sixty concubines (2 Chron. 11:21). This was a common way to form political alliances in the ancient Near East, but it was also an act of rebellion against God's commands (Deut. 17:17).

Third, family division and sibling rivalry are also intensive with each generation. David has some tensions with his brothers (1 Sam. 16–17). One of his sons, Absalom, murders his brother Amnon in revenge for raping his sister. The family is terribly divided as a result. Eventually, Absalom grows bitter and proclaims himself king, conquering Jerusalem and setting out to kill his own father. Civil war breaks out, and twenty thousand men die (2 Sam. 18:7).

Solomon's son Rehoboam carries this pattern even further as his family disintegrates. Finally, the once-united twelve tribes of Israel split apart into a northern kingdom with ten tribes and a southern kingdom with two. It is now only a matter of time before the "split family" is carried into exile.

Sin is passed on from generation to generation. God allows this story to be recorded to sober us to take a deep, hard look inside (cf. 1 Cor. 10:6). The implication for church life is clear. It is impossible to help people break free from their past apart from understanding the families in which they grew up. Unless we grasp the power of the past on who we are in the present, we will inevitably replicate those patterns in relationships inside and outside the church.

> It is impossible to help people break free from their past apart from understanding the families in which they grew up.

Abraham, Isaac, and Jacob

Tracing the family history of Abraham, Isaac, and Jacob in Genesis 12–50 is another powerful example of generational blessing and sinful patterns being passed on. The blessings are so significant that they reach to us today! Few readers, however, note the sins and emotional immaturity that are also passed on from generation to generation.

Look at the adapted genogram on page 97.

Again, at least three common patterns are evident by looking at the genogram. First, a pattern of lying is evident in all four generations, increasing in intensity with each. Fearful, Abraham lies twice about Sarah, denying she is his wife. Rebecca and Isaac's marriage is also dominated by lies and trickery (Gen. 27). Their son Jacob then increases the level of manipulation by lying consistently to almost everyone with whom he is in relationship. In fact, his very name means "deceiver." By the fourth generation, ten of Jacob's sons fake the death of their younger brother Joseph. They go through all the motions of a wake, funeral, and time of mourning to maintain such a lie.

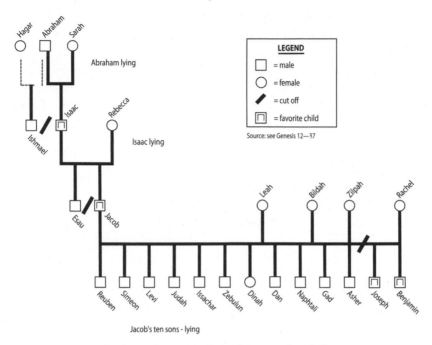

Abraham, Isaac, Jacob, and Generational Sin

A second common pattern is the way at least one parent in each generation has a "favorite" child. Abraham favors Ishmael, but Sarah wants him removed from the family. Isaac favors Esau and wants him to receive the powerful family blessing. And Jacob favors Joseph and later Benjamin, the youngest of his twelve sons.

Third, sibling rivalry and relational cutoff between brothers cause tensions that show up through three successive generations. The friction of Ishmael and Isaac eventually leads to them being cut off from one another. (This division and tension continues today in the Middle East tensions between Arabs and Jews.) Esau and Jacob become open enemies, once Jacob steals Esau's blessing. Finally, Joseph is cut off from his ten older brothers for most of his adult life.

1. Identifying How Your Family Shaped You

Part of our mentoring, leadership development, and discipleship at New Life Fellowship now includes leading people to do a simple genogram of the family in which God placed them. Except in rare instances, our family is the most powerful, influential group that has affected who we are today.

The following are the kinds of questions we ask to attempt to get beneath the surface at how the past might be impacting the present. We ask people to fill out the genogram through the eyes of their childhood (as if between eight and twelve years old).

1. Describe each family member with two or three adjectives (parents, caretakers, grandparents, siblings, children).
2. Describe your parents' (caretakers') and grandparents' marriages.
3. How was conflict handled in your extended family over two to three generations? Anger? Gender roles?
4. What were some generational themes (e.g., addictions, affairs, losses, abuse, divorce, depression, mental illness, abortions, children born out of wedlock, etc.)?
5. How well did your family do in talking about feelings?
6. How was sexuality talked or not talked about? What were the implied messages?
7. Were there any family "secrets" (such as a pregnancy out of wedlock, incest, or major financial scandal)?
8. What was considered "success" in your family?
9. How was money handled? Spirituality? Holidays? Relationships with extended family?
10. How did your family's ethnicity shape you?
11. Were there any heroes or heroines in the family? Scapegoats? "Losers"? Why?
12. What kinds of addictions, if any, existed in the family?
13. Were there traumatic losses in the past or present, such as sudden death, prolonged illnesses, stillbirths/miscarriages, bankruptcy, or divorce?

The exercise, while painful, leads us to ask three essential questions if we are going to lead others with integrity.

1. What one or two patterns might emerge of how your family has impacted who you are today?
2. In what area(s) might you be shaping your life and your ministry according to your past rather than Christ's family?
3. What "hard work of discipleship" might you have before you?

Each of the people we serve need to ask these hard questions to be free in Christ. That implies, however, that we as leaders/mentors are asking them first and leading out of the work of God in our own lives.

2. Discerning the Major Influences in Your Life

Outside of one's family of origin, it is important to consider what have been the other major influences in a person's life. For example, I was greatly influenced by evangelical Christianity in college. It gave me a rich appreciation for the grace of God in the gospel. At the same time, it reinforced an ascetic, active way of life characterized by Jesus' words, "Whoever wants to be my disciple must deny themselves and take up their cross daily and follow me" (Luke 9:23). It has taken me a long time to balance my theology with pieces that were missing.

Other people are shaped by significant events such as a divorce, sexual or emotional abuse, an addiction, a lengthy period of unemployment, a particular betrayal, or a friendship. The question to ask is, "What are a few events or people that have impacted who I am today and that will help me understand 'what makes me tick'?"

Let's look at some examples.

> What are a few events or people that have impacted who I am today and that will help me understand "what makes me tick"?

- Understanding that a turning point in her life was a certain rejection in junior high school was important for Joan's discipleship. It had led her into a life of drug addiction. Narcotics Anonymous played a large role in her recovery.
- Charlotte and Nathan were impacted by the trauma of war in their home countries. Panic attacks and outbursts of anger are just two of the outcomes of those experiences that had to be addressed in their discipleship.
- Pierre's experience of being wrongly classified as "mentally challenged" instead of dyslexic marked his self-image and caused him to struggle with trusting God and others.
- Ken's involvement as a soldier in Vietnam embittered him toward authority.

- Ron's fight to make it as a professional musician in the dog-eat-dog world of jazz contributed to his relentless perfectionism with himself and others. He battles to receive God's unconditional love and grace in Christ.
- Ted's twelve years at boarding school in New England make intimacy and family life difficult for him even now as a middle-aged adult.
- Kathy's autistic son has made her sensitive to families with a disabled member.

All the above people are in different places in their journey with Christ, but a critical part of growing into maturity in Christ needs to include addressing these issues and how they impact who they are in the present, both positively and negatively.

The New Birth into a Spiritual Family

It is most important to remember that while we may have a disposition toward a certain behavior, there is another possibility and reality for "reparenting" us: a spiritual family.

Jesus describes becoming a Christian as a new birth (see John 3:3–5). Picture yourself as an apple tree, but you would really like to bear peaches. You can be pruned, or someone can attach peaches with wire to your branches, but apples will keep coming. If you want peaches, you have to dig up the apple tree and plant a peach tree.

> Only by a direct intervention of God can you or I be changed. We require a complete change at the root or base of who we are.

New roots are needed for new fruit. All we do is modify the same tree when we make resolutions and commitments to pray more, go to church more consistently, or resolve to stop bad behavior. The root needs to be pulled up. A new tree is needed.

Jesus declares that only by a direct intervention of God can you or I be changed. We require a complete change at the root or base of who we are. The new birth can be described as the action of God whereby his very life and power are implanted in the base of your heart so the root is transformed. The seed then grows, blossoms, and produces fruit from this new supernatural seed. We receive a new heart, a new nature, and a new spirit (Ezek. 36:25–27).

The New, First Family of Jesus

The New Testament describes becoming a Christian as a spiritual rebirth through which we are adopted into a new family—the family of Jesus. Once this occurs, we become brothers and sisters to a worldwide family that crosses racial, cultural, economic, and gender barriers (see Gal. 3:28). We are birthed into a new family tree.

In one instance, Jesus' mother and brothers arrived at a house where he was teaching. When the crowd sitting around him told Jesus they were outside, he replied, " 'Who are my mother and my brothers?' ... Then he looked at those seated in a circle around him and said, 'Here are my mother and my brothers! Whoever does God's will is my brother and sister and mother' " (Mark 3:33–35).

The church, for the believer, is now our "first family."[2] In fact, family is the most significant metaphor used in Scripture to describe the church. Anderson and Guernsey say it best:

> The church is the new family of God ... Through spiritual rebirth, we each become brother or sister of Jesus Christ through adoption into the family of God. Consequently we are brother and sister to each other. Husbands and wives are first of all brother and sister in Jesus Christ before they are husband and wife. Sons and daughters are also brother and sister to their father and mother before they are sons and daughters.[3]

3. Becoming Reparented through the Church

Paul illustrates the gospel by using the profound truth of Roman adoption when a child was taken out of his previous status and placed in a new, permanent relationship with his new father. Old debts were canceled. The child was given absolute stability, assurance, security, and authority with his sonship. He or she could now use the term "Abba" ("Daddy"), a strong but intimate word used only by children with their father.

The critical factor that most significantly determines my new identity as a Christian is not the blood of my biological family but the blood of Jesus. We are given a new name (Christian), a new inheritance (freedom, glory, hope, resources a hundredfold), and new power (the Holy Spirit) to live in this new life. We become partakers of the divine nature (2 Peter 1:4), able to enjoy the absolute security and stability, freedom, intimacy, and confidence in prayer (Luke 11:5–13) of children in God's family. There exists a new dynamic in the life inside me, the life of Jesus.

Without hesitation, Jesus called men and women to himself over their biological families, saying that "anyone who loves their father or mother more than me is not worthy of me" (Matt. 10:37).

The New Testament world is unable to imagine living out healthy family life apart from the context of a healthy church life. The local church becomes the place where I am, in a very real sense, reparented.

> The local church becomes the place where I am, in a very real sense, reparented.

The question, then, is why isn't this happening? Why is it that most people in our churches seem to be radically different on one level from their neighbors — they pray, read the Bible, go to church, give money to church — but on another deeper level, they are similar?

The Importance of Process

To become a Christian and to be adopted into God's family with the new name of "Christian" does not erase the past. God does not give us amnesia or do emergency emotional/spiritual reconstructive surgery. God does forgive the past, but he does not erase it. We are given a new start, but we still come in as babies drinking milk and are expected to die daily to the parts of our lives that do not honor God and follow Jesus.

> To be adopted into God's family with the new name of "Christian" does not erase the past.

We all come into the family of Jesus with broken bones, wounds, and legs shot up in the war of life. God's intention is to heal our brokenness and patch up our wounds. He allows the scars and weakness to remain. We are then to go out and heal others as wounded healers.

Discipleship, then, must include honest reflection on the positive and negative impact of our family of origin as well as other major influences in our lives. This is hard work. Following Jesus is a process that takes time. But the extent to which we can go back and understand how it has shaped us will determine, to a large degree, our level of awareness and our ability to break destructive patterns, pass on constructive legacies, and grow in love toward God and people.

God's invitation is to welcome him into those areas so we might break free to live life as joyfully and freely as he intends.

Working through the Church

To work this principle through the discipleship of the church, as with all the others in an emotionally healthy church, the leaders must begin to integrate it into their own lives.

As the senior pastor, I had to begin to break the power of my past on the present by taking a serious look at it. This was then followed by our staff and board.

The words of an old Hasidic rabbi on his deathbed are true:

> When I was young, I set out to change the world. When I grew older, I perceived that this was too ambitious so I set out to change my state. This, too, I realized as I grew older was too ambitious, so I set out to change my town. When I realized I could not even do this, I tried to change my family. Now as an old man, I know that I should have started by changing myself. If I had started with myself, maybe then I would have succeeded in changing my family, the town, or even the state — and who knows, maybe even the world![4]

Doing a simple family genogram to help people begin to gain an awareness of critical issues of their past became part of our leadership development and mentoring. Personal formation classes and tracks became part of our equipping at the church.

When I preach through Scripture on a weekly basis, I constantly ask myself the question: "How does this differ from the way I was shaped, either in my family growing up or by other influences?" For example, in a series I did on James, one of the messages had to do with showing partiality (James 2:1–13). As part of my application of the text, I wrestled with how my family growing up ranked people. How did we view people with great wealth or education? People who were poor and uneducated? How did we talk or treat people from different cultures, races, ethnic groups, or political persuasions? How was this different from how God views the rich and poor, and people from different social classes, cultures, or races? Now that I am in Christ's family, what needs to change in the way I view and treat people? This self-examination models the proper role the Word of God is to play in our lives — reparenting us according to God's ways.

Our church does not simply offer small groups and seminars/workshops around Scripture, but also around emotionally healthy skills and relationships. We focus on topics, such as speaking and listening, handling anger constructively, fighting fairly (conflict resolution), faulty thinking, expectations and breaking the power of the past (genograms). We recognize that both spiritual practices (prayer, Bible study, giving, fellowship) and emotionally healthy practices (listening, speaking, fighting fairly) are essential if we are to mature in Christ.

We do a lot of work with married and premarital couples at New Life. Like many churches, we have blended families. In all the retreats, counseling, and married-couple small groups, the issue of how their family of origin has shaped their understanding of marriage and family is by far the most powerful and critical to address. We apply this principle equally to singles, especially as it relates to their relationships with the opposite sex.

At New Life we have people from all corners of Asia, Europe, Africa, and the Middle East, not to mention many other ethnic groups from the United States. Some come from a Hindu background, others Muslim or Buddhist. In our discipleship, it is important to help them become aware of how their families and cultures understand spoken and unspoken loyalties to parents. What debts do children have toward their parents and families? What positive legacies do they bring into our church family that we want to integrate? What are the parts of their ethnicity that contradict the call of the gospel (Matt. 10:21)?

Finally, when we discern the possible presence of a biological component (such as severe depression, bipolar disorder, substance or alcohol addiction, a severe personality disorder, or abuse), we get people in touch with professional counselors who are able to take them to a level of work on their past that is beyond our expertise as a local church.

4. Leading a Church Family Like My Own Family

It takes great courage to begin looking at your family of origin with any objectivity. I know it was extremely difficult for me to begin noting areas of weakness in our Italian-American family. Loyalties run deep, and to question unspoken family rules that go back generations felt like betrayal. Once I started this journey, however, it became obvious how my past was negatively impacting the church family I was leading. I found three major areas of impact.

First, throughout my childhood I had been, along with my brothers, the confidant of my mother, who seemed very unhappy in her life and marriage. I spent a lot of those years wanting nothing more than for her to find the joy and happiness my father seemed to have kept from her. It was almost as if I had been her loving parent, dreaming of a glorious time when she would be fully grown up and living happily ever after. I had internalized a sense of responsibility to fix all the family's problems.

I had become accustomed to that role; and when I became a pastor, it was a perfect fit. Now I would solve everyone else's difficulties and make their lives happier and better. I did learn a great deal about how to care for and listen to others through my family. But I knew little about how to allow others to care for me and how to do appropriate self-care.

Is it any wonder that I struggle with taking on too much responsibility for people in the church? When someone was having a personal difficulty in the church, I considered it my job "to make that person feel better." After becoming aware of how I did this for most of my childhood in my family growing up, it became much easier to change. I was also able to shift to a five-day, fifty-hour workweek, allowing the rest of the church to function in a more balanced way.[5]

Second, my dad, a baker, loved his work. He had been supporting his family since he was twelve when his father died suddenly during the Great Depression. His work was his life. He did it intensely and was one of the best Italian bakers in the New York City region. His goal for his four children was for us to get the education in college that he had been denied.

Thus he passed on to me a driving passion to work, to be the best, to "make it" in America. I too began my marriage with little time for leisure and family. My work also became my life. I think it would have been such whether I had gone into law, medicine, teaching, or church leadership. Wherever I went, I was following in his footsteps.

I passed on to the leadership of our church a driving passion to grow bigger, better, and stronger every year. The pace was exhausting, much like my dad's. I attributed it to the opportunities for God's kingdom to expand. In fact, I was seeking to find value and worth in the church, not in Christ. In the process I neglected the people closest to me — much like my father.

> I was seeking to find value and worth in the church, not in Christ.

Only through this commitment to reflect seriously on my own family history in light of the values of the gospel have I been able to get off the "fast track" of working and producing. Instead, slowly, I am learning to follow him in Sabbath rest, contentment, joy, peace (Rom. 14:17), prayer, and reflection.

Third, and perhaps most important, I carried with me into leadership a fear of being abandoned. I had struggled with rejection issues as a child, and thus it was embedded in the foundation of who I was. As a result, when people would be dissatisfied or leave the church (a common occurrence for any local church pastor), I would be devastated.

This power of the past in my life caused a great deal of chaos in the New Life family. Everyone's vision became my vision. I knew that if I spoke what I really wanted to do, some people would leave. For years, I fudged the truth. Worse, I rarely confronted people about their shortcomings, inadequacies, and sins — especially if I did not think they were receptive. I withdrew from conflict and would gladly take on myself all the blame for anything wrong, as long as everyone was happy and we could move on. My pattern bore the terrible fruit described in the opening chapter, when the Spanish pastor left us so divisively.

Conflict is a normal part of life. People tend to resolve it in one of five ways: escalating, withdrawing, attacking, assuming things are worse than reality, or triangling (i.e., instead of A going to B to resolve a conflict, A would talk to C to relieve the anxiety). In my family growing up, I tended to withdraw. I learned to internalize the conflicts and attempted to smooth over differences. I then carried that pattern into the church family, something Christ never intended.

> Conflict is a normal part of life … I learned to internalize the conflicts and attempted to smooth over differences.

At the same time, the family I grew up in, even though tarnished by the fall like all families, gave me a number of gifts for which I am eternally grateful. Through them God gave me a great sensitivity to other people. I am easily able to enter into their pain and express sincere compassion. I also learned how to comfort others in ways that are meaningful, not perfunctory. God also used my family to give me a love for reading and learning, a passion for people, and a love for music and the arts. God used all of my past—both positive and negative—to uniquely shape me into the way I serve and lead as a pastor today.

God commands us to honor our parents. As an adult, I believe this means we respect and thank God for them. I would broaden that to include thanking God for our story, for our past, and for the place, time, and family into which we were born.

Every one of us in leadership, however, must ask repeatedly before God the difficult question: How much of my family history might be running the church or ministry God has entrusted to my care?

5. Remember How Many People Are at the Table

I am often asked why it takes maturity in family issues to give pastoral leadership in a church, be it at a pastoral board meeting, in small group ministry, or in administrative issues. Part of the answer involves the idea of reparenting. No matter what kind of ministry you lead, most of the people involved will bring emotional "baggage" from their families. When you are in a meeting with six other people, there are really many other invisible people present at that table.

On the next page is a graph of a church board meeting as they deal with the difficult issue of whether to hire an executive assistant for you as the senior pastor. You have requested the board to authorize payment, beginning in two weeks. It is going to make their financial situation tight for the rest of the budget year because of other financial commitments the board has made. Each of the six people at the meeting come from a family system with certain unspoken rules, values, and ways of doing things.[6]

Joe, the chairman of the board, is a high-powered executive with a software company. He loves risk and has already decided in his head that he will work overtime to make up the budget difference. He won't say anything to the rest of the board about this decision, lest he come across as proud. His wife will not be happy, but then again she is always complaining.

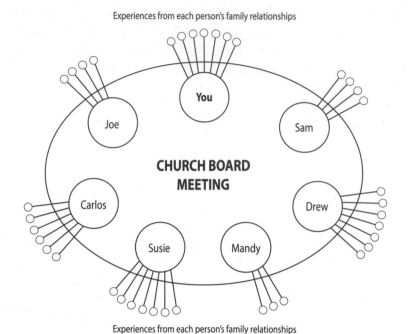

Experiences from each person's family relationships

You

Joe

Sam

CHURCH BOARD MEETING

Carlos

Drew

Susie

Mandy

Experiences from each person's family relationships

Seven Families Attend the Board Meeting

Carlos runs the struggling family hardware store in town. He thinks hiring an executive assistant for the senior pastor is reckless. He doesn't like the idea of the church not having money in the bank. He would never run his business that way. At the moment he is dealing with the possibility that Home Depot, a competitor, may move into town and bury his business. He has a pit in his stomach as he listens to the pastor. He is thinking of his father turning over in his grave at such recklessness. Fearful of being honest about his true feelings, Carlos suggests the group pray to get a word from God about this step of faith.

Jane has a law degree and is presently a stay-at-home mom with two children. She is embarrassed and ashamed. She is smoking almost a pack of cigarettes a day (nobody on the board knows), and her oldest son has recently quit high school. Isn't a board member's family supposed to be in order? She feels alone and needs all the friends she can get. "Whatever you want, Pastor," she advises confidently.

Mandy is a single professional, a pediatrician with a thriving practice. She now has three other doctors and five nurses working with her. They recently bought a building and are expanding their practice. She joined the board last year at the pastor's request, but she made it clear that, if she joined, she was expecting growth and change. A high risk-taker, Mandy is the first woman in her family to earn an advanced degree. She also won a sexual harassment lawsuit while in medical school. She is so glad the pastor is finally taking some initiative to get this church moving!

Drew functions in two roles. He is one of the associate pastors and also an elder. This puts him in a particularly powerful role. He likes that. He is perturbed, however, with the senior pastor, who he feels has had everything handed to him on a silver platter. Drew was raised by a single mom and was forced to work full time through college and seminary. He is angry that the pastor is getting another perk. He is sitting at the table thinking, "God, doesn't anything ever go my way? Why does this guy get everything he wants?"

Finally, Sam is sitting at the table angry. The pastor seemed to take a critical shot at single people during his sermon three weeks ago, especially single men. *Why didn't he have the courage to come to me face-to-face?* Sam wonders. Sam has not talked with the pastor about his feelings. Instead, he is thinking of leaving the church when summer comes. That is the way conflict was always dealt with in his family growing up. You "burn the bridge" and move on. Sam is not in favor of this expenditure of funds.

Needless to say, if you as the leader are going to bring mature spiritual leadership to that table, you need to consider at least three issues:

1. You need to take a deep, inside look at your own motivations, reasons, goals, plans, and family dynamics (past and present) as you take this next step of expansion. You need to know what you are feeling and thinking and then be able to express that clearly, directly, and respectfully to the board.
2. You must lead the members of the group in such a way that they can honestly express their concerns and feelings. A great deal is underneath the surface at this meeting. I would suggest the board wait on the decision and have a meeting where they talk about what is going on inside each one of them and in their relationships.

   The leader needs to give strong leadership and direction in that meeting. He needs to create a safe environment for them to share honestly. This will probably include the setting of certain guidelines and boundaries for the sharing. For example, each one should speak in the "I," not the "you" or "they." It may be appropriate to ask each group member, "What is the biggest thing impacting your life right now?" Then give each person ten minutes ... and pray for one another.

3. You need to meet with the board either one-on-one or as a group to serve them to mature in their walk with God. Remember that Jesus, while he led the multitudes, focused on three, then twelve, in whom he invested his life. I began by giving myself to the staff and elders of our church in order to bring about change in the larger church.

It can be overwhelming to think of the church as a place where all these individuals are bringing their entire family histories with them. This is, however, a fairly accurate picture. It also helps us understand the enormous complexity of leading a church.

The church will never mature beyond the leadership. Hopefully they can model and support a way of life where members of the body take the log out of their own eye first (Matt. 7:1–5) and work on their own material.

Gustavo and Nancy

New Life Fellowship took a major leap forward when the lights came on that there was a connection between the families we grew up in and our present Christian lives. I've seen innumerable people mature as a result of having taken a deep look at how their past has impacted their present. The following is one example.

Gustavo and Nancy had been in our small group for the last four years. Gustavo came from a family where his mother, the youngest of ten children, was determined that each of her three children would always be the top of the class, always be right, and always know the most. They would work as hard as possible through life. Sharing emotions and weakness was not allowed. If you had a setback or failure (such as falling off your bike), the response was, "Get up. Don't dwell on it and move on." There was little experience of feeling or sharing emotions.

Gustavo had also been falsely accused at his previous place of employment and lost his job in disgrace, causing him to trust others with his inner life even less

Imagine Gustavo's bringing this way of relating to the team he was leading at work and to the New Life small group. He was rarely vulnerable or weak, and the love and unity among his team was shallow. He taught the content of the Bible well, but he frequently carried resentments because he was so infrequently honest or assertive. He couldn't say no to the newest projects and expansion opportunities at work. He always said yes to new places to serve at church. He was exhausted.

Nancy, by contrast, came from a loving and giving family. She served alongside Gustavo, always expecting the best from themselves as a couple. She too was poor on setting limits and saying no. She was the oldest of three children and was drawn to her dad, identifying with his emotions of anger, guilt, worry, and hurt. She took on the responsibility to make sure her dad felt better. If he didn't seem to be recovering from his negative feelings, she felt guilty. She would try to rescue him, always trying to do "the right thing."

Nancy naturally transferred this way of relating to her marriage and into her service for Christ at church. She was the great caretaker, fixing everyone and making sure everyone was doing okay. There was little time for Nancy to feel, think, or be her own separate person. She was tired, exhausted, and lonely.

It wasn't until they looked honestly at how their past family systems impacted their present relationships at work, home, and church that they were able to make some dramatic changes. It was difficult initially because they both considered their families so well adjusted — especially when compared to many other people.

The sad truth, however, is that the family dynamics in which they grew up were more dominant in their daily lives than their new family — the family of Jesus. They lived as if their loyalty was first to their parents, then to God's kingdom.

It required a painful denial of self (Luke 9:23) for Gustavo to begin to express weakness to others at work and in our small group. It was a step of faith in God for him to begin to assert himself when something bothered him, to begin to feel and not function as a machine.

It also required a painful denial of self for Nancy to stop being responsible

> We need to make sure ... that we are dying to the right things.

for everyone at home or church, to let them each carry his or her own burdens (Gal. 6:5), and to recognize she doesn't have to meet everyone else's need. Taking care of herself as an infinitely valuable child of God, resting, and having "fun" caused her to feel (at least initially) as if she was betraying an unspoken, invisible rule from her family. For Nancy, it felt like a death.

The great news, however, is that in the kingdom of God, when we die, it brings life. We need to make sure, then, that we are dying to the right things.

6. We Never Finish Going Back

People sometimes say to me, "I've done a genogram. I know all about my family." When I hear this, I realize they don't get it. Each human being is infinitely complex and unique. We will never fully grasp the depth of our icebergs.

We don't go back to our pasts for the sake of going back. We go back when we are stuck, unable to go forward.

As I mentioned in the previous chapter, I found myself stuck in my leadership at New Life Fellowship Church. I couldn't seem to go forward. Our church was growing and I found myself avoiding a number of the large leadership issues. I avoided making personnel decisions, managing staff and key volunteers, writing job descriptions, taking time to plan for meetings, or following through on project details. I wanted someone else to do it.

"That's all administration," I told myself. "That's something that someone else should do. It's just not me." Truth be told, I was afraid of being misunderstood, losing friendships, or having people leave the church.

I finally reached a point of utter frustration. The inner workings of our staff were not reflecting the message I was preaching. The problem, however, was not them but me. The following are two of the family of origin dynamics I needed to break in order to move forward.

First, my mother's family has owned a business since 1923. It is marked by confusion and chaos. I simply assumed that I too did not have the executive skills to lead a large organization well. I never invested the time to learn. I was afraid I couldn't do it, so I always delegated that to others. I finally broke the script my family handed down to me and chose to learn the skills of leadership. This growing process has been wonderful, both for me and for our church.

Second, my Italian-American heritage places a high value on loyalty in the family. I remember my father sitting me down repeatedly to lecture me on the topic. So when it came time for me to let go of paid staff, it was difficult. I was betraying a family commandment that said, "Once you work for me, you are in the family. You are in for life!" Yet as senior pastor, my role, under our elder board, is to steward the church's resources in order to fulfill our mission. The fit of what the church needs and desires may change over time. Thus, our status as employees is subject to the direction God is taking the church, her resources, and the effectiveness of the staff person.

I have been working on my genogram now for fourteen years. And I continue to discover new things as I encounter new situations in my journey with Christ. Remember, you will never finish going back.

The next chapter takes us into what happens when anyone takes a deep, hard look inside himself or herself, especially inside your own story. You become vulnerable, transparent, and broken.

CHAPTER 7

PRINCIPLE 3: LIVE IN BROKENNESS AND VULNERABILITY

❧

In emotionally healthy churches, people live and lead out of brokenness and vulnerability. They understand that leadership in the
kingdom of God is from the bottom up, not a grasping, controlling, or
lording over others. It is leading out of failure and pain, questions and
struggles — a serving that lets go. It is a noticeably different way of life
from what is commonly modeled in the world and, unfortunately, in
many churches.

Storm-Proofing Your Life

Over Labor Day weekend in 1900, many residents on Galveston
Island, Texas, sought relief from the unusually hot September weather
by wading in the cool waters of the Gulf of Mexico. None suspected that
almost half the 37,000-resident population was about to die or become
instantly homeless, pummeled by the most deadly hurricane on record.
Yet later that fateful Saturday night, a hurricane with sustained winds
of more than 125 miles an hour and gusts up to 200 miles an hour
slammed directly into Galveston. In the language of today's National
Weather Service, what struck them would be called an extreme hurricane or X-storm.

The official forecast in the Galveston News had said, "Rain Saturday,
with high northerly winds; Sunday rain, followed by clearing." Yet suddenly the tempest appeared. By 1:00 p.m. the rains became a storm, by

5:00 p.m. winds reached hurricane velocity, and by 8:30 p.m., water levels stood as high as twenty feet above normal. During that short time frame, most of the island's homes became submerged, barely visible, or blown away.

Reports of a distant tropical storm had reached Galveston's weather bureau earlier that week, but they caused no great alarm. "The usual signs which herald the approach of hurricanes were not present in this case," wrote Isaac M. Cline, Galveston's veteran and senior weather bureau official. Isaac himself lived three blocks from the beach, but, tellingly, didn't see any need to evacuate his pregnant wife (who was drowned), his brother, or either family's children.

Why? Isaac Cline himself had predicted that no hurricane could seriously damage the city. "An absurd delusion" is how he had characterized the fear that any hurricane posed a serious danger to the burgeoning city of Galveston.

Based partly on Cline's expert opinion, Galveston had dismissed a proposal to erect a seawall, claiming it a needless, wasteful expense. As a result, many people in that beautiful city grew in confidence that they could withstand any storm. They never anticipated gusts of two hundred miles an hour that would be like thirty tons slamming against a house wall, crumbling it as if the timber were match sticks. They never anticipated waves fifty feet long and ten feet high with a static weight of eighty thousand pounds. These were waves with destructive power beyond measure. Moving at thirty miles an hour, they generated a forward momentum of two million pounds, powerful enough to dislodge strong artillery emplacements.[1] So many people were drowned that bodies washed back on shore for months. Isaac Cline, the weatherman, never anticipated a storm of this intensity.

In the same way that Isaac thought he had built a stable, well-anchored house that could withstand storms, so I too went to great lengths to prepare myself for leadership as best I could. I accumulated knowledge, skills, and experience from a vast array of Christian arenas. My hope was that no person, trial, difficulty, or circumstance would break me, regardless of the force of the hurricane. I sought to live in the reality

> My preparation left out ... brokenness and weakness. As a result, when the really big storms hit, I wasn't ready.

that the same power that raised Jesus from the dead was now in me (Eph. 1:19–23). I reminded myself that greater is he who is in me than he who is in the world (1 John 4:4). I prayed like David, "With your help I can advance against a troop; with my God I can scale a wall" (2 Sam. 22:30).

I was determined to remain stable, firm, consistent, and faithful. God had given me zeal, talents, and a lot of experience. I was going to be a warrior, a soldier, and a servant for God and his church.

My preparation, however, both formal and informal, left out one of *the most important biblical pathways* to grow in spiritual authority and leadership—brokenness and weakness. As a result, when the really big storms hit, I wasn't ready.

1. Developing a Theology of Weakness

After Adam and Eve sin in the garden of Eden, God lovingly pursues them and makes a way for them to come back to him and to one another. He goes out looking for them, "walking in the garden in the cool of the day" (Gen. 3:8). He provides them with clothes to cover their shame (3:21). He promises that one day he will overcome the serpent whose lies they believed (3:15).

Because of the fall, God also builds the curse of "thorns and thistles" (Gen. 3:18) into the fabric of life as we know it even today. God explains how all of life, from that point forward, will be painful, difficult, and frustrating. He breaks the curse down into two primary areas: our relationships (3:16) and our work (3:17–19).

Relationships, God says, will now be marked by pain and misunderstandings. We will be disappointed with people in our marriages, families, churches, and workplaces. Intimacy will be replaced with manipulation, power struggles, put-downs, seductions, defensiveness, and the withholding of relationship. Loneliness will reign.

We may have been built to engage the earth and to work, but now frustration and failure will be our lot. In essence, the ground will be hard. Thorns and thistles will mark our work. We may reach our goals and accomplish things, but we will never feel completely satisfied. A sense of restlessness and incompleteness will always accompany our work on earth. In this life all symphonies remain unfinished.[2]

Why does God do this? He releases the curse in order to drive us to our knees and to seek him to recognize our need for a Savior

(Gal. 3:21–25). The problem is instead of being broken by the thorns and thistles of life and thus coming to Christ, we either flee, fight, or hide.

a. Flee. Some of us flee by burying our pain in some form of addictive behavior, avoiding life by focusing on only a small part of it. Many Christians suffer pain, but they run away from it or anesthetize it. How many pastors numb the pains of life by becoming addicted to building their church? How many people zealously put their energy into a church ministry as a way of avoiding certain unpleasant relationships at home? How many

> God releases the curse in order to drive us to our knees and to seek him, to recognize our need for a Savior.

females will bury themselves in caring for the children as a way of not looking honestly at other broken areas of their lives? How many men pour their life energy into succeeding at their professions while failing miserably at home?

b. Fight. Others of us become angry, bitter, and/or violent because life is not going our way. How many Christians need to deal with an anger that is close to their soul but instead put on the veneer of a spirituality — "a righteous indignation like Jesus," as they wrongly describe it? They take out their anger on misguided politicians and doctrinally imperfect Christians. Rather than be broken by the difficulties of life, I meet many in our churches who are angry at God for not answering their prayers or ruling the world in a way that seems wise.

c. Hide. Still others of us build our lives in ways that cover up how damaged, cracked, fractured, frail, limited, and imperfect we are. That's what I did for years. The most poignant example occurred several years ago when, for a brief time, I traveled to different parts of the country and spoke at church-growth conferences. I spoke about our church's successes, focusing on what I did right. I conveyed a sense of mastery and control of how to lead a church and build an infrastructure of small groups. I was the center of attention, sharing my expertise freely over breaks and meals.

However, I glossed over disappointments and setbacks, both personally and in the church. I also found myself exaggerating more than I like to admit. On the surface it appeared that I was succeeding. Some of the exploits were true. But, as I would later understand, focusing on my success was my tool to avoid looking honestly at how damaged, cracked, imperfect, and limited I really was. It also gave me a false sense of worth and value that left me empty.

I remember getting an invitation to speak at a church-growth conference in Tennessee because a plenary speaker had gotten sick and they needed someone to fill in. The honorarium was significant. But I knew I could no longer go. Something in my soul was dying at those conferences when I spoke. I had an uncomfortable feeling that I was not telling the whole truth. God had done a number of great things, but there was another side to the story and to me.

Everyone is broken, damaged, cracked, and imperfect. It is a common thread of all humanity — even for those who deny its reality in their life.

Two Types of Churches

The following chart describes two very different ways a church lives out her spirituality. The first, for lack of a better term, is characterized by pride and defensiveness; the second is marked by brokenness and vulnerability. Which column best describes you and your church?

PROUD & DEFENSIVE	BROKEN & VULNERABLE
1. I am guarded and protective about my imperfections and flaws.	1. I am transparent and weak; I disclose myself to appropriate others.
2. I focus on the "positive," strong, successful parts of myself.	2. I am aware of the weak, needy, limited parts of who I am, and I freely admit failure.
3. I am highly "offendable" and defensive.	3. I am approachable and open to input.
4. I naturally focus first on the flaws, mistakes, and sins of others.	4. I am aware of my own brokenness. I have compassion and am slow to judge others.
5. I give my opinion a lot, even when I am not asked.	5. I am slow to speak and quick to listen.

PROUD & DEFENSIVE	BROKEN & VULNERABLE
6. I don't get close to people.	6. I am open, soft, and curious about others.
7. I keep people from really seeing what is going on inside of me.	7. I delight in showing vulnerability and weakness, that Christ's power may be seen.
8. I like to control most situations.	8. I can let go and give people opportunity to earn my trust.
9. I have to be right in order to feel strong and good.	9. I understand that God's strength reveals itself in admitting mistakes, weakness, and statements that "I was wrong."
10. I blame others.	10. I take responsibility for myself and speak mostly in the "I," not the "you" or "they."
11. I often hold grudges and rarely ask forgiveness.	11. I don't hold people in debt to me, and am able to ask others for forgiveness as needed.
12. When I am offended, I write people off.	12. When I am offended, I ask questions to explore what happened.
13. I deny, avoid, or withdraw from painful realities.	13. I honestly look at the truth underneath the surface, even when it hurts.
14. I give answers and explanations to those in pain, hoping to fix or change them.	14. I am present with people in their pain, and am comfortable with mystery and with saying, "I don't know."
15. I have to prove I am right when wronged.	15. I can let things go.
16. I am demanding.	16. I assert myself respectfully and kindly.
17. I am highly self-conscious and concerned about how others perceive me.	17. I am more aware of God and others than the impression I am making.
18. I see people as resources to be used for God.	18. I see people as gifts to be loved and enjoyed.

Paul's Spiritual Authority and Weakness

The apostle Paul is arguably the greatest Christian to have ever lived. He wrote almost half the books of the New Testament and expanded Christianity in the first century in a way that remains unsurpassed to this day. Even so, Paul's authority and position as an apostle was seriously challenged on more than one occasion. The primary reason for this was related to his understanding of weakness and brokenness.

A case in point is Corinth. "Super-apostles" had come to the church with a ministry of signs and wonders that surpassed Paul. They also spoke of revelations and experiences with God that made Paul's seem ordinary. They arrived with extraordinary speaking gifts. Claiming a special, unique authority from God, they gradually drew the congregation's loyalty to themselves and away from the apostle Paul. Embracing weakness and imperfection was not on their radar screen when developing leadership qualities.

People in Corinth were much like we are today. This city in Greece was strategically located on the Aegean Sea. It had exploded into one of the world's largest and most powerful cities. People went there to make it in the big city. Densely populated, multiethnic, sexually cut loose from traditional moorings, it was a combination of New York City, Las Vegas, and Los Angeles.[3]

Twenty-first-century culture measures strength in terms of power. If you are a celebrity, a physically beautiful or wealthy individual, a professional athlete, an accomplished lawyer, a doctor, or a successful politician, you are considered strong. Brilliant people dazzle us with their intellectual and verbal abilities. Contemporary church culture has largely bought into the world's definition of power and strength. We look for building, finances, numbers of people, and large budgets to demonstrate the strength and success of our churches and ministries.

Yet in 2 Corinthians 12, Paul argues for the authenticity of his leadership by appealing, not to his visions and revelations from God, not to his successes and gifts, but instead to his weakness! He writes about how God had allowed a "thorn in his flesh" in his life to humble him.

> Paul argues for the authenticity of his leadership by appealing ... to his weakness!

Scholars are not sure whether this "thorn" was a physical ailment (such as an eye problem, speech defect, or epilepsy), the agony of people constantly opposing and misunderstanding him, or a spiritual temptation (perhaps a tendency to bitterness or a terrible temper). In ancient times, thorns were used as stakes in the ground during battle to slow an enemy's progress. This stake was cutting through Paul into the center of his being.

Whatever it was, it "tormented" Paul. It seriously discouraged him. Even so, Paul referred to it as a gift, saying:

> Three times I pleaded with the Lord to take it away from me. But he said to me, "My grace is sufficient for you, for my power is made perfect in weakness." Therefore I will boast all the more gladly about my weaknesses, so that Christ's power may rest on me. That is why, for Christ's sake, I delight in weaknesses ... in hardships ... in difficulties. For when I am weak, then I am strong. (2 Cor. 12:8–10)

For Paul, his great weakness was his badge of apostleship and authority from God—so much so that he boasted in it, arguing that this is when the real power and glory of Jesus flowed through him. It made him feel so weak that it forced him to be dependent on God.

If Paul were preaching at a pastor's conference and received the opportunity to speak of his work as an apostolic leader, his topic first would not be how he planted twenty-one churches in Asia Minor. Nor would his opening message be titled, "Six Steps to Raise Up Leaders from within the Church." He would perhaps speak first of how God did not answer his prayers for personal healing. He would describe how weak, difficult, fractured, and broken he was. "There is a message in this, friends," he might add. "If God can use me, he can use anybody! It really is about Jesus in us, not our own abilities and talents. The kingdom of God is about his power, his strength, not ours! Be encouraged!"

Paul did not want to lead out of weakness. He repeatedly told God, "I can't take it." God knew he would be unbearable without this "thorn." Can you imagine what he might have been like? Undoubtedly the flow of God's

> It really is about Jesus in us, not our own abilities and talents.

power would have been seriously diminished through Paul if he were arrogant or full of himself.

2. Accepting Your Gift of a Handicap

What might be the "gift of a handicap" God has given you? (That's how *The Message* translates "thorn in the flesh.") A child with special needs? A struggle with an addiction that forces you to be vigilant every day and attend meetings regularly? Emotional fragility with a tendency to depression, anxiety, severe isolation, or loneliness as a single person or widow? Scars on your soul from an abusive past? Childhood patterns of relating to other people that cause you to feel desperate for change? A physical disability? Cancer? Real temptations to anger, hate, resentment, or judgmentalism?

Our world treats weakness and failure as terminal. It says, "You are a loser." God says, "This is a universal human experience, cutting across all ages, cultures, races, and social classes. It is my gift specially crafted for you so you can lead out of weakness and brokenness, not your own strength and power."

My understanding was that God wanted to heal my brokenness and vulnerabilities completely. Few consider brokenness as God's design and will for our lives!

Paul's growth in Christ parallels his increasing sense of weakness and sinfulness.

- In Galatians 2:6, written in AD 49, after being a Christian for fourteen years, he writes about the apostles this way: "As for those were held in high esteem — whatever they were makes no difference to me." He appears proud and headstrong.
- Six years later, in AD 55, he writes the Corinthians in a more humble manner: " I am the least of the apostles" (1 Cor. 15:9).
- Five years after that, in about AD 60 and twenty-five years after becoming a Christian, he proclaims, "I am less than the least of all the Lord's people" (Eph. 3:8).
- Finally, two years before his death and perhaps after walking with Christ for thirty years, he is able to see clearly, "I am the worst [of all sinners]" (1 Tim. 1:15).[4]

What happened? Paul had grown in his understanding of the love of God in the gospel. He had become stronger in Christ by becoming weaker: "For when I am weak, then I am strong" (2 Cor. 12:10).

Walking as a Cracked Pot

A story I heard wonderfully illustrates this countercultural truth.

There once lived a water carrier in India. He used two large pots for his task. He suspended a pole across his neck and attached a pot at each end of the pole. One of the pots had a big crack in it while the other pot was perfect. The perfect pot always delivered a full portion of water from the stream to the master's house, while the cracked pot arrived only half full each day.

For two years this water carrier made the same journey. The perfect pot became proud of its accomplishments. The cracked pot was ashamed of its imperfection and miserable that it was able to accomplish only half of what it had been made to do. Finally, one day by the stream, the cracked pot spoke to his owner about his bitter failure, "I am ashamed of myself, and I want to apologize that I have only been able to deliver half my water to your house. There is a crack in my side which causes water to leak out. Because of my flaws, you don't get full value from your efforts."

Then the water carrier replied, smiling, "As we return to the master's house, I want you to notice the beautiful flowers along the path."

On that trip from the stream, the cracked pot looked around.

"Did you notice there are flowers only on your side of the path, but not on the other pot's side?" the water carrier commented. "That's because I have always known about your flaw, and I took advantage of it. I planted seeds on your side of the path, and every day while we passed these spots, you watered them. Now for two years I have been able to pick those beautiful flowers to decorate my master's table. Without you being just the way you are, I would not have this beauty to grace his house."[5]

It is the way God works.

Lou's Descent to Humility

Many people read books on humility but are not humble. Others preach messages and teach Bible studies on the topic but remain impenetrable. Like myself, Lou, one of my staff pastors, was one of those people.

I was sitting at my kitchen table with my wife, and we were trying to stop the marital free fall that Lou and his wife, Susan, were experiencing. We were trying desperately to help them listen to one another with respect. At one point in the conversation, Lou, frustrated, burst out, "I understand that it's not just Susan, that I have problems too. But my problems are more like having a broken leg, and Susan's problems are more like having cancer."

It was easy, almost natural, for Lou to look at and focus on his wife's defects of character. But it was difficult, almost impossible, for him to look at his own weaknesses and flaws. It was the fateful combination of Lou's inborn temperament, family of origin, early discipleship training (through a campus ministry that prided itself on practicing "the basics"), and church culture that made it seemingly impossible for Lou to see his own brokenness. Lou loved books and always thought that knowledge or more knowledge was the answer to everything.

We tried unsuccessfully to get Lou to listen to his wife. He could fix, solve, arrange, and control just about everything. If you had a problem, Lou could "teach" you the solution. But he couldn't control Susan's desperation and misery in their marriage. I recommended he go to a professional marriage counselor.

Who? Me? Lou thought to himself. *That is ridiculous!* He was shamed and devastated. Gradually, for the first time in his life, he came face-to-face with his inability to resolve the problems with his own wife. He slowly began to open up about the parts of himself that were radically broken.

Lou doesn't have as many answers as he used to. He says "I don't know" a lot more. His teaching at New Life does not carry the self-sufficient, "together" quality as previously. He receives correction from others with humility. Most important, perhaps, is how people are beginning to seek him out when their lives fall apart. Lou is actually becoming known as a "safe" person. One of his unique strengths now at New Life is his ability to listen to and counsel people who are hurting. His teaching ministry now also carries an aroma of brokenness that was never present before.

3. Transitioning to a Church Based on Weakness

It Began with Me

A seismic shift began at New Life when, after almost eight years of leading out of my "strengths" and "successes," I admitted to the congregation (and not merely to the board) that my personal life and marriage were out of order. I then made the decision, along with my wife, to go public with our struggle and journey of healing and restoration.

I began to speak freely of my mistakes, vulnerabilities, and failures. I now was able to say in meetings, "I don't know what to do." I talked openly about my insecurities, my disappointments, and my shattered dreams. I shared feelings that, previously, I tended to be ashamed of—anger, jealousy, depression, sadness, despair.

If you listen to my sermon tapes before and after 1996, you will notice a sharp difference. Prior to 1996 I may have admitted to some weakness about myself or shared a struggle. I did so because it sounded good and worked well into the point I was making in the sermon. Pretense and protection still characterized my leadership.

> I began to speak freely of my mistakes, vulnerabilities, and failures.

I made the decision during a three-month sabbatical in 1996 that I would preach out of my failures, weaknesses, and struggles, not my successes. This vulnerability, while uncomfortable at first, revolutionized my preaching and New Life Fellowship. I began to wrestle with texts and my own difficulties in obeying them before I applied them to everyone else. Now I shared these struggles openly in my sermons. We were all now on equal footing, wrestling to obey God's Word in our lives.

I remember Geri and I doing our first marriage retreat, sharing painful details of our story as a couple. One person left the room crying, saying, "I never expected to see anyone, let alone my pastor, that naked!" (By that she meant "vulnerable.") A wave of such brokenness had come into our lives that we had nothing left to hide.

Not only did I not feel worse as I initially feared, I felt more alive and clean than I had in years. My illusions of pretense and protectiveness were dissipating. And I began to sense God's love in Christ and the Holy Spirit's power in an entirely new way.

> I began to sense God's love in Christ and the Holy Spirit's power in an entirely new way.

It Rippled through the Leadership

One of the exceptional qualities of New Life is that leaders, on all levels, share their weaknesses freely and speak often of God's mercy. As one of our pastors recently said, "It's really hard to get fired off staff unless you refuse to be broken and humble." An expectation exists to be teachable, correctable, and willing to do ongoing work on your own issues. There are no Christian heroes here. Just people.

Worship, ministry, and small group leaders are encouraged to tell their stories of weakness and brokenness as they lead others. It is perhaps the one indispensable quality for successful service at New Life.

Adam is a young, gifted leader who moved to New York City a couple of years ago. The following is his account, in his own words, of his cultural clash and journey.

> I had life all figured out. Ministry? I had it all figured out too. I was young, I was confident, I was invincible. I had been a Christian for a little over a decade, and in my mind, there was no question too complex or circumstance too deflating to knock me from the top of Christendom. I was told that I had lots of gifts, a number of natural leadership abilities, and a knack for influence.
>
> As a result, I was a defensive, feisty, and often unteachable Christian who masqueraded as the humble hero. I would listen to people, but not really listen. I was often impatient with others, and I tended to give advice to anyone and everyone, just because I thought that was my duty and "gift" to them. I valued strength more than weakness, dogma more than grace, perfection more than brokenness. I was confident in the abilities God had given me.
>
> I lived out my parents' advice to me as a young boy: "You can be messy, but just don't show it to others."
>
> Coming to New Life and hearing about vulnerability and brokenness was shattering. It seemed too risky — nice enough to sound good and idealistic, but at the same time a little too dangerous and improbable. To be honest, it was a bit terrifying.
>
> But it was liberating. It gave me a fresher, newer way of seeing the gospel, of understanding grace, and of appreciating and worshiping the humble King as I never had before. I learned to trust him even when I didn't have the answer to everything, and I learned to listen. I learned to say "I don't know" when really, I didn't know. I learned to see people

through a new lens, a lens of grace and sympathy, a lens of compassion and humility.

I learned that leadership is not always being the strong one; instead, it is being the weak one who is made strong by God alone. I have come to realize that oftentimes, I could learn a lot from other people if I wasn't so insistent on being right.

In a nutshell, I learned that I was not as whole as I thought I was. In an odd and mysterious way, I learned that I could only become whole as a leader, a friend, and a student by being broken and weak and vulnerable before God ... and, yes, before others too.

That too was liberating.

It Filtered into the Wider Culture

We use every opportunity for people to give testimony about how God meets them in their failures and frailties. We want people to acknowledge the cracks in their soul—whether they come to church as a result of their own sins or of sins committed against them. Thus, we use Sunday worship services, marriage and singles retreats, small groups, baptisms, and other events to give opportunity for people to tell their stories.

> I learned that leadership is not always being the strong one; instead, it is being the weak one who is made strong by God alone.

It is common to hear from a recovering heroin and crack addict who now leads worship and from a self-righteous, respectable, middle-class father of three struggling with pornography in the same service. We invited a former transvestite to give his story on a Sunday morning (with accompanying pictures of his life before Christ, I may add). The same theme runs through every person's story. We are all broken; we each compensate in different ways.

We constantly remind people that the only kind of people God uses are those who do not depend on their own gifts or resources.

- Moses stuttered.
- David's armor didn't fit.
- John Mark deserted Paul.
- Timothy had ulcers.

- Hosea's wife was a prostitute.
- Amos's only training was farming.
- Jacob was a liar.
- David had an affair, murdered, and abused power.
- Naomi was a widow.
- Paul was a persecutor.
- Moses was a murderer.
- Jonah ran from God's will.
- Gideon and Thomas both doubted.
- Jeremiah was depressed and suicidal.
- Elijah was burned out.
- John the Baptist was a loudmouth.
- Martha was a worry wart.
- Noah got drunk.
- Solomon was too rich, and Jesus was too poor.
- Abraham was too old, and David too young.
- Peter was afraid of death, and Lazarus was dead.
- Moses had a short fuse (so did Peter, Paul, and lots of Bible heroes).

God has always used cracked pots to "show that this all-surpassing power is from God and not from us" (2 Cor. 4:7).

We forget that David, one of God's most beloved friends, used his power as king to ensure the details of his colossal failure (adultery and murder) were published in the history books for future generations! In fact, David wrote a song about his failure to be sung in Israel's worship services and to be published in their worship manual, the Psalms. David knew that "my sacrifice, O God, is a broken spirit; a broken and contrite heart you, God, will not despise" (Ps. 51:17).

It doesn't mean we encourage people to stay the way they are. Admitting the truth about ourselves, however, is the key starting point for change. My wife and I often remark that the day we admitted we were not loving people was the day we began to be loving toward others.

4. Following the Prodigal Son as the Model

One of the turning points in shifting our church culture occurred, however, when I preached a seven-part series on the prodigal sons of Luke 15:11–32. Using Rembrandt's painting called "Return of the

Prodigal Son," I projected it on a large screen as I preached through the text. God met us in an extraordinary way.

Rembrandt's painting is taken from Jesus' parable in Luke 15, offering a magnificent visual aid to help us choose the pathway towards brokenness, weakness, humility, and vulnerability. The younger son is kneeling, resting his head on the father's bosom. He is bald, seemingly exhausted and emaciated, without his cloak, wearing only one tattered shoe, and disheveled. He is a picture of a life that has been broken.

According to the parable, the younger son demanded his percentage of the estate (one third) and ran away from home. In traditional Middle Eastern culture, for a son to ask for his inheritance while his father is still alive is the same as saying, "Father, I am eager for you to die. I want to live now as if you are dead."

> The younger son is ... a picture of a life that has been broken.

He shames his father and disgraces his family. But things go badly for him until eventually he is tending pigs. For

**Rembrandt's Painting of the Return of the Prodigal Son
Shows the Father's Incredible Love**

a Jewish listener in Jesus' day, the younger brother has fallen into the cesspool of cesspools. Jews who touched pigs were four times as unclean as those who visited a prostitute.

Finally, he comes "to his senses" (Luke 15:17) and turns back toward home. He gets up and turns around. As he walks toward home in shame, the father runs toward him (the father's sprint is the Greek word for athletic games). The father does not tap his foot and say, "This better be good," nor does he simply wait on his porch. He runs and throws himself on his son before the son can finish his prepared speech. He cuts him off and declares, in effect, "You are my son" (Luke 15:20–22).

Then the unimaginable occurs. "He kissed him" (Luke 15:20). No other religion describes a God like this. He reinstates his son's position of authority by stripping off the old, torn, foul-smelling clothes, places the best robe on him, gives him a signet ring of legal authority, and outfits him with the shoes of a free man who belongs in the house. The father then throws a joyful party with music and dancing.

The message is powerful because the father represents our heavenly Father. God dances with his shattered, broken child.

The Younger Son — Knowing His Neediness

Take a moment, once again, and look at the painting on page 129. The younger son's brokenness is the picture of the Christian life. I must live there intentionally. Otherwise I will end up being the older brother standing erect to the right.

The key word is "intentionally." That kneeling, disheveled son resting in his father's chest, with the father's large hands upon him, is the call to you and me to go against the forces that fight against us choosing this path. He is kneeling because he cannot do life on his own. He is seriously dependent. He is very, very needy. We all are. We often forget that truth when things are going our way.

Henri Nouwen, in his classic book about Rembrandt's painting entitled *The Return of the Prodigal Son*, describes leaving home as moving out of the place of the Father's love where I hear in the center of my being, "You are my son whom I love, upon you does my favor rest." Nouwen writes:

> Yet over and over again I have left home. I have fled the hands
> of blessing and run to faraway places searching for love! This
> is the great tragedy of my life and the lives of so many I meet

on my journey. Somehow I have become deaf to the voice that calls me the Beloved ... There are many other voices. The dark voices of my surrounding world try to persuade me that I am no good and that I can only become good by earning my goodness through "making it" up the ladder of success.[6]

The result is many of us in leadership are trying hard to please people, achieve success, and be recognized. We end up lost.

When I get depressed after someone graciously corrects a comment I make in a sermon, or I find myself envying other people's success, or I am unable to say no without feeling guilty, I realize I am lost. I have left my home of resting and soaking in the love of God for me in Christ. I am searching for unconditional love where it cannot be found.

When I am caught up in games, manipulations, self-delusions, power struggles, and distortions, and I forget the voice of the Father that says to me, "You are my son, Pete, whom I love," then I know I have left home. I am lost and need to make the long, hard journey back.

When I attempt to exercise control and power by not greeting a church member who has slighted me, I have strayed from the embrace of the Father.

When I discipline my children, not out of a desire to help them grow but because they embarrass me to my friends, I am lost.

When my views are challenged and I feel threatened, and then I defend myself vigorously rather than say, "You've given me some good things to think about," I am lost.

> When I attempt to exercise control and power ... I have strayed from the embrace of the Father.

When I need a certain size ministry, position, or salary to feel valuable, I am lost.

I have two copies of Rembrandt's picture. One is in my home above the piano; the other is in our church office. I recognize I am the younger brother, always running away from home. This picture keeps me centered, focused.

The younger brother, kneeling with his head resting on his father's chest and receiving the warm embrace of the father's worn hands, is where I want to live. When I do, fully aware of how broken and fragile I am, I gain a small glimpse into "how wide and long and high and deep is the love of Christ, and ... know [experientially] this love that surpasses knowledge" (Eph. 3:18–19).

The younger brother comes home and receives the father's love. He does not get executed or dismissed. He is not shamed. He receives life.

The extent to which I am in touch with my "lostness" and brokenness is the extent to which I grasp the glory of the gospel and am able to revel in the Father's love.

Older Brother — Picture of Lostness

What does it look like when I stray from weakness and brokenness? The older brother shows us. He is the climax of the parable for those to whom Jesus is speaking. In Rembrandt's painting, he is well-clothed in a gold-embroidered garment like his father, judging, annoyed, looking down at the father's lavish reception of his youngest son who has so disgraced the family and squandered the family fortune.

Yet he is more lost than his younger brother. Why? Because he cannot see his lostness! His respectability and morality have blinded him.

He is living with the father but is far from the father. He serves as a warning to me that it is possible to obey God's commands and be lost. I can be leading in the church, praying, reading the Bible, serving, or witnessing and be lost. As I work for God, I can appear to be near God and yet actually be very far from him.

His response to the lavish love of the father on the lost younger brother is, "All these years I've been slaving for you" (Luke 15:29). He doesn't understand what the father is doing.

How Do I Know If I Am the Lost Older Brother?

It is important always to keep the older brother before us in this parable. When I am not intentional and purposeful about leading out of weakness and brokenness, I become like him.

I watch for three signs.

First, when I hold on to my anger rather than process it, I am the lost older brother. There is no dance in the heart of the older brother. He is angry. It is understandable. His younger brother has humiliated the family, squandered large amounts of money, and probably created more work over those years for him, the older brother. The issue is what he does with it.

He doesn't own his anger, wrestle with it, or bring it humbly to his father. Some of us stuff our anger and eventually explode. We save up bits and pieces of offenses until we can take it no more and begin slamming doors, throwing things, or attempt to get back or get even. Others of us take our anger from one place, such as the office or home, and bring it into the church. How many times have I directed my anger from a nasty New York City traffic jam toward my "slow" children, who are taking so long to get into bed?

Sometimes, we turn it so strongly inward that our souls are forced to swallow thousands of hours of anger until it turns into depression or ulcers or insomnia or tension headaches. Still others of us are passive-aggressive. We unconsciously try to defeat the person with whom we are upset by showing up late, forgetting birthdays, or withholding love or respect.

Anger is an important, complex emotion, especially for those of us in leadership. There are so many people and situations coming at us that at times I am not sure why I am even angry or upset. The key is for me to kneel before the Father and humbly ask, "What is this anger all about? Where is it coming from? Does it remind me of something in the past? What will it mean for me to be assertive and not aggressive, deliberate but not impulsive, prompt but not rushing in to speak with the person who evoked these angry feelings?"

Second, when I find myself grumbling and complaining a lot, I am the lost older brother. The older brother grumbles to his father, "This son of yours." He won't admit the younger son is his brother, back in the family. He is condescending, proud, and fault-finding. When my heart and posture toward people are not like the father in the painting, I know I have wandered from home.

> Anger is an important, complex emotion, especially for those of us in leadership.

There is a place for the older brother to process his sadness and disappointment over the younger brother. But we sense in this parable that he is only resentful and angry.

The older brother hears the music and immediately responds, "Why wasn't I informed? What is this all about?" He is afraid of being excluded. He lacks any sense of lightheartedness or spontaneity. He is high-strung, "heavy," grumpy, and discontent.

When I find myself crabby and envying others, it is a sign that I have moved from the younger son's position of humility to the older brother's position of pride.

Third, when I have a hard time letting go of offenses, it is a sure sign I am the lost older brother. Forgiveness is a process that I will discuss more fully in the next chapter on grieving. The foundation, however, for moving forward is to grasp the enormity of my debt, which is far greater than I could ever imagine. Again, I run to kneel before the Father.

Becoming the Father

The great fruit of choosing the unpopular, countercultural path of brokenness and weakness is that people will be drawn to us, just as they were drawn to Jesus. He never compromised his holiness, what he believed in, or what he stood for. He did not mince his words, nor did he ever sin. Yet the refuse of society, such as prostitutes and financial scoundrels (called tax collectors), knew that Jesus loved them even while they were still living in their sin. They wanted to be with Jesus. He welcomed their presence with him.

> The great fruit
> of choosing
> the unpopular,
> countercultural
> path of brokenness
> and weakness is
> that people will be
> drawn to us, just as
> they were drawn to
> Jesus.

Spend a few minutes meditating on the father in the painting. Notice his hands, his expression, his unconditional love, what it has cost him in terms of tears and love. This parable teaches me much about the love of God that treats each one of us as his favorite. But it also points to the kind of men and women he is calling us to be.

The church is full of younger sons running away every time God or someone else does not meet their expectations. It is also full of older brothers who are angry and grumpy. I know. I am both. The great need of our day, however, is for you and me to press on to grow into being mothers and fathers of the faith.

People are desperate to be with others who will incarnate God's love in a practical way, who can do what the father does in this painting—embrace, love, empathize, be present, and forgive freely. It is a love without conditions, something the world knows little of. It is supernatural.

Once I began this shift to sharing and leading out of my vulnerabilities, many more people found they could trust me. Why? There was nothing they could say that could surprise me. They could sense it.

I related to everyone's heart that was an abyss. How? I had begun to know my own.

My struggle is not with my sexual orientation, yet I can empathize with those in our congregation who do. I do not have a mentally challenged child, yet I can relate with those who do. I did not spend twenty years on heroin on the streets, contracting the HIV virus, yet I understand. I have not raped or murdered or committed adultery with my body, but I know the murder and adultery of my own heart (Matt. 5:27–30).

A Prayer

Here is a prayer God has used to encourage me on this new journey of brokenness and vulnerability:

I asked God for strength that I might achieve,
I was made weak that I might learn humbly to obey.
I asked for health that I might do great things;
I was given infirmity that I might do better things.
I asked for riches that I might be happy;
I was given poverty that I might be wise.
I asked for power when I was young that I might have the praise
    of men;
I was given weakness that I might feel the need for God.
I asked for all things that I might enjoy life;
I was given life that I might enjoy all things.
I got nothing that I asked for,
But everything I had hoped for.
Almost despite myself, my unspoken prayers were answered.
I am, among all people, most richly blessed.[7]

Embrace All Your Humanity

The choice to live in brokenness and vulnerability challenges us in profound ways to let go of what other people think and to surrender to God's love and mercy. I tend to perfectionism and don't like to make mistakes. I like to "get it right" the first time.

The problem is that I am human. Very human. I do make mistakes. I am not above the rest of the human race. I can be honest and trustworthy and show great integrity. I can also be a liar, not follow through on what I say, and violate my own integrity in a heartbeat. Both are true. I am a saint and sinner. So are you.

In fact, after thirty years of following Jesus, I now see the depth of my own sinfulness with greater clarity. The hole in my soul is much deeper and more frightening than I ever realized. Yet from that abyss bloom seeds of potential and new life.

I realize now that few of us descend down into that black hole for fear of never coming up. I would have preferred that God make me an angel, absent from the mess of my humanity. I suspect most of you would like the same thing.

Yet our light as leaders shines most brightly from the very backdrop of our own brokenness and vulnerability. This is our greatest gift to the people we serve. We help create a safe environment for others to come out of hiding and be themselves. Our churches truly become communities of grace. Then we can all boast, like Paul, that God's power really is made perfect in weakness (2 Cor. 12:9). This brokenness leads us to embrace the gift of our limits, the theme of the next chapter.

CHAPTER 8

PRINCIPLE 4:
RECEIVE THE GIFT OF LIMITS

E motionally healthy people understand the limits God has given them. They joyfully receive the one, two, seven, or ten talents God has so graciously distributed. As a result, they are not frenzied and covetous, trying to live a life God never intended. They are marked by contentment and joy.

Emotionally healthy churches also embrace their limits with the same joy and contentment, not attempting to be like another church. They have a confident sense of God's "good hand" on their church "for such a time as this" (Est. 4:11–14).

The Dilemma of the Bridge

Rabbi Edwin Friedman tells the story of a man who had given much thought to what he wanted from life. After trying many things, succeeding at some and failing at others, he finally decided what he wanted.

One day the opportunity came for him to experience exactly the way of living that he had dreamed about. But the opportunity would be available only for a short time. It would not wait, and it would not come again.

Eager to take advantage of this open pathway, the man started on his journey. With each step, he moved faster and faster. Each time he thought about his goal, his heart beat quicker; and with each vision of what lay ahead, he found renewed vigor.

As he hurried along, he came to a bridge that crossed through the middle of a town. The bridge spanned high above a dangerous river.

After starting across the bridge, he noticed someone coming from the opposite direction. The stranger seemed to be coming toward him to greet him. As the stranger grew closer, the man could discern that they didn't know each other, but yet they looked amazingly similar. They were even dressed alike. The only difference was that the stranger had a rope wrapped many times around his waist. If stretched out, the rope would reach a length of perhaps thirty feet.

The stranger began to unwrap the rope as he walked. Just as the two men were about to meet, the stranger said, "Pardon me, would you be so kind as to hold the end of the rope for me?"

The man agreed without a thought, reached out, and took it.

"Thank you," said the stranger. He then added, "Two hands now, and remember, hold tight." At that point, the stranger jumped off the bridge.

The man on the bridge abruptly felt a strong pull from the now-extended rope. He automatically held tight and was almost dragged over the side of the bridge.

"What are you trying to do?" he shouted to the stranger below.

"Just hold tight," said the stranger.

This is ridiculous, the man thought. He began trying to haul the other man in. Yet it was just beyond his strength to bring the other back to safety.

Again he yelled over the edge, "Why did you do this?"

"Remember," said the other, "if you let go, I will be lost."

"But I cannot pull you up," the man cried.

"I am your responsibility," said the other.

"I did not ask for it," the man said.

"If you let go, I am lost," repeated the stranger.

The man began to look around for help. No one was within sight.

He began to think about his predicament. Here he was eagerly pursuing a unique opportunity, and now he was being sidetracked for who knows how long.

Maybe I can tie the rope somewhere, he thought. He examined the bridge carefully, but there was no way to get rid of his newfound burden.

So he again yelled over the edge, "What do you want?"

"Just your help," came the answer.

"How can I help? I cannot pull you in, and there is no place to tie the rope while I find someone else who could help you."

"Just keep hanging on," replied the dangling man. "That will be enough."

Fearing that his arms could not hold out much longer, he tied the rope around his waist.

"Why did you do this?" he asked again. "Don't you see what you have done? What possible purpose could you have in mind?"

"Just remember," said the other, "my life is in your hands."

Now the man was perplexed. He reasoned within himself, *If I let go, all my life I will know that I let this other man die. If I stay, I risk losing my momentum toward my own long-sought-after salvation. Either way this will haunt me forever.*

As time went by, still no one came. The man became keenly aware that it was almost too late to resume his journey. If he didn't leave immediately, he wouldn't arrive in time.

Finally, he devised a plan. "Listen," he explained to the man hanging below, "I think I know how to save you." He mapped out the idea. The stranger could climb back up by wrapping the rope around him. Loop by loop, the rope would become shorter.

But the dangling man had no interest in the idea.

"I don't think I can hang on much longer," warned the man on the bridge.

"You must try," appealed the stranger. "If you fail, I die."

Suddenly a new idea struck the man on the bridge. It was different and even alien to his normal way of thinking. "I want you to listen carefully," he said, "because I mean what I am about to say."

The dangling man indicated that he was listening.

"I will not accept the position of choice for your life, only for my own; I hereby give back the position of choice for your own life to you."

"What do you mean?" the other asked, afraid.

"I mean, simply, it's up to you. You decide which way this ends. I will become the counterweight. You do the pulling and bring yourself up. I will even tug some from here."

He unwound the rope from around his waist and braced himself to be a counterweight. He was ready to help as soon as the dangling man began to act.

"You cannot mean what you say," the other shrieked. "You would not be so selfish. I am your responsibility. What could be so important that you would let someone die? Do not do this to me."

After a long pause, the man on the bridge at last uttered slowly, "I accept your choice." In voicing these words, he freed his hands and continued his journey over the bridge.[1]

How Best to Help People Who Jump off Bridges

This fable reminds me of the dilemmas of Christian leadership. You and I became pastors, board members, small group leaders, ministry coordinators, and active members of our churches because we want to help people who have fallen off the bridge. For years I pulled people up, often at great personal expense emotionally and spiritually, only to find out they purposefully would fall off (or jump off) another bridge the next month.

For years I reluctantly took the rope. Once I had the rope and they were dangling, I felt guilty if I let go. How could I? I was a Christian. Wouldn't Jesus pull them up? If I did not pull them up, was I being selfish? For how long would I need to place my visions, dreams, desires, hopes, and plans on hold? Did they matter anyway since I was a servant of Christ? And where was everyone else?

I, like many others who serve in urban areas or overseas, had become resentful and bitter toward the rest of the church for not "suffering" for God. It took a great deal of work for me to take responsibility for my choice to walk on the bridge.

> I ... had become resentful and bitter toward the rest of the church for not "suffering" for God.

In one parable Jesus told, the good Samaritan came upon only one person on the side of the road (Luke 10:29–37). I felt as if I had fifteen at a time lining up on the bridge, each placing a rope in my hands.

I had many moments when I wished I didn't see all those people hanging from the bridge. Merely knowing them caused me to feel like the rope was in my hands. If only I had avoided seeing or hearing their problems—then I wouldn't feel so guilty!

A few years ago, a single mom with six children under ten years old from five different fathers lived across the street. My wife and I would sometimes give her a break and take care of her children. What about the next day? And the next? How about their schooling? Their finances? What about mentoring them? Helping them find a future? Where was it appropriate to stop? Wasn't this my neighborhood? It took me a long time to learn that each day we could decide what we would like to do, or not do, for her in the name of Christ.

Four houses down lived a church leader with his family. Out of compassion they took in a single mom with a small baby. The mom did not pay for her rent or for groceries. Resentment slowly began to build from her hosts. Then, without asking, the young mother began regularly to leave her baby for twelve hours at the house while she went out with her friends. They were beside themselves. How could they possibly put her and her baby out on the street?

Understanding and respecting our boundaries and limits is one of the most important character qualities and skills leaders need in order to be long-term lovers of God and others. This is important for all of life—be it the workplace, parenting, marriage, single relationships with the opposite sex—but especially in this "new family," the local church into which we have been adopted by God's grace.

For this reason, at the heart of many problems in our churches is conflict over properly respecting and understanding limits in this "new family" called the church.

1. Questioning the Church without Limits

It takes great maturity for a church to identify opportunities and to choose not to take advantage of them. Each church, like each small group, ministry, and individual, has God-given limits. How many services should we have on Sunday? What about a Saturday night service? Others are doing it successfully and growing. If we are two hundred people, why not become four hundred or eight hundred or ten thousand?

I always assumed continued numerical growth for every local church was God's will. It is not.

Multiplying Small Groups

In our early years we expected each small group to multiply within one year. Every leader was to have at least one apprentice in training. Goals would be set accordingly. In addition, each group was expected to have worship, Bible study, prayer, fellowship, and outreach to their neighbors. Groups met weekly. Leaders and their apprentices were expected to attend monthly training gatherings. Along with early morning prayer meetings three days a week, we met once a month for a half night of prayer. The pace was exhausting.

I remember one of the groups that we led. I was constantly harried and rushed, with too much to do in too little time. The wife of our apprentice always seemed annoyed with her husband and would make sarcastic remarks about him to the group. Another woman made critical, cynical remarks throughout the Bible study and fellowship time about other people. The hostess was tired of having all of us in her house each week. You could predict the same two people would take up most of the sharing time.

Additionally, we did not weigh the impact of having a mentally challenged person in our group. His limitation was something to conquer, not a gift to be received. The only problem was we didn't know how to draw out his story; thus, we treated him as if everything was normal, as if he wasn't mentally handicapped.

Something was wrong. Most of us attended each week out of guilt. We all felt uncomfortable. But we didn't know how to go beneath the surface in our meetings (principle 1). We didn't know each other's history or story—how the past impacted our present (principle 2). And we didn't know it was biblical to be broken and admit our failure as a group (principle 3). Lastly, we saw limits as an obstacle to overcome, not a gift to receive (principle 4). We felt pressure to grow and to multiply like the rest of the small groups in the church.

Fortunately, the group died.

Tired Workers in the Church

Fran was single, gifted, and a compelling leader. She was a magnet for needy people and seemed to have gifts in many areas—administration, teaching, evangelism, pastoring, and hospitality. The church was growing rapidly and the opportunities to touch people's lives seemed endless. Saying no was not considered a godly act. Fran rarely said no.

What happened? Like the rest of us serving in the church, she could keep up the pace only for so long until she had to get out of leadership completely to regain some balance in her life. She left, but we kept up the feverish activity, ignorant of the Bible's teaching on limits and boundaries. For that we paid a high price, both personally and in our families.

2. Recognizing That Jesus Embraced Human Limits

I spent a large part of my years as a leader trying to be someone I was not. I attended conferences and read books that peddled "ecclesiastical pornography," to use Eugene Petersen's term.[2] They promised a church free from the problems of regular sinners like ours. The best and the brightest programs and people were highlighted. If only I would be and do as their leaders, so our church would be equally large and prosperous.

The problem was that God has not given me the abilities and capacities he has given those other leaders. I bring other strengths to the task of leadership. My unwillingness to accept reality led me down paths that God never intended. For years, I attempted to live

> I spent a large part of my years as a leader trying to be someone I was not.

out a script for my life that was not mine. While the script needed an actor, I was the wrong person auditioning for the part.

God has given me two or three, perhaps five talents. He did not give me eight or ten. My parents told me I could be anything I wanted in life—a doctor, musician, professor, writer, a professional athlete. I tried to play basketball like Michael Jordan in high school. I couldn't. We lost most of our games.

Yet I didn't get the message. I could not do anything I wanted. Yes, I had gifts and potentials. But I also had limits given to me by God as a gift.

Jesus, Limits, and Spiritual Warfare

As far as we know, Jesus did not do any miracles the first thirty years of his life. He was a faithful son, employee, and participant in his community and synagogue. He apparently joyfully embraced the limits given him by his Father in heaven.

> Jesus apparently joyfully embraced the limits given him by his Father in heaven.

At the time of his baptism, he was affirmed by God the Father, "You are my Son, whom I love; with you I am well pleased" (Mark 1:11). After about thirty years of obscurity, he was affirmed to begin a brief three-year public ministry.

Immediately after his baptism, Jesus was thrust into the desert to be tempted by the devil. The essence of the temptation was to transgress or cross over the limits God had placed around him. This continues to be a central spiritual warfare issue for most of us who are actively seeking to do God's work with our lives.

Jesus had to learn obedience through what he suffered (Heb. 5:8). That included setting limits and watching needs that remained unmet.

In his temptation, the devil begins, "If you are the Son of God, tell these stones to become bread" (Matt. 4:3). Jesus is at a point of weakness. He has not eaten for forty days. It is as if Satan says, "Do something. If you don't eat, you will die, and nobody will experience salvation. Look at your life—born in a cave, a refugee in Africa, an obscure family, many other hardships. You have needs and wants not being met by God. How can you be the Son of God and have so many problems? You're a loser."

Jesus accepts the gift of limits, and the rocks remain rocks. No manna from heaven appears, although it is in his power to do so.

In the second temptation, Satan takes Jesus to the highest point in the holy city and invites him to jump off, demonstrating to the multitudes that God is really with him. "Let the people see you. Let them see you have something. They think you're nothing, a nobody." He must make a decision to wait on God for his timing.

Jesus accepts God's limits and walks down the temple steps, and there is no miracle. He doesn't do anything sensational to prove himself to anyone.

The third temptation, I believe, is close to home for us serving in leadership. Jesus is taken to a high mountain and shown all the earth: the crowds and brilliance of Athens, the glory of Rome, the treasures of Egypt, all Jerusalem, magnificent Corinth, along with all the kingdoms of this world. If Jesus would only cross this limit and bow to Satan for just a single moment (then he can repent), the world will be saved, and millions of people will be helped now.

If Jesus would simply skip over the God-given limit of suffering and the cross, the work of God would happen so much more quickly!

The frightening truth is we can sometimes pass through our God-given limits and end up doing God's work without God!

I know.

Limits as a Deeply Spiritual Issue

Receiving the gift of limits touches the core of our relationship with God.

Adam and Eve's original sin of rebellion against God was all about limits. God gave them enormous freedom in the garden of Eden. Then, without explanation, God set a boundary before them. "You are free to eat from any tree in the garden; but you must not eat from the tree of the knowledge of good and evil, for when you eat of it you will certainly die" (Gen. 2:16–17). The tree confronted them with God's authority. They were to trust and surrender to the goodness of God. They were to bow humbly before his incomprehensible ways. The fallout from their refusal to do so remains with us to this day.

John the Baptist, on the other hand, models wonderfully for us what it means to embrace our limits. Crowds that formerly followed John for baptism switched their allegiances once Jesus began his ministry. They began leaving John to follow Jesus. Some of John's followers were upset about this dramatic turn of events.

John understood limits and replied, "A person can receive only what is given from heaven" (John 3:27). He was able to say, "I accept my limits, my humanity, my declining popularity. I am not the center of the universe. I am not God."

Jesus' Limits amidst Enormous Needs

Jesus did not heal every sick and demon-possessed person in the hospital. He did not build a great church in Capernaum when he was begged to remain in that city (Mark 1:21–45). He refused to let certain people follow him, such as the Gadarene demoniac who had been delivered. He prayed all night and chose only twelve to be closest to him (Luke 6:12–16). Others were undoubtedly disappointed. Jesus did not run after the crowds when they defected from him after he delivered a difficult teaching about his body and his blood (John 6:22–71).

Jesus did not go in person to meet the needs of everyone in Europe, Africa, Asia, or the Americas. Yet he prayed at the end of his life, "I have … [finished] the work you gave me to do" (John 17:4).

Why, then, did I always feel as if there was too little time and too much to do? Why did I feel chronically pressured and restless in my interior? Why did my life have so little margin or flexibility? Why did I never feel "finished" meeting needs? I was spending time in prayer and the Word. I worked on my priorities and time management. I attended countless seminars to help me manage and delegate more effectively. What was the problem?

I did not understand the powerful principle of limits as a gift from the hand of God.

My lack of understanding how boundaries and limits applied to serving Christ almost caused us to leave the pastorate. I know many others who started out enthusiastically serving others, but later quit because they didn't know how to walk on the bridge with people trying to hand them ropes or people screaming below. So they chose to purchase earplugs to avoid listening altogether while they lived their own lives. Or they decided the church is full of hypocrisy and pathology, resolving never to trust or serve needy people again.

> My lack of understanding how boundaries and limits applied to serving Christ almost caused us to leave the pastorate.

Limits as Our Friend

While our culture resists the idea of limits, it is critical that we embrace them. They are like a fenced-in yard that protects young children. They are the hands of a friend, keeping us grounded so that we don't hurt ourselves, others, or God's work.

Parker Palmer tells the story about when he was asked to be president of a college. Initially he was very excited and gathered a group of trusted friends together to help him discern if it was God's will. About halfway through the evening, someone asked, "What would you like about being president?" He answered, "Well, I wouldn't like having to give up my writing and teaching. I would not like the politics of the presidency, never knowing who your real friends are. I would not like ..."

The person who asked the question repeated one more time the question: "What would you like most about being president?" Palmer fumbled, "I would not like giving up my summer vacations. I would not like having to wear a suit and tie all the time. I would not like ..."

Finally, he gave the only honest answer he possessed: "I guess what I'd like most is getting my picture in the paper with the word 'President' under it."[3] He finally realized that for him to take that position would be a disaster for himself and for the college. He withdrew his name from consideration.

Palmer quotes the old Hasidic tale that points out our tendency to want to live out someone else's life instead of our own and the "ultimate importance of becoming one's self." Rabbi Zusya, when he was an old man, said, "In the coming world, they will not ask me: 'Why were you not Moses?' They will ask me, 'Why were you not Zusya?'"[4] The true vocation for every human being is, as Kierkegaard said, "the will to be oneself."[5]

3. Learning to Discern My Limitations

Look at your personality. Do you get more energy from being with people (extrovert) or from doing tasks (introvert)? Are you more spontaneous and creative, or controlled and orderly? Are you more easygoing and relaxed, or tense and anxious? On boldness and risk-taking I scored a ten on a scale of one to ten (with ten being the highest). I was willing to be Robin Hood and take on Nottingham for a grand vision. At the same time I scored a ten on sensitivity. The latter would qualify me to be a counselor or social worker, not a CEO or union president. Much of that was shaped by my childhood and the family I grew up in. At New Life we like to give the 16PF (Personality Factor) test to help people discern their personalities better. Myers-Briggs and Performax-DiSC are also helpful tools.

Look at your season of life. Your season of life is also a God-given limit. Ecclesiastes teaches us "there is a time for everything and a season for every activity under the heavens ... a time to plant and a time to uproot ... a time to weep and a time to laugh ... a time to be silent and a time to speak" (Eccl. 3:1 – 8).

Parenting has seasons. There are seasons when we need to be home with small children. Then these children become teenagers and leave home, thrusting us into a different season of life. There are times when, because of health reasons, our families need us. There are seasons of financial prosperity and times of struggle. There are times to be studying intensely and preparing. There are times for great activity. There are times to grieve a loss and wait.

It is critical we do not judge other people's seasons or impose our season on others. Little is permanent in life.

Look at your life situation. Your life situation is also a limit. When we age physically, we find our bodies cannot do what they used to. When we are young and without much life experience, certain doors may remain closed to us. If we have a physical or emotional disability or a sickness, we may find this keeps us from going down a path we may have planned.

If you are married, Paul considers that a limit (1 Cor. 7:32 – 35). Singleness is a different kind of limit. Each child, while a gift from God, now constitutes a limit in what, where, and how you use your life to serve God. If you have a special-needs child or an aging parent, that too affects your life course.

Look at your emotional, physical, and intellectual capacities. Your emotional, physical, and intellectual capacities are also a God-given gift. I have a large capacity for people and complexity in my work. At the same time, if I work all day with people for more than two days consecutively, I find myself lethargic and depressed. I need time to read, pray, and reflect. I also need three to five minutes for transitioning from one meeting to another at church in order to be centered and fully attentive.

I have a pastor friend who is able to work seventy to eighty hour weeks, six days a week with ease. God bless him, but I cannot do likewise physically, emotionally, and spiritually. It is so freeing as a leader for me to utter the words "I can't." When we don't respect God's limits in our lives, we will often find ourselves overextended, stressed, and exhausted.

Look at your "difficult" emotions. Anger, depression, and rage, for example, often function as oil lights in our lives, informing us that something is not right on the inside of the engine of our lives. This is often one of the ways God stops me and gets my attention.

Look at your scars and wounds from your family past. They are also God-given limits and gifts. If we will look for the hand of God moving in our family history, even in the most painful moments, we will find golden nuggets in that rocky soil. Abuse, neglect, abandonment, poverty, oppression, and so on may cause us to feel we are "behind," always trying to catch up. God sees it differently.

The limits I inherit from my family turn out to be gifts, once I embrace them. I find myself more dependent on God, more sensitive, and less judgmental of others. I love others better as I encourage them to joyfully live within their God-given limits.

Nicholas — Tsar of Russia

Nicholas II found himself at the age of twenty-six installed as tsar of Russia, ruler of almost one-sixth of the world. A reluctant leader, forced by the death of his father into a role for which he was ill-equipped, Nicholas seemed to be just the opposite of his aggressive, strong father, whom he called a "father beyond compare."[6] He lacked his father's experience, authoritative manner, and majestic physical stature.

Instead, God had given Nicholas a tender temperament, a deep love for his family, and a sensitive nature. He was continually accused of having an un-tsar-like nature because he was soft-spoken and kind. One historian noted: "In office, the Emperor's gentleness and his lack of self-assertiveness had been weaknesses ... With his family ... they were strengths."[7]

The demands of ruling never suited his personality. He was more suited to be a tailor than an emperor. He much preferred to be with his wife and children in private at home or at one of their summer residences. Meanwhile, the storm clouds of World War I were swirling around him as was Lenin's Bolshevik revolution of 1917.

Out of a sense of duty he persevered but, eventually, tsarist Russia crumbled. If Nicholas had dared to break with the life script handed to him and let someone else become leader, history may have turned out differently.

Faithful to Your True Self

Ask yourself these questions: Does the way in which I am living my life fit my God-given nature? Does it fit my true self (to use Thomas Merton's terminology in his *Seeds of Contemplation*)?[8] Am I being faithful to my God-given talents, my unique story, my weaknesses?

Maturity in life is when someone is living joyfully within their God-given limits. I find most of us resent limits — in ourselves and in others. We expect far too much from ourselves and each other and often live frustrated and angry lives. Much of

> Maturity in life is when someone is living joyfully within their God-given limits.

burnout is a result of giving what we do not possess. Henri Nouwen summarizes our challenge well:

> No two lives are the same. We often compare our lives with those of others, trying to decide whether we are better or worse off, but such comparisons do not help us much. We have to live our life, not someone else's. We have to hold *our own* cup. We have to dare to say: "This is my life, the life that is given to me, and it is this life that I have to live, as well as I can. My life is unique. Nobody else will ever live it. I have my own history, my own family, my own body, my own character, my own friends, my own way of thinking, speaking, and acting—yes, I have my own life to live. No one else has the same challenge. I am alone, because I am unique. Many people can help me live my life, but after all is said and done, I have to make my own choices about how to live.[9]

God invites us to do life, to work from a place of rest. I watch carefully for signals that I have strayed from my God-given life. I know I am off center, when:

- I am anxious.
- I am rushing or hurrying.
- My body is in a knot.
- I am doing too many things.
- My mind cannot stop racing.
- I am driving too fast.
- I am not able to be fully present with people.
- I am irritable about the simple tasks of life, like having to wait in line at the supermarket.
- I am skimming over time with God.

These are a few of my warning signs. You may want to delete some or add others that apply to your particular temptations and vulnerabilities. Most important, we must be brutally honest with ourselves when we are straying from the center of God's will and the unique life he has called us to live.

4. Integrating the Gift of Limits into the Church

In talking with pastors and leaders, I find this principle to be the most difficult one to apply in the church. In fact, one of the great tasks of leadership is to help others accept their limits. There are at least four ways that we have intentionally worked the gift of limits into New Life: emphasizing self-care of leaders, setting limits on invasive people, giving people freedom to say no, and intentionally teaching boundaries throughout the church.

Emphasize Self-Care of Leaders

As with all the principles of an emotionally healthy church, this one too begins with the leadership. We seek to model the priority that our personal lives and family come first, not the church. Staff, board members, and leaders are expected to do appropriate self-care and set boundaries based on who God has made them to be and on their particular family situation.

Understanding the gift of limits enables us to affirm self-care. It is one of the great challenges for those who serve others. As Parker Palmer says, "Self-care is never a selfish act — it is simply good stewardship of the only gift I have, the gift I was put on earth to offer to others. Anytime we can listen to true self and give it the care it requires, we do so not only for ourselves, but for the many others whose lives we touch."[10]

This is so vital to the health of our church that we have crafted a "Rule of Life" for our pastoral staff that includes weekly Sabbath-keeping, a day alone with God each month, and a commitment to pause for "Daily Offices" (often called "Fixed-Hour Prayers") each day.[11] God has a unique combination of activity and contemplation for each of us. He has made each of us different. The question is how much time we each need alone *with* God so that Christ's life flows out of us. When we are able to help both ourselves and those around us with this delicate balance, we find ourselves so deeply rooted in God that our activity *for* him becomes marked by a rich peace and joy.

> Understanding the gift of limits enables us to affirm self-care. It is one of the great challenges for those who serve others.

Everyone on our staff or in volunteer leadership understands that if their family or personal life is out of control, we will ask them to step down from leadership. This isn't a punishment; it is an act of love and concern. The fruit of this is that our people now rarely feel used.

Set Limits on Invasive People

A critical issue for a church is to create and maintain a climate of love and respect for each person in the community. That requires intentionally teaching limits and boundaries as well as reparenting invasive people. I am referring to those who take up too much space at the expense of others, who don't allow others to express themselves, who manipulate and use people for their own purposes, or who damage the community by approaching situations and people in ways that are not biblical.

Often in churches, the most demanding, complaining members set the agenda. Like cancer cells, they kill healthy ones by invading other people's spaces. They seem unable to learn from their experiences and are unwilling to change.

An emotionally healthy church has a vision from God about its uniqueness and calling. It is not trying to be another church. It has its own values and goals. It seeks to function as Jesus did. He was empathetic to the twelve disciples, the religious leaders, and the crowds, but he maintained a clear sense of God's plan for his life. His highest priority was not to avoid conflict but to do God's will.[12]

Give People Freedom to Say No

We teach members to use their spiritual gifts in the church and to serve in at least one ministry outside of their gifting. At the same time, we applaud some people for saying no, especially those who work tirelessly. For those of us who feel guilty when we see an unmet need, it takes great courage and strength to not volunteer. For us, it is denying our sinful self (that wants to be God) and following Jesus. It is trusting that God will meet that need through others.

Is it more difficult to get people to serve at New Life now than in previous years? Yes. Without shame, guilt, or pressure, people are free to say, "No, thank you." The result, however, is that the quality of what we are doing is more loving. People are less cranky and cantankerous, and they tend to serve for a longer period of time because they are internally motivated. They love and give love freely.

Perhaps most important, they feel loved and not used to build the church.

Teach Boundaries 101 and 102

Adam and Eve were the first boundary breakers. They crossed the line God had set up for them, eating from the forbidden tree and then running from God. From that time forward we have been breaking boundaries and crossing lines with God and one another. The fall distorted for the rest of human history our sense of separateness, boundaries, and responsibility. We have been confused, ever since, about where we end and someone else begins.[13]

Boundaries, simply defined, are the realization that I am a separate person, apart from others. They represent "what is me and what is not me." Boundaries show where you end and someone else begins. With proper boundaries I know what I am and am not responsible for.

People with poor boundaries feel compelled to do what others want even though it is not what they want to do. They are afraid of disappointing someone or being criticized. They want others to like them, and they surely don't want to be seen as selfish. You hear them making statements such as the following:

- "I said I would lead the usher ministry because the pastor asked. I know I don't have the time right now with all the pressure at work and the needs of my family, but I just couldn't say no."
- "I have to go to prayer meeting on Wednesday night. People really expect me to go. I know Pastor Joe and the others would be let down if I didn't show up."
- "Honey, we have to go to dinner at the Martinezes'. I know we don't want to and our kids will complain because there is nobody their age to play with, but what are we going to do? Do you know how upset they would be? They are just trying to be nice."

The problem with each of the above scenarios is each person does not know where they end and the other person begins. Each person does not have a life apart from the other. That is the crux of what boundaries are all about: "Where do I end and where does someone else begin?"

I must define and protect my boundaries with anything that breathes. Our boundaries get tested numerous times each day — by spouses, friends, coworkers, church members, salespeople, and children. People simply want what they want. That is not a bad thing. People will always want things from you and me, such as time, emotional support, money. This is normal.

The problem is that the world's needs are far greater than my personal supply. And I must now discern what is the best response in the long run rather than what is the easiest to do right now. I was recently asked, for example, to take significant leadership in a large overseas missions project. The person leading the initiative visited my office and presented me with a strong case for my involvement. My personal supply of time and energy, however, are limited by my commitments to God, Geri, my daughters, and to New Life Fellowship Church as senior pastor. Saying yes would have negatively impacted at least one of those commitments.[14]

Not setting boundaries often leads to numerous other problems, such as anxiety, depression, anger, panic, and feelings of powerlessness. It is seen most destructively when people allow themselves to be physically, sexually, emotionally, or spiritually abused.

Boundaries 101: Learning to be together yet separate. The following chart is simple to understand but extremely difficult to live. Each circle represents two different people. Each one has thoughts, opinions, feelings, values, hopes, fears, beliefs, abilities, desires, likes, and dislikes. Each one is inside one circle, yet each is within the property line of the person. That is why it is so critical we pay attention to what we are thinking, feeling, desiring, and so on and become more and more aware of who we are.

The Bible calls us as a family to be connected to one another in relationship in such a loving way that the world will know that Jesus is real and alive (John 13:34–35). This connection, however, to others is to happen without us losing our individuality or separateness.

Each one of us is a unique individual made in the image of God. He has crowned us with glory and honor (Ps. 8:5). He has stamped onto us uniqueness, sacredness, preciousness, and value. Each individual life is a miracle.[15]

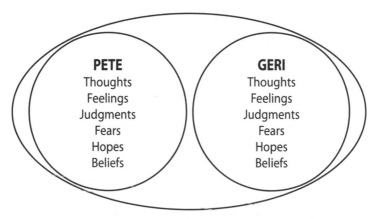

Learning to Be Together Yet Separate

In our small groups, equipping classes, and seminars on boundaries, we also teach that most of us are also notorious for crossing other people's boundaries. We sometimes don't take no for an answer, or we might say to other people, "You've got to do this!" or "You must see this issue the way I do!"

What, then, is the balance of separateness and togetherness? How do I work out the tensions inherent in this?

Boundaries 102: Respect in our togetherness yet separateness. The problem with most churches (and marriages, too, by the way) is there is not enough separateness. I have crossed people's boundaries more than once by making judgments on why they were not attending New Life anymore or did not want to serve in leadership. I never respected them enough to ask why. I was too "enmeshed" with that person.

Many of us in leadership also need to respect ourselves more and declare clearly what we think and feel. Out of fear and a desire for "peace," we often allow our individuality to be diminished. "Pastor, I am really mad about the lack of a midweek service. I really need it." In my better moments, I respond, "I'm sorry we don't have a midweek service. Check out one of our small groups. They're great."

Christian leaders all too often allow themselves to be disrespected, allowing people to speak to them and about them in ways that are inappropriate. They think that this is the "Christian way." But for a healthy community to thrive, there must be a foundation of respect. By respect, I am referring to how we treat one another, not how we feel about each other. We have a right to be different, a right to be taken seriously, a right to be heard, and a right to disagree. Take away any of those and you have relationships dominated by one or more persons at the expense of another.

> Christian leaders all too often allow themselves to be disrespected.

5. Growing through Our Limitations

At the same time we must regularly ask ourselves: Are there limits that God is asking me to break through because they are a result of my character flaws?

As I mentioned earlier, I was stuck for years around the issue of my organizational abilities as a pastor. Making personnel decisions, managing budgets, following through on details, and writing job descriptions were difficult for me. I excelled in vision-casting and teaching. I was told: "You don't have those gifts, so play to your strengths and hire people to your weaknesses. Spend your time in the Word and prayer. Let others run the church."

We tried different staff configurations, hiring from the outside, hiring from the inside, dividing the job between different people. Each time we hit a wall. Nothing seemed to work long-term. Tension remained until I was willing to confront my own character flaws.

While it is true that my primary calling is not to be an executive pastor, the real issue related to my character. I preferred the easy thing (preaching and praying) to the hard thing of managing people. I did not like to invest the time needed to thoughtfully prepare for staff meetings and wrestle with strategic planning. It was easier to be impulsive and "vision-driven" than to look at hard facts. Who wanted to confront a nonperforming volunteer when I could be spending that time preaching and receiving praise from the congregation?

The issue for me, as it is for many lead/senior pastors I meet, did not revolve around my God-given limitations, but my weakness in character. We have since formed a director team to do some of that work. The difference now is that I am not doing executive functions to avoid growing up in Christ.

6. Watching God Work through Our Limitations

Before closing this chapter, I must emphasize that God, at times, will take us beyond our limitations in supernatural ways.

- Sarah was ninety and Abraham "as good as dead" (Rom. 4:19). Yet God made them a mother and father to nations.
- Elijah and Jeremiah were prone to bouts of depression and yet were mightily used by God.
- Moses was eighty years old when God set him on a task that required the physical and emotional stamina of a forty-year-old. He also had a major speech impediment that, in his opinion, disqualified him. God saw it differently.
- Timothy, apparently fearful and shy by nature, was called upon by God to lead the large, difficult church at Ephesus, which was

beset by divisions, problems, and conflicts. Paul reminded him that God had not given him a spirit of fear (2 Tim.1:7).

Hebrews 11 provides us with a sampling of the biblical heroes who, by faith, conquered kingdoms, shut the mouths of lions, and became powerful in battle, routing foreign enemies (Heb. 11:32–33). For this reason we must regularly ask ourselves: Which are the limits God is asking me to break through by faith so that others might know and trust him, that I might become the person he intends? And which of the limits, external or internal, do I need to receive as a gift, as God's invitation for me to surrender in trust to him?

Sometimes it can seem as if living within boundaries and limits is not in the best interest of the church. It appears that obeying God could lead to disaster, both for us and for those around us. Will anything get done? Will the church ever grow? Will everyone become self-absorbed narcissists living in isolation from one another if I teach this?

King David was overwhelmingly grateful to God for all his goodness to him. Everything was going right. His power had been consolidated. Jerusalem was established as the capital with the ark of God's presence at its center. David was riding a wave of popularity and was regularly publishing powerful songs and hymns of worship to God.

He desperately wanted to build God a temple for nations to know God. Nathan the prophet encouraged him to go for it. God, however, said, "No." God set a clear limit.

This was one of the most critical moments in King David's life. It would either qualify or disqualify him as a true king with a heart for God. These moments and decisions are equally critical for us.

I cannot imagine the depth of David's disappointment or embarrassment. What would all the other pagan kings around him think? They had all built magnificent temple structures to their gods. David looked foolish and weak by comparison.

David, the Bible says, sat down and prayed. By the time it was over, he submitted to God's limit, trusting an infinite plan he could not see. "Our God is in heaven; he does whatever pleases him" (Ps. 115:3). "The secret things belong to the LORD our God" (Deut. 29:29). David realized God is God and he was not.

David wrestled with the core spiritual issue for us if we are to be faithful to living within our God-given boundaries and limits: Is God good and is God really sovereign?

God is so staggering that, like David, we can't even imagine where he is going and what he is doing in and through our lives. David accepted that his breadth of knowledge was too narrow to perceive God's intent. Only time would strip away his shallow understandings of what was going on and why God said no to his plans. God was painting on a vast canvas over a long period of time. Only in eternity would he understand.

Meanwhile, David, like us, was to be faithful to his God-given limits and prepare the materials for Solomon, his son, to build the temple in the next generation. That required a radical faith and trust in God. In the same way, people in emotionally healthy churches trust in God's goodness by receiving his limits as gifts and expressions of his love. At times this involves grieving the loss of dreams and expectations we may have for our lives, a reality that leads us to the next principle of emotionally healthy disciples and churches: the ability to embrace grief and loss.

CHAPTER 9

PRINCIPLE 5:
EMBRACE GRIEVING AND LOSS

In emotionally healthy churches, people embrace grief as a way to become more like God. They understand what a critical component of discipleship grieving our losses is. Why? It is the only pathway to becoming a compassionate person like our Lord Jesus.

I covered over my losses for years and years, unaware of how they were shaping my current relationships and leadership. God was seeking to enlarge my soul and mature me while I was seeking a quick end to my pain. Pastors and leaders, in particular, experience a large number of losses due to our unique position in the body of Christ. Often, when we wonder if we are regressing and going backward spiritually, God is doing his most profound work of transformation in us.

The Soul Grows Larger through Suffering

In the fall of 1991 Jerry and Lynda Sittser, along with his mother and their four children ranging from ages two to eight, were driving in their minivan on a lonely stretch of highway in rural Idaho. They had been visiting a nearby Native American Indian reservation as a school project for their two oldest children. They seemed, as friends described them, like the "two-million-dollar" family. They felt as if they were "living on top of the world."

Ten minutes into their drive home, Sittser noticed a car traveling toward them extremely fast. He slowed down at a curve but the

159

oncoming car, traveling at eighty-five miles an hour, crashed head-long into their minivan. The driver was drunk. In one moment Sittser lost three generations — his mother, his wife, and their four-year-old daughter. He writes, "In one moment my family as I had known and cherished it was obliterated."[1] Sittser sat on that lonely highway watching them die.

The driver of the other car was eventually declared not guilty and set free because it could not be proven, beyond the shadow of a doubt at the trial, that he (not his pregnant wife, who had died in the accident) had been driving the car.

Sittser wrote a book about his descent into an abyss of grief and incomprehensible pain that changed his life. Under the title *A Grace Disguised: How the Soul Grows through Loss*, he writes:

> *Catastrophic loss by definition precludes recovery. It will trans-form us or destroy us, but it will never leave us the same.* There is no going back to the past … It is not therefore true that we become less through loss — unless we allow the loss to make us less, grinding our soul down until there is nothing left. *Loss can also make us more.* I did not get over my loved ones; rather I absorbed the loss into my life until it became part of who I am. Sorrow took up permanent residence in my soul *and enlarged it* … One learns the pain of others by suffering one's own pain, by turning inside oneself, by finding one's own soul … How-ever painful, sorrow is good for the soul … The soul is elastic, like a balloon. *It can grow larger through suffering.*[2] (emphasis added)

At the same time as I was wrestling with this strange process called grieving and its relationship to spirituality, I was given a book enti-tled *Lament for a Son*, by Nicholas Wolterstorff,[3] a Yale professor and theologian. The small book is filled with his reflections and struggles over God's allowing the death of his twenty-five-year-old son, Eric, in a mountain-climbing accident in Austria.

He doesn't have any explanations or answers for why God would have allowed such a tragedy. Who does? At one point, however, he con-cludes with a profound insight, "Through the prism of my tears I have seen a suffering God. It is said of God that no one can behold his face and live. I always thought this meant that no one can see his splendor and live. A friend said perhaps it meant that no one could see his sorrow and live. Or perhaps his sorrow is splendor."[4]

Let Grief Develop Maturity

Few Christians in North America and Europe understand sorrow and grieving, especially as it relates to God, ourselves, and its vital importance to living in a healthy community. But the degree to which I learn to grieve my own losses is in direct proportion to the depth and quality of my relationship with God and the compassion I can offer to others.

Think with me for a moment about the vast array of losses we accumulate in a lifetime. There are devastating losses that include, for example, the death of children, the premature death of a spouse, a disability, divorce, rape, emotional or sexual abuse, irreversible cancer, infertility, the shattering of a lifelong dream, a suicide, someone we love who betrays us, or the discovery that one of our role models was corrupt.

Sometimes our sense of loss comes from cataclysmic events that happen nearby us. On September 11, 2001, when the two planes filled with suicide bombers and innocent people flew into the largest buildings in our city, killing almost three thousand people, our community experienced daily trauma for over a year. In situations like this, we normally give permission to people to grieve — at least for a season.

Other losses are considered "insignificant," yet it is equally important to grieve over them. Stuffed down and denied, they gather in our souls like heavy stones that weigh us down. Unattended to over time, they prevent us from entering into walking freely and honestly with God and others.

> Other losses ... unattended to over time, prevent us from entering into walking freely and honestly with God and others.

I am referring to what some call our "natural losses." You graduate from high school or college and lose your financial or emotional security. Your youthful skin begins to wrinkle and age. You move away and your former friendships fade away. Relationships don't work out the way you hoped. Your children become less and less dependent on you as they grow older. Leadership changes in the church. Your small group ends. Your church constructs a new building. A grandparent dies. A fire destroys your cherished photographs. A faithful pet is run over by a car.

Other losses are more hidden and difficult to classify, such as a stillbirth, a miscarriage, or an abortion.

The most important issue is not calculating where a particular loss is on the continuum of public to private, or sudden to gradual. Loss is loss. It is the norm of life, not the exception.

God has made us all unique. Our temperaments and histories are different. What may be an insignificant loss for you may be catastrophic for me. Each of us will respond differently. For example, when a pet dies, it is a great loss for one family member while another is hardly affected by it.

When a person leaves the church disgruntled, the response of different pastors on our staff is strikingly different. A few of us feel it deeply. Others are able to accept it and move on quickly. We are each built uniquely.

Because others are not affected by the loss in the same way you are, it does not change the fact that this is your experience. Geri, for example, grieves the raising of our children in New York City, a city of over eight million people. While there are many benefits to raising our children in this densely populated city filled with peoples from all over the world, she knows they are missing out on the rich experience of the small-town community life that she experienced growing up. I don't have that same sense of loss.

Two former members of our church (now living in Florida), Martin and Carol, were engaged to be married and filled with anticipation for their future when Martin's only daughter, age eleven, was murdered in broad daylight. She was on her way to meet some friends at a skating rink. It has been seventeen years, and only recently have authorities indicted the murderer. The landscape of their lives was shattered by the explosive effect of this senseless act.

> We all experience sorrows and are invited to grieve and grow through them.

I have not experienced any sorrow near that magnitude in my life. Yet I can enter, on some level at least, into their experience because I have chosen to enter into my own sorrows and grief. What is universal is that we all experience sorrows and are invited to grieve and grow through them.

Grieving Is Not an Interruption

I used to believe that grieving was an interruption, an obstacle in my path to serve Christ. In short, I considered it a waste of time, preventing me from "redeeming the time" (Eph. 5:16 KJV) for God. "Just get over it," I would mutter silently to myself.

"Forgive and forget, that's what the Bible says ... as God does!" I would say.

One of the great obstacles to grieving, at least for me, was that I had created the situations that were now causing such pain for me and others in the church. I was "reaping what I had sown." "So what good is being sad over it going to do?" I'd remind myself. "Let's fix it and move on." After all, what right did I have to feel the sadness and frustration of the mess I had made?

I was also uncomfortable with the lack of control I might have if I allowed myself to feel the depression, the anger, the sadness, and the doubts about God. At times I wondered if God had let go of the steering wheel in the car of my life while it sped off a cliff. So I moved on. Unable to mourn, I covered over my losses for years and years. I hated the notion of losing control and having to wait so helplessly for God. One of the reasons I resisted stopping from all my busy activity is I did not want to face the sadness that was waiting for me.

We commonly avoid God's interruptions of loss in our churches as well.

> I was also uncomfortable with the lack of control I might have if I allowed myself to feel.

For example, the church moves into a new place and a new building, yet there is a group of people struggling with the move. They don't feel right, interpreting that as a sign from God they shouldn't have moved. In actuality, however, they needed time and an opportunity to grieve leaving a place where God had done many wonderful works. Instead of going room by room in the old building, remembering the youth who had experiences with God in a certain back room, the babies dedicated, and weddings celebrated in the small sanctuary, their feelings are seen as rebellion or a lack of willingness to participate in this next "move of God." In fact, what they need is the opportunity to pray, to express thanks to God for all the good things he has done, and to say goodbye.

We celebrate Mother's Day and forget to be sensitive to the infertile couples or single women who find this the most difficult Sunday of the year as their dreams for children slip away, more and more, each year.

People lose a child through miscarriage, and we admonish them to get back into life as it was as soon as possible.

Good, faithful members of our community move far away, and we feel guilty about our sadness and grief. We share it with our small group, and people quote Philippians 4:4 ("Rejoice in the Lord always. I will say it again: Rejoice!") or 1 Thessalonians 5:18 ("Give thanks in all circumstances").

A person goes through a painful divorce and quickly finds another companion, thinking, "Isn't it wonderful that all things work together for good?" (Rom. 8:28), without ever grieving the enormity of the loss. We are not sure what to say or do.

A young man in his twenties begins to explore his past (principle 2) and, for the first time, faces the abuse and abandonment he suffered as a foster child in the city system for eighteen years. He is encouraged immediately to forget about it and focus on his intimacy with his heavenly Father and new adoption into God's family. As a result, he misses a wonderful opportunity to remove a blockage in his spiritual and emotional growth.

Avoid Superficial Forgiveness

Forgiveness is not a quick process. I do not believe it is possible to truly forgive another person from the heart until we allow ourselves to feel the pain of what was lost. People who say it is simply an act of the will do not understand grieving.

When Jesus forgives us, he does not say, "Well, they did their best. They couldn't help it." He is not detached and void of emotions. Rather, Jesus truly feels our rebellion, our waywardness, our unwillingness to receive him as he hangs there alone

> Forgiveness is not a quick process.

on the cross and cries, "Father, forgive them, for they do not know what they are doing" (Luke 23:34).

The process of forgiveness always involves grieving before letting go—whether you are the person giving forgiveness or asking for it.

I remember clearly when the Spanish congregation I pastored had split and two hundred people whom I had shepherded for four years left the church. I had invested a great deal of love, sweat, energy, and prayer into the planting of the congregation. Not only was there no time or space or understanding of grieving my loss, but I found that the more I tried to forgive the leader through sheer force of the will, the more my feelings of anger intensified. I was moving on, preaching, teaching, leading, building the church, but inwardly I was under an oppressive guilt over my inability to forgive him.

I remember one of our members confronting me with my own theology: "Pastor Pete, you taught us that unless we forgive our enemies, God in heaven won't forgive us. Why don't you just forgive him and move on?"

I was so distraught! I didn't understand that there might be a process to forgiving. I didn't understand it was important that I own the pain first so that I could forgive maturely and not superficially. I didn't understand that it was a journey, and the deeper the wound, the longer the journey. I didn't understand that forgiveness from the heart is very, very difficult, that it often takes a miracle from God. Denying the painful, horrible reality of what had happened surfaced in a growing resentment toward the church and God.

Lewis Smedes sums up the dangers of superficial forgiveness: "We will not take healing action against unfair pain until we own the pain we want to heal. It is not enough to feel pain. We need to appropriate the pain we feel: Be conscious of it, take it on, and take it as our own ... I worry about fast forgivers. They tend to forgive quickly in order to avoid their pain."[5]

> Some people in grief commit reckless sins ... to escape the pain of their present situation.

I understand now why some people in grief commit reckless sins. They don't know what else they can do to escape the pain of their present situation. They haven't learned to grieve.

1. Phase One: Paying Attention as Part of the Grieving Process

Elizabeth Kübler-Ross has made famous five stages of response to death: denial, anger, bargaining, depression, and acceptance.[6] While this is helpful, I recommend we learn from David and his response to grief and loss as a model, dividing the process into three distinct phases: paying attention, waiting in the confusing in-between, and allowing the old to birth the new. Each needs to be understood in relation to the other and as part of something larger and more complex that we can ever fully understand.

David, the Lamenting Psalmist: A Man after God's Own Heart

David is well known for being a man after God's own heart (1 Sam. 13:14; Acts 13:22). What few realize is how closely this characteristic is related to the way he repeatedly paid attention to loss, disappointment, and threats of death. Unlike how I handled my grief about the staff betrayal, David spoke and sang all the time about his different sadnesses.

For example, David had a deep love and respect for King Saul even though Saul felt threatened by David's popularity with the people and hunted him down for ten to twelve years. David was also best friends with Saul's son Jonathan. They had a beautiful friendship for many years, based on their mutual love for God and the truth.

During David's time in the wilderness, Saul and Jonathan were killed in battle with the Philistines. This marked the end of Saul's forty-plus-year reign as king and the beginning of David's. When David heard of their deaths, he did not move to the next event in God's plan (receiving the throne of Israel). Instead, he grieved. He could not bear to think of the Philistines rejoicing.

So he writes a song, a poem — a moving, beautiful, detailed lament of the horror that has occurred (2 Sam. 1:17–27). "Your glory, O Israel, lies slain on your heights. How the mighty have fallen ... Saul and Jonathan, in life they were loved and gracious" (vv. 19, 26 NIV). He anguishes over the catastrophe three times: "How the mighty have fallen!" David, consumed with grief, addresses Jonathan directly, "I grieve for you, Jonathan my brother."

Teach the Lament to God's People

David actually orders the people to join him in singing the lamentation he has written: "O daughters of Israel, weep for Saul." Can you imagine? David expects others to join him in pouring out grief with tears about the enormous loss Israel now faces. He recognizes that something precious in Israel is gone and will never return.

David also orders that his song of lament be taught to the thousands of men of Judah (2 Sam. 1:18). He wants them to learn it, to memorize it, and to sing it as their experience, not simply his.

> David expects others to join him in pouring out grief with tears about the enormous loss Israel now faces.

When is the last time your church sang a lament like this in Sunday worship to God? In fact, when have you ever been taught the importance of grieving and loss and how to integrate it into worship to God? When is the last time you preached or heard a message on grieving or lamenting?

Why does David force the people to stop and pay attention? Why does he want them to express sorrow over the deaths of Saul and Jonathan? Isn't there a lot of work to do now that there will be a transition to a new government?

David understands how indispensable grieving is to spiritual maturity. David knows we are deepened by taking the time to grieve our losses before moving on. He knows how important it is for the people to stay connected to reality and not to run from pain.

At New Life this has meant we needed to slow down. When my role as the leader of the pastoral staff team was given to another, I thought nothing of it. He was more gifted than I was to lead and manage them. I was positive the staff would be thrilled. I forgot that after many years they had grown accustomed to my leading and attending all the staff meetings. It was a loss — greater for some than for others, depending on how long they had been on staff and on their own particular history.

We have learned that when people leave the church or move away, it is important to pause and feel the loss. When a ministry dream or opportunity does not work out, it is crucial that we pay attention to our inner life beneath the surface and feel the disappointment before God.

When people have a vision to do a new program or ministry and cannot, they need to grieve their limits and humanity before God.

> When a ministry dream or opportunity does not work out, it is crucial that we pay attention to our inner life beneath the surface and feel the disappointment before God.

Pay Attention in the Book of Psalms

Throughout history, Psalms has been the most popular book of the Bible. And for good reason, for there is a "psalm for every sigh." This longest book in the Bible includes psalms of adoration, psalms of thanksgiving, psalms of wisdom, psalms of repentance, and even psalms expressing doubt.

The majority are far from cheerful. As Bernard Anderson writes, "Laments far outnumber any other kind of songs in the Psalter."[7] More than half of the 150 psalms are classified as laments. Most were written by David, according to tradition.

The laments pay attention to the reality that life can be hard, difficult, and sometimes even brutal. They take notice of the apparent absence of God. They notice when circumstances seem to say that God is not good. They cry out to God for comfort and care.

Laments wrestle with God's loyal, faithful love (ḥesed in Hebrew).

- "Tears have been my food day and night." (Ps. 42:3)
- "Why must I go about mourning, oppressed by the enemy?" (Ps. 43:2)
- "Has his unfailing love [ḥesed] vanished forever? Has his promise failed for all time? Has God forgotten to be merciful?" (Ps. 77:8–9)
- "You have put me in the lowest pit, in the darkest depths. Your wrath lies heavily on me; you have overwhelmed me with all your waves." (Ps. 88:6–7)

Psalms ask the difficult question: Since God is good and loving, why is he not doing something?

Pay Attention to Pain

Many of us have taken on our culture's pain-denying view of grieving. Perhaps the most popular way in our culture of not paying attention to our losses and pain is by medicating ourselves through an addiction. People use work, TV, drugs, alcohol, shopping or food binges, busyness, sexual escapades, unhealthy relational attachments, *even serving others at church incessantly* — anything to medicate the pain of life.

Year after year we deny and avoid the difficulties and losses of life, the rejections and frustrations. People in our churches minimize their failures and disappointments. The result is that for many today, at least in prosperous North America, there is a widespread inability to face pain. This has led to an overall feeling of superficiality and a lack of profound compassion.

Our culture trivializes tragedy and loss. Every night on the news we are given pictures of crimes, wars, famines, murders, and natural disasters. They are analyzed and reported, but there is no lamenting.

Our national capacity to grieve is almost lost. We are too busy with trying to keep everything as it is and getting our own way. When a loss enters our life, we become angry at God and treat it as an alien invasion from outer space. Is it any wonder that so much depression exists in our culture? Is it any wonder there has been such an explosion of drugs prescribed for depression and anxiety?

This is unbiblical and a denial of our common humanity. The ancient Hebrews physically expressed their laments by tearing their clothes and utilizing sackcloth and ashes. Jesus himself offered up prayer and petitions with loud cries and tears (Heb. 5:7). During Noah's generation, Scripture indicates God was grieved about the state of humanity (Gen. 6). Jeremiah had six confessions or laments in which he protested to God about his circumstances. After the fall of Jerusalem, he wrote an entire biblical book called Lamentations.

"There is a time for everything, and a season for every activity under the heavens," including "a time to mourn" (Eccl.3:1, 4). To reject God's seasons for grief and sadness as they come to us is to live only half of our lives. What makes this particularly tragic is that Jesus Christ came to set us free to engage life fully, not escape from its reality.

Follow How Jesus Grieved

Imagine Jesus, the "man of sorrows" (Isa. 53:3), in the following situations:

- At the tomb of Lazarus, what if Jesus had not wept (John 11:35) but instead said: "Come on, everyone! Please stop all the moaning. Get a grip. I'll take care of this."

- What if his prayer over Jerusalem had gone like this: "I wanted to gather you as a hen gathers her chicks, but you made your decision, you turned against God. It's too bad. I am moving on without you."
- Or, when Jesus was on the cross, instead of crying, "My God, my God why have you forsaken me?" what if he had shouted out over the crowd, "God is great! He will be victorious! Praise him!"

Hebrews 5:8 tells us "He learned obedience from what he suffered." So do we.

> In Scripture, the Godlike response is ... for us to deal honestly and prayerfully with our losses and disappointments.

In Scripture, the Godlike response is neither a spin nor a cover-up. The model and teaching is for us to deal honestly and prayerfully with our losses and disappointments (big and small) and all their accompanying confusing emotions. Scripture commands us to pay attention. Grieving is indispensable for a full-orbed spirituality.

I suspect David (the psalmist) and Jeremiah (the author of the book of Lamentations) understood this tendency not to let difficult, painful realities into our lives. Knowing, however, how indispensable losses are for us to change and grow, they wrote songs and poems of lament for us to sing from generation to generation.

Pay Attention to Deaths from Our Past

Jesus defined the growth process in these words: "Unless a kernel of wheat falls to the ground and dies, it remains only a single seed. But if it dies, it produces many seeds" (John 12:24). Jesus characterizes the Christian life as one of dying so that a new door can open to a radically new life.

Death, however, must come first. That death begins participating in the sometimes excruciating process of paying attention. If we pay attention to them, however, something new will be birthed.

Bianca, for example, was tormented from a young age through her dreams. She remembers sexual nightmares at age eleven. She would toss and turn, feeling dirty. She was still too young to know her nightmares were the result of years of molestation and rape by a much-loved relative.

She grew older without noticing that she was anxious, that she was uncomfortable with her sexuality and the sexuality of others. Throughout the years Bianca shared what had happened to her with three people. None asked questions. One commented, "Well, maybe he was just experimenting."

She was conscious of her sexual abuse. She hadn't buried it. She didn't have to remember it; it was always there.

In 1989, she started working for the Board of Education in the largest school district in New York City, in a school where 95 percent of the population was below the poverty line. Her nightmares returned with a vengeance. The lack of protection and safety in the life of some of her students evoked horrible images of her own childhood. Her dreams became filled once again with violence, rape, and anxiety. Insomnia set in.

By then, she had already been a Christian for twelve years, faithfully attending Bible studies and prayer meetings. Nonetheless, the sense of sadness that had always permeated her life became overwhelming.

The church was interested in her strength and her service. She was gifted in so many ways. But she couldn't share that she was dying on the inside. No one in leadership had modeled vulnerability, weakness, confusion, or extreme pain. Everything was "Praise God, for he is good."

She was serving a God she did not trust, a God she felt was distant and only interested in her strengths. On many Sundays she would cry long and hard, thinking her children would have to visit her under some viaduct because she would end up a prostitute. She questioned how a life so broken could ever be put together again. She secretly wondered how God could have looked upon those nights of death and abuse and not be moved to protect her?

Out of desperation Bianca went to a safe place to talk about her grief, through a friend finding a Christian counselor. Here she began to explore and grieve the devastation to her wholeness as a little girl. She entered the chaos and darkness of the death of her childhood at the hands of this relative. The floodgates were now open. Things seemed only to get worse as her feelings and frozen rage exploded into anger and depression.

She responded to an altar call at her church for people with sexual brokenness in their past. She began to share her abyss with some close, trusted friends in the body. She stopped working so hard to earn God's approval and began to grasp the love and grace in the gospel. These events have taken years.

Bianca has a hole in her soul that will never go away. Something died for her at the hands of her abuser that she cannot get back. She is on a journey, however, toward wholeness. It is a process. Issues related to her sexual abuse come up every so often, and sometimes she stalls a little. Injustices toward children sometimes stir in her painful memories.

But Bianca is walking, loving, and serving Christ. Her journey has given her a depth and clarity about the gospel like few others possess. She carries teachings and insights in many small, powerful ways at New Life — through dance, participation in small groups, and gifts of wisdom, so that "our theology might be clean," as Bianca describes it.

2. Phase Two: Waiting in the Confusing In-Between

There exists, however, in the pattern God established for us in the person of Jesus an "in-between" time. This is the time between the cross of Good Friday (i.e., Jesus' death) and Pentecost (i.e., the unfolding of the new day). The disciples were confused and bewildered, even after the resurrection. Their understanding of God, his plans, and their own futures was undergoing a radical transformation. They were dying to the old to make way for the new.

Theology professor and author Walter Brueggemann has said the psalms can be divided into three types — orientation, disorientation, and reorientation. (1) The first are songs of *orientation*, where we enjoy God and his creation and blessings, delight in his goodness, and enjoy a rich sense of well-being and joy in him. (2) The second are songs of *disorientation*, seasons of hurt, suffering, and dislocation, written when the bottom falls out and we wonder what is happening. This is the confusing in-between, when we so often feel doubts, resentment, isolation, and despair. (3) Third are psalms of *reorientation*, when God breaks in and does something new. This is when joy breaks through our despair.[8]

> The psalms can be divided into three types: orientation, disorientation, and reorientation.

These movements are not once and for all but repeated countless times throughout our life. Bianca sings all three, over and over again.

Concretely, what does this look like?

New Life Fellowship Church, for almost four years, had saved and prayed to buy the building we had been renting for eight years. It was a 60,000-square-foot Elks Lodge in the center of Queens, New York City. Strategically, it seemed perfect for our mission. The church was doing wonderfully. But at the final hour, a large developer came in to offer a deal we could not match. Suddenly, we went from having a glorious future with dreams to serve New York City and beyond, to possible homelessness with only a six-month window to find a new location. The blow came like a sledgehammer to our congregation, in particular to those of us in leadership who had invested much time and energy in the purchase.

Many people were confused, angry, hurt, and disappointed in God. My first reaction was to spiritualize the situation and to control it. I wanted to "fix" the pain of this interruption. Where was God? Why didn't he answer our prayers? Where was his answer to our prayers?

The church entered into many months of a "dark night of the soul"[9] of disorientation. I remembered the words of Leighton Ford, one of my mentors, saying: "Pete, remember that the most important time is *between* the dreams, not the dreams themselves."

During that time a weariness, a helplessness, a sense of failure and defeat descended on us. Our prayers no longer seemed to work. We could no longer see what God was doing, and there was little visible fruit. We were forced, against our will, to wait.

Another building—larger, cheaper, and with more parking—came up for sale during this time. We prayed as an elder board and realized it would take us out away from our calling in the heart of the more difficult part of Queens. We waited.

Throughout this experience God did something profound in us. He purged a bit more "self-will" and stubbornness out of us and led us to a deeper place of true peace and rest in his will. Eventually, the developer's deal with the Elks collapsed, and we were able to buy the building two years later.

We thought waiting was a parenthesis. It was not. God was working, only we couldn't see it.

Sometimes, we rebel during confusing in-between periods rather than embrace the waiting period in which we find ourselves. The temptation to flee from God, to quit, or to fall into despair is great when it appears God is absent. The good news is that even then, God will find us and meet us.

Grieving and Discipleship in the Church

The first, and always the most important, way to integrate this new paradigm about grieving is for you to *stop* and *pay attention* to your losses, large and small, both in the past and present. If you are new to this, I recommend you take a day away on a retreat with God to journal and pray about significant events in your past that, perhaps, you have not grieved. Give yourself permission to feel. Slow down the pace of your life. Remember, your losses are not something "to get over" but are of great value to God and your spirituality.

Second, begin to equip people, particularly those helping and serving others, to identify and reflect on losses in their lives and the lives of others. The church is uniquely positioned, among all the helping professions, to be with people at critical junctures in their lives — deaths, weddings (loss of singleness and past family alignments), serious illnesses, birth ceremonies, divorces, retirements, and geographic moves. These are discipleship moments to aid people in stepping out of our culture's numbing of pain to allow themselves to feel the disorientation in their lives. Sadly, many people who have suffered abuse in their past have never been given permission to grieve their pain.

> *Stop* and *pay attention* to your losses, large and small ... Give yourself permission to feel.

Third, teach the psalms to give people a biblical basis and framework for grieving. I preached a fourteen-week series on different types of songs in the Psalter. We sang and studied psalms of adoration, psalms of thanksgiving, psalms of lament, psalms of wisdom, psalms of trust, and psalms about the poor and oppressed. I then invited everyone in the congregation to write their own psalms or poems out of their experiences with God through life. Not surprisingly, we received a large number of laments written to God.

Finally, in your mentoring of people, one-on-one or in a small group, make a simple timeline with them from birth to the present. Ask them to identify and describe significant difficult or sad events in their lives. In one sitting you may learn more about their soul and life in God than you might have in one year.

Remember the Compost Pile

What now enables me to remain faithful in the disorientating "in-between" times is the powerful truth that God uses all things for our benefit, his glory, and others' good.

John Milton in *Paradise Lost* compares the evil of history to a compost pile—a mixture of decaying substances such as animal excrement, vegetable and fruit peels, potato skins, egg shells, dead leaves, and banana peels. If you cover it with dirt, after some time it smells wonderful. The soil has become a rich, natural fertilizer and is tremendous for growing fruit and vegetables—but you have to be willing to wait, in some cases, years.

> God transforms evil into good without diminishing the awfulness of the evil.

Milton's point is that the worst events of human history that we cannot understand, even hell itself, are only compost in God's wonderful eternal plan. Out of the greatest evil, the death of Jesus, came the greatest good. God transforms evil into good without diminishing the awfulness of the evil.

3. Phase Three: Allowing the Old to Birth the New

Some people embrace grieving more readily than others. I don't like to grieve. In fact, I tend to avoid it. But the overwhelming benefits encourage me to take the ancient paths of the great saints of old.

Changes That Come through Mourning

Startling shifts and inner changes result in us as we take this strange path downward into mourning. It becomes apparent why Jesus taught, "Blessed are those who mourn, for they will be comforted" (Matt. 5:4). As a result of grieving, we experience new, inner births or changes:

- We have a greater capacity to wait on God and surrender to his will. Grieving breaks something in our fearful self-will that wants to run the universe for God.
- We are kinder and more compassionate. Sadness softens our defense and people find us safer. Henri Nouwen rightly says that the degree to which we grieve our losses is the degree to which we

are compassionate. "There is no compassion without many tears ... To become like the Father whose only authority is compassion, I have to shed countless tears and so prepare my heart to receive anyone, whatever their journey has been, and forgive them from the heart."[10] Absorbing our own pain, we are able to enter the pain of others.

- We are less covetous, less idolatrous. Life is stripped of its pretense and nonessentials. We are more apt to rid ourselves of the unimportant things in life that others so desperately want.
- We are liberated from having to impress others. We can follow God's plan with a new freedom because we are not as motivated to please people.
- We are able to live more comfortably with mystery when it comes to God and his plans. We are not afraid to say, "I don't know," and live in a "holy unknowing."
- We are characterized by a greater humility and brokenness.
- We enjoy a new, vivid appreciation of the sacredness in all of life — the changing seasons, the wind, the falling of the leaves, the holidays, other people.
- We have fewer fears and a greater willingness to take risks.
- We sense the reality of heaven in a new way, understanding more fully that we are only aliens and sojourners on earth.
- We have a greater sensitivity for the poor, the widow, the orphan, the marginalized, and the wounded. We understand them.
- We are more at home with ourselves and with God.

Grieving our losses transforms us in remarkable ways that make the process worthwhile. Layers of our counterfeit self are shed. Something truer — that is, Christ in and through us — slowly emerges. New possibilities become possible — for us and for all those we touch with our lives.

Magda Embraces Grief and Loss

Magda is a Filipina woman in her sixties. She radiates the warmth of Christ in a way that is nothing less than extraordinary. Her pathway there, however, has been long and arduous.

A child during World War II in the Philippines, she witnessed great atrocities that scarred her little soul — starvation, torture, bombings. She vividly remembers as a six-year-old fleeing from the Japanese across mountains for weeks at a time. Given away to an aunt, she suffered unmentionable losses.

Marrying at age twenty-two, she gave birth to nine children. Desirous to give her children a better life in the United States, she left them back home while she moved here to be a nurse. Her hope was to bring them over within a year. Ten years later she was still battling to have her immigration papers approved. She saw her children, ages six to fourteen, an average of one time every two to three years. Eventually they were all able to emigrate.

In 1987, while on the Ohio Turnpike with her twin daughters and future son-in-law, the driver momentarily fell asleep and crashed. Her twenty-one-year-old daughter—who was planning to go overseas on a youth ministry mission—died instantly as did her other daughter's fiancé. Magda herself was in critical condition for weeks. She begged the doctor to let her at least see a video of the wake and funeral of her daughter, but he refused because she was too weak.

Then in 2001, another son, age thirty-six, also died unexpectedly during a physical training exercise in the army, leaving a wife and three children. He had been in the U.S. Navy for seventeen years and was planning to become a pastor when his time with the Navy finished.

Magda describes how she survived so many catastrophic losses: "I look at Jesus on the cross, and he suffered more than I have. He withstood such pain and sorrow because he loved humankind. I can too. I want to give something back. God has made me more sensitive to the pain and suffering of people who have experienced death, and I can be his loving hand. I say, 'Lord, help me to say what you want to say and let me be your mouthpiece and hands so people will know you more in their sorrow.'"

Today she leads a bereavement group and serves many others, both inside and outside the church. She enters their pain, leading them in how to grieve properly and connect, not only with themselves, but most importantly to God.

Following the Thread that Leads to Godlike Compassion

This path of biblical grieving is a great gift we can give both to ourselves and to others. It can often feel, however, as if it is only going to make things worse—as if we shouldn't be going down this road. Let me encourage you to follow the thread, to follow God's way. It leads to life.

George MacDonald, in his book *The Princess and the Goblin*,[11] tells the story of a little eight-year-old princess living alone in a little palace on a large mountain. Inside the mountain are a race of goblins who hate the king (her father) and his descendants (the princess). They plot to kidnap and destroy her.

> Biblical grieving is a great gift ... Let me encourage you to follow the thread, to follow God's way. It leads to life.

Her very old grandmother, however, knows she is in grave danger and gives her a ring with a thread attached to it. The princess can't see the thread, but she can feel it.

"But, remember," instructs the grandmother, "it may seem to you a very roundabout way, indeed, but you must not doubt the thread."

The thread consistently leads the opposite of what the princess expects. It begins by directing her up the mountain into a hole, into total darkness. As she crawls "farther and farther into the darkness of the great hollow mountain" and through narrow passages, she wonders, *Will I ever get out of here?*

Finally she is led to a huge heap of stones. She cries. She wails. The thread goes into the stones so she finally begins to remove them one by one when she finds her good friend trapped behind them. As they try to find their way out of the maze inside the mountain, he argues that she is leading them in directions by which they will never escape the darkness.

The princess whispers, "I know that, but this is the way my thread goes, and I must follow it." Even though it goes against her natural instincts, she obeys and follows the thread. She has no fear of danger but is content and calm. Why? She knows her all-knowing grandmother is guiding her with the thread. Eventually the goblins' plans are exposed and defeated.

> God assures us that he will ... lead us into new resurrections.

As I've said earlier, doing the work of grieving goes counter to our culture. Yet it is the thread outlined to us by

God in Scripture. It is very different from our culture and very different from the way most of us have lived our lives in God. But if we do, God assures us that he will defeat the goblins on our behalf and lead us into new resurrections.

Most important, the church, having learned to absorb and grow through pain, will bear the rich fruit of Godlike compassion toward others. The ability to embrace our losses and grief will equip us to love others as Jesus did. We will then be able to model our lives effectively and authentically on the incarnation.

This leads us to the next chapter — making the incarnation of Jesus our model for loving well.

Chapter 10

Principle 6:
Make Incarnation Your Model
for Loving Well

In emotionally healthy churches, people intentionally follow the model of Jesus. They focus on loving well, recognizing that the indispensable mark of spiritual maturity is not about recognition, numbers, spiritual gifts, or biblical knowledge. The essence of a genuine spiritual life is to love — God, ourselves, and other people.

They commit themselves to follow the three dynamics of incarnation found in the life of Jesus in order to love other people: entering another's world, holding on to yourself, and hanging between two worlds.

Now Is the Time

The year is 1963. The city is Birmingham, Alabama. Schools, restrooms, parks, drinking fountains, and buses are all racially segregated by law. The Reverend Martin Luther King Jr. has arrived in the city to lead a peaceful, nonviolent demonstration against racial injustice in the city. The city's sheriff, however, has secured a court injunction making the march illegal.

Martin Luther King Jr. knows the cost of marching. He does so anyway and is taken to jail. On Tuesday, April 16, 1963, he is given a copy of the *Birmingham News*. It contains a letter addressed to him

180

from eight pastors and a rabbi. They argue that he should have been more patient. His response, a now-famous part of American literature, is called "Letter from a Birmingham Jail":

> I guess it is easy for those who have never felt the stinging darts of segregation to say "wait." But when you have seen vicious mobs lynch your mothers and fathers at will and drown your sisters and brothers at whim; when you have seen hate-filled policemen curse, kick, brutalize, and even kill your black brothers and sisters with impunity; when you see the vast majority of your 20 million Negro brothers smothering in an airtight cage of poverty in the midst of an affluent society; when you suddenly find your tongue twisted and your speech stammering as you seek to explain to your six-year-old daughter why she can't go to the public amusement park that has just been advertised on television, and see tears welling up in her little eyes when she is told that Funtown is closed to colored children, and see the depressing clouds of inferiority begin in her little mental sky, and see her begin to distort her little personality by unconsciously developing a bitterness toward white people ... when you take a cross-country drive and find it necessary to sleep night after night in the uncomfortable corners of your automobile because no motel will accept you; when you are humiliated day in and day out by nagging signs reading "white" men and "colored"; when your first name becomes "nigger" and your middle name becomes "boy" (however old you are) ... and when your wife and mother are never given the respected title "Mrs."; when you are harried by day and haunted by night by the fact that you are a Negro, living constantly at tip-toe stance never quite knowing what to expect next, and plagued with inner fears and outer resentments; when you are forever fighting a degenerating sense of "nobodiness";—then you will understand why we find it difficult to wait.[1]

Dr. King's goal is clear: He is seeking desperately and passionately to get the white Christian leaders from that city to walk in the shoes of an African American. You have heard the Native

> Incarnation ... is a difficult lesson for anyone to learn.

American saying, "To truly understand other human beings, we must first walk a mile in their moccasins." Dr. King understands others must first remove their own moccasins before they can understand what life is like for an African American in the United States in 1963.

He is seeking to teach them about incarnation. It is a difficult lesson for anyone to learn.

Moving to New York City

With a desire to incarnate, Geri and I moved almost twenty-five years ago to New York to raise our family. We bid farewell to what might have been a comfortable, middle-class suburban life and moved into the complex, multiethnic, heavily congested world of Queens.

On the small block we have lived for the last thirteen years, we have had as neighbors drug addicts, prostitutes, orphans, widows, widowers, single moms, a fifty-five-year old man acting as an extra for movies, African Americans, Cypriots, Koreans, Chinese, Hispanics, singles, married couples, and retirees. For most of their lives our children have been a racial minority at church, in school, and in their neighborhood.

We believed in the incarnation of Jesus Christ, who was fully God and fully man. But we never understood, really, what it meant to incarnate—until only a few short years ago. Geri and I didn't grasp how to do it with one another, let alone with our neighbors or in the church.

It is my experience that virtually all Christian leaders I have met believe, as I did, that they understand incarnational ministry.

St. Basil, the bishop of Caesarea in the fourth century, once wrote: "Annunciations are frequent, and incarnations are rare." In other words, bold announcements of what God is doing or saying are common. People who follow the humble way of Jesus are much more difficult to find.

I now understand why. It is much more costly and countercultural, even among fellow Christians.

Seeing Jesus' Love as Incarnation

What it means to be a disciple can best be understood around the unfathomable mystery of the incarnation. God took on human flesh. The infinite Creator and Sustainer of the universe limited himself to the confines of history and a human body. "The Word became flesh and made his dwelling among us" (John 1:14). Or as *The Message* translates it, "The Word become flesh and blood, and moved into the neighborhood. We saw the glory with our own eyes."

God invaded our planet and forever changed it. God became incarnate. He took on human flesh in a way that is shocking, concrete, raw, and physically tangible. God knew there was no better way to show human beings than by fully entering their world—physically and emotionally.

> God invaded our planet and forever changed it. God became incarnate.

God took on skin and flesh for us. Ronald Rolheiser powerfully illustrates why:

> There is a marvelous story told about a four-year-old girl who awoke one night frightened—convinced that in the darkness around her there were all kinds of spooks and monsters. Alone, she ran to her parents' bedroom. Her mother calmed her down and, taking her by the hand, led her back to her own room, where she put on a light and reassured the child with these words: "You needn't be afraid, you are not alone here. God is in the room with you."
>
> The child replied, "I know that God is here, but I need someone in this room who has some skin!"[2]

God knows we needed his skin, not simply the knowledge that he is everywhere. People today are desperate for "skin"—to be loved, for someone to incarnate with them. For this reason, people will pay $100 to $150 an hour to a therapist as someone to love them, to enter and to care about their world.

Today, God still has physical skin and can be seen, touched, heard, and tasted. How? Through his body, the church, in whom he dwells. We are called, in the name of Jesus and by the indwelling Holy Spirit, to be skin for people all around us.

Easier Said Than Done

A neighbor came by to talk with me as I was working on this manuscript. She was depressed, with suicidal thoughts. In her mid-twenties, she did not have a high school diploma, a job, or a social life. She was wondering if she would be alone the rest of her life. She was terribly bored with everything. She had a physical disability and was beginning to realize how trapped she was in her unhealthy home environment. She cried on our couch for a while.

The more she talked and I listened, occasionally asking questions, the more I was able to see the jagged, broken parts of her world and feel the depth of her agony. I didn't even know where to begin to "fix" her or solve her problems. But she wasn't asking for advice. She longed for me to join her and see how hard the world looks when I put her shoes on. For her that world looked overwhelming and scary. She longed for me to listen and be available.

She had accepted Christ in the last year and was now regularly attending Bible study and church. I am sure the small group is grateful she is there. They are undoubtedly, as am I, proud she has become a Christian.

But does anybody have any idea what is going on in her life—the pain, the agony, the loneliness? Does anybody care? The larger question is: Do I really care? I was reminded of that stinging voice who once said to me in so many words, "Pete, as long as your God is not warmth and touch and compassion, I think I will remain an agnostic."

Conflict between the Contemporary Church and Incarnational Ministry

When I became a Christian, I felt an overwhelming sense of burden that my friends and family would come to know the love of God in Christ. The message of free forgiveness and God's unconditional love set my heart on fire.

What started out so purely became partially polluted over time. I learned about prayer, Bible study, evangelism, and disciple-making. I eventually learned about leadership, preaching, pastoring, and multiplying other leaders. I shepherded people to Christ as best I could and sought to lead people into the truth about God.

However, my emphasis was on "going to make disciples" and growing the church. I needed people to respond. It wasn't so much that they were "scalps," but there was something I needed them to do and be so that I could get Christ's mission done more effectively. There was an entire world out there in need of Jesus Christ—churches to be planted, people to be trained, poor folks to be fed.

It became difficult to distinguish between loving people for who they are versus using them for how they could join with the mission. Did I need these people to be converted to Christ in order to build the church or my program? Or could I simply delight in them as created beings made in the image of God? I was so deeply involved in getting Christ's work done that the line became impossible to distinguish. Regardless, I didn't have time to sort it out anyway. There was simply too much to do!

I don't remember the incarnation ever being held up as the defining model of what it meant to be a Christian or as a model of leadership. I didn't know how to do it, what it meant, or what it might look like practically. It was not on the seminary curriculum. The emphasis was to learn so I could teach others. Thus, "teach and instruct," not "listen and learn," were the dominant behaviors expected of trained leaders. I was going to enter other people's worlds only enough to change them, not necessarily to love them.

> It became difficult to distinguish between loving people for who they are versus using them for how they could join with the mission.

The distinction may seem slight but actually is enormous. Prior to his death, Roman Catholic priest Henri Nouwen articulated, I believe, the struggle for many of us. One voice says to succeed and achieve. It is the voice Nouwen says he spent most of his life heeding. He taught at Notre Dame, Harvard, and Yale. He averaged writing more than a book a year. His speaking schedule and ministry constantly threatened to suffocate his spiritual life. The other voice was God's, telling him he was unconditionally loved. He had nothing to prove. This voice told him the goal of ministry was to recognize the Lord's voice, his face, and his touch in every person he met. Only in the last ten years of his life, he said, did he truly listen to that second voice. The transition for Nouwen occurred when he resigned his professorship from Harvard and accepted a position as pastor of L'Arche Community of mentally handicapped people near Toronto, Ontario, Canada.[3]

With the multiple demands and constant pressure on our overloaded schedules, it is difficult to hear that second voice.

Doing More Than Physically Entering Other People's World

I spent three years on staff with InterVarsity Christian Fellowship, a Christian organization working among African Americans and Hispanics, attending churches where I was the minority and trying to understand their world.

I spent four months in the Philippines working with university students in the early 1980s and a year in Costa Rica, Central America, in 1985. My understanding of incarnation, at the time, was applied, for the most part, to cross-cultural contexts.

I went, totally immersed myself in the culture, and became "one" with the people. When Geri and I moved to Costa Rica, we did incarnate. We ate their food — rice and beans three times a day and meat once a week. We learned their language. We celebrated their customs and traditions and lived in a poor community like the common people. Our room was small and spartan. We lived with a large family, sacrificing our privacy and everyday wants for space. It was above a carpentry shop that spewed its sawdust through the holes in the floor promptly at 6:00 a.m., Monday through Saturday.

We physically and culturally left our world. We left what was comfortable and familiar. Geri would frequently say, "This is hard and all I did was leave the United States. Jesus left heaven for earth!"

At the time, however, we did not understand the principles of emotional health as outlined in this book. This severely limited our ability to enter anyone's world.

- We didn't know how to look beneath the surface of our lives (ch. 5). How were we going to share parts of ourselves we had never explored?
- We were unable to articulate our own respective stories growing up and how they impacted our present (ch. 6). How were we going to probe and explore other people's unique journey when we had not seriously considered ours?
- We were not walking in our own brokenness and vulnerability (ch. 7). We were loaded with defenses.
- Our lack of understanding of limits and boundaries caused us to go beyond what God asked, often leading to resentment toward others (ch. 8).
- And we didn't know how to grieve with people in their pain and loss. We had never grieved our own (ch. 9).

Learning to incarnate is the sixth principle of emotionally healthy churches because it assumes progress on the other five. To the extent I am maturing in the first five principles is the degree to which I will be able to love well.

The Three Dynamics of Incarnational Life

On one level the incarnation calls us out of our literal, physical comfort zones to meet people where they are. For this reason our church remains in a densely populated area like Elmhurst, Queens. Sixty percent of our community does not have medical insurance. Many live below the poverty line. This led us, over the years, to invest large amounts of time, energy, and money in the creation of a medical clinic, a food pantry, and a variety of other ministries to serve our community. We have also emphasized taking our ministry to the streets, whether this is in the form of worship events, children's programs, or outreach events.

This level, however, is actually the easier side of practicing incarnation. The life of Jesus teaches us the three dynamics of what it looks like to incarnate in order to love other people: entering another's world, holding on to yourself, and hanging between two worlds.

All three, while distinct, happen simultaneously. So for true incarnation to be taking place, whether it is with a neighbor, coworker, friend, fellow board member with whom we disagree, a spouse, a parent, or a child, all three components must be present.[4]

> The incarnation calls us out of our literal, physical comfort zones to meet people where they are.

1. Entering Another's World

Our own experience into more authentic and heart-wrenching incarnation happened unexpectedly.

I actually learned it in my tenth year of marriage. Geri and I had learned a simple listening technique called reflective listening. (I learned something similar in college but didn't apply it. Now I understand why: It is simple to understand, difficult to do.) The purpose is to provide a safe, respectful structure for two people to share honestly, freely, and, hopefully, more clearly.

Reflective listening is simple. One person has the floor, speaking a few sentences at a time. You don't go on and on. Then the listener repeats back to him or her exactly what has just been said. The person listening attempts to enter into the world of the person speaking, laying aside questions, agendas, defenses, and simply seeks to understand the other person's experience.

As we learned this technique, on one level it appeared robotic and infantile. Initially, we couldn't do it without defending ourselves or getting angry. Gradually, we learned and grew.

I can remember the week Geri and I actually did successfully incarnate with one another. After eight years of rapid fire, "machine-gun" communication where we finished each other's sentences, we gazed at each other in astonishment. Never had we felt so loved and valued by one another. As we matured in this, it became clear to us that we were experiencing a taste of the kingdom of God on earth, a taste of his love. How could I have been so blind to what is the indispensable element to loving people: listening?

> How could I have been so blind to what is the indispensable element to loving people: listening?

Annie Dillard tells about some British explorers in their search for the North Pole in the 1800s. They knew it would be a two- to three-year journey, yet each sailing vessel carried only a twelve-day supply of coal. Instead of bringing more coal, each ship made room for a 1,200-volume library, a hand organ playing fifty tunes, china place settings for officers and men, cut-glass wine goblets, and sterling silver flatware. They carried no special clothing for the Arctic except the uniforms of the Queen's Navy. When the Eskimos came across their frozen remains, the men were all dressed up, pulling a lifeboat full of sterling silver and chocolate.

I felt equally foolish. I had lots of excellent theological and practical training. I had experience as an urban church planter, was a pastor of a growing church, and had a variety of cross-cultural experiences overseas. But I didn't have the coal! I didn't know how to listen in such a way as to be able to feel what someone else was feeling. I often heard only part of what was said, framing my reply rather than entering their world. Like many others, I was often too busy contradicting, correcting, judging, or rebutting to really understand what other people meant or were feeling—especially if I was rushed or under stress.

Give yourself this little listening test. Circle all the statements you can affirm.

1. I make a great effort to enter other people's experience of life.
2. I do not presume to know what the other person is trying to communicate.
3. My close friends would say I listen more than I speak.
4. When people are angry with me, I am able to listen to their side without getting upset.
5. People share freely with me because they know I listen well.
6. I listen not only to what people say but also for their nonverbal cues, body language, tone of voice, and the like.
7. I give people my undivided attention when they are talking to me.
8. I am able to reflect back and validate another person's feelings with empathy.
9. I am aware of my primary defensive mechanisms when I am under stress, such as placating, blaming, problem solving prematurely, or becoming distracted.
10. I am aware of how the family in which I was raised has influenced my present listening style.
11. I ask for clarification when I am not clear on something another person is saying rather than attempt to fill in the blanks.
12. I never assume something, especially negative, unless it is clearly stated by the person speaking.
13. I ask questions when listening rather than mind-read or make assumptions.
14. I don't interrupt or listen for openings to get my point across when another is speaking.
15. I am aware when I am listening of my own personal "hot buttons" that cause me to get angry, upset, fearful, or nervous.

If you checked 12 or more, you are an outstanding listener; 8–11, very good; 5–7, good; 4 or fewer, poor—"you are in trouble." If you want to be really brave, after you score yourself, ask your spouse or closest friend to rate you as a listener. You may be surprised.

David Augsburger has summed this up well: "Being heard is so close to being loved that for the average person, they are almost indistinguishable."[5]

Learning to Listen, Learning to be Present

The Gospels are filled with accounts of Jesus' interactions with individuals—Matthew, Nathaniel, a prostitute, Nicodemus, a blind man, a Samaritan woman, and many others. When the rich young ruler came up to him, Jesus "looked at him and loved him." He listened. He was present, never in a rush or distracted. He took the time to explore stories.

> Jesus listened. He was present, never in a rush or distracted.

When is the last time someone said to you, "Let me tell you about those Christians—they are fantastic listeners! I have never seen a group of people more interested to know my world, curious, asking questions—listening to me!"

People who enter into other people's world are available and present. One of my favorite thoughts comes from Henri Nouwen:

> To care means first of all to be present to each other. From experience you know that those who care for you become present to you. When they listen, they listen to you. When they speak, they speak to you. Their presence is a healing presence because they accept you on your terms, and they encourage you to take your own life seriously.[6]

Incarnation in the Church's Discipleship

The first and by far the most important change in New Life related to this principle has been to teach people, intentionally, how to listen.

Like many people, I had heard many sermons on the need to listen well and be slow to speak (Prov. 17:27–28; James 1:19). But listening does not come naturally to anyone I have met thus far. Few of us have ever had the experience of being truly listened to.

When I began to listen—really listen—to the people's stories and hearts, many of them cried. They felt valued, worthy, and loved.

Initially it was difficult not to give advice or to react when I became uncomfortable. Gradually, however, I learned to not spout off advice until I had incarnated on some level.

The following are three basic listening/speaking exercises we teach at retreats, leadership forums, small group sessions, and equipping classes. They now form an indispensable part of our life as a church community committed, above all else, to loving well.

Incarnational Listening

First, we taught incarnational listening, actually coaching people to ensure they complied with the guidelines. The following is a sample explanation:

How to begin...

Decide who will speak first and who will listen first.

When you are the speaker...

1. Speak using "I" statements (rather than "you" statements). In other words, talk about *your own* thoughts, feelings, and desires.
2. Keep your statements brief.
3. Stop to let the other person paraphrase what you've said.
4. Include feelings in your statements.
5. Be honest, clear, direct, and respectful.

As the listener...

1. Give the speaker your full attention (don't be thinking about your rebuttal).
2. Step into the speaker's shoes (feel what they are feeling; then get back out).
3. Avoid judging or interpreting.
4. Reflect back as accurately as you can what you heard them say (paraphrase).
5. When you think they are done ask, "Is there more?"
6. When they are done ask them, "Of everything you have shared, what is the most important thing you want me to remember?"

You may want to set a seven to ten minute time limit on the speaker to begin. Or you may keep going until your partner says, "No, there's nothing more."

Validation

A second listening exercise we teach is called simply "validation." Validation is not necessarily agreeing with the other person but saying something like:

- "I can see how you would see it that way [even if I don't agree]."
- "From your perspective that makes sense."
- "I can understand that."
- "That makes sense."

Again the key is to say it and mean it, truly entering into that person's world.

This takes a lot of humility. Imagine Josephine coming to you after she has not been at your women's fellowship meetings or church for the last three months. She blurts out in frustration, "I have felt such rejection from you. You never hugged me before or after the meetings as you did the other women." You could say, "That's ridiculous. It never even entered my mind" and turn the problem back to her. Validation says, "From your perspective, I can see how you might feel that way." That takes humility.

Exploring

Exploring, put simply, is to function as a good news reporter and ask questions. "Tell me more. Help me understand. How did you draw that conclusion?" The goal is to set aside any need to respond, defend, or correct the other person. This is especially challenging when you are feeling attacked, annoyed, afraid, or angry. Exploring tests your ability to remain nondefensive. Again, you are not to think about what you are going to say next but are attentive to their world and reality.

For example, imagine a person approaching you after leading a small group meeting and saying, "Gee, Henry, I sure didn't get anything out of that meeting tonight." Your first reaction will probably be to take their head off somehow, either verbally or physically. Exploring requires you to ask calmly, "That's interesting. Tell me what made it an unfruitful evening for you."

Most Christians, especially those of us in leadership, talk much more than we listen. Doing one of the above listening techniques can be extremely difficult. That is why we often provide a third person to serve as a coach in the early stages as people are learning these skills.

Outside of our modeling incarnation as a leadership, nothing has caused this principle to ripple through our church more powerfully than the above, apparently wooden and humiliating, listening techniques.

2. Holding On to Yourself

The great challenge in incarnation, for most of us, is to hold on to ourselves and not to lose ourselves when we enter another person's world. To do so is to be like Jesus. The apostle John records that prior to Jesus' washing his disciples' feet, he "knew that the Father had put all things under his power, and that he had come from God and was returning to God" (John 13:3). Jesus never ceased to be God when he took on human flesh and became one of us.

At New Life, we have people from over sixty-five different countries. Almost one-third are African American and West Indian. Another third are Asian (Chinese, Korean, Indonesian, Filipino, etc.). The rest are Hispanic, Jewish, Eastern European, African, and Anglo. I am a second-generation Italian American. While I am called to go into other people's worlds, it is necessary that I do not lose my God-given self in the process.

In order to be an emotionally and spiritually mature disciple of Jesus, this second dynamic is perhaps the most difficult, challenging principle to apply. Without this, you end up a chameleon like Leonard Zelig.

> While I am called to go into other people's worlds, it is necessary that I do not lose my God-given self in the process.

Woody Allen, in his movie *Zelig*, traces the life of a human chameleon named Leonard Zelig. He becomes a celebrity in the 1920s due to his unique power and ability to look and act like whoever is around him—black, Indian, obese, Chinese, Scottish—you name it, and Zelig becomes it. This human chameleon has no identity or "self" of his own. He becomes whomever he is around. He jokes with prizefighter Jack Dempsey. He is with Hitler on the speaker's platform at Nuremberg.

Zelig assumes whatever strong personalities he meets up with. With the Chinese he is straight out of China. With rabbis, he miraculously grows a beard and side curls. With psychiatrists, he repeats their jargon

and strokes his chin as if he were a wise man. At the Vatican he is part
of Pope Pius XI's clerical attendants. As a chameleon, he changes color,
accent, and shape as the world around him changes. Everywhere he
simply conforms. He wants only to be safe, to fit in, to be accepted, to
be liked. He is famous for being nobody, a nonperson.[7]

At times we empathize *too* much. Out of fear we do not assert our
preferences and point of view, and we lose ourselves in the process.
Remember, Jesus is our model. He became fully man, but he remained
fully God.

The following are a few illustrations to help give a picture of what
it looks like practically to hang on to yourself.

Donna and Allison

Two women in our church who were friends recognized there was
tension in their relationship. Donna was upset with Allison. Whenever
she asked Allison to do something, she always "seemed" to turn her
down. But when Allison suggested an activity, Donna was always willing and available. Finally, annoyed, frustrated, and angry, Donna confronted Allison.

Allison, however, had slowly been learning to "hold on to herself."
In the past she would have always gone out with Donna because of
guilt. She would have felt like a "bad" person for saying no. Now she
was respecting herself enough to realize she had a choice to say yes
or no. She acknowledged she was introverted and not able to be with
people as much as Donna, a high extrovert.

What then did she do? First, she listened empathetically to Donna's
disappointment, sadness, and anger without reacting or defending herself. After Donna felt heard, Allison, holding on to herself, honored her
feelings and desires, saying, "Allison, I very much appreciate you as a
friend. I enjoy spending time with you. I just need the freedom to say no."

Let's say Donna did not respond favorably. If Allison then loses
her self and begins to go out with Donna all the time, she will probably
grow resentful and the relationship may end anyway. Loving herself and
Donna well requires Allison to do the hard work of holding on to herself.

Wilson and Jack

Wilson was a small group leader with whom it was difficult to
disagree. It was usually "his way or the highway" (although he was

unaware of it). Jack had been attending Wilson's small group for the last year but was ready for a change. He wanted to join the worship team choir at church and to begin some new relationships. After the group one Thursday night, he shared his plans with Wilson. Wilson's response was clear, "If you leave this small group, you are out of God's will." For Wilson it was a biblical issue of Jack's inability to sustain close relationships in the body of Christ.

Needless to say, this was a difficult situation for Jack. What would it mean for him to follow Jesus and model the incarnation here? In most similar scenarios, he would either disappear from the small group or the church to avoid the pain, or at least remain in any relationship with Wilson.

Jack, fortunately, had been learning about incarnation. So, first, he listened to Wilson's heart and fears for his spiritual safety and development. It was difficult for Jack since he didn't agree with some of Wilson's conclusions and assessments. He listened respectfully and did not react. Second, he held on to himself, respecting his own legitimate interests and desires. He thanked Wilson for all that he had learned in the group and for their relationship. He seriously considered all that Wilson shared. He then shared that he hoped to visit occasionally. He asked if they could do some kind of healthy termination with the group. Again, Wilson was not happy but chose to respect Jack and his decision.

Shouldn't We Have a Prayer Meeting Like ...

"Pastor," she began adamantly, "we need a strong Tuesday night prayer meeting. God moves in answer to prayer. I visited a church recently that has built their entire ministry out of that prayer meeting. You should build the prayer ministry first and then do small groups."

I immediately felt cornered. Her tone of voice made it feel more like a demand than a suggestion. I used to feel guilty, defensive, and angry when people would come to me with radically different ideas like this that were working so well in another church.

What could I say? Who doesn't believe in the need for prayer?

The reality was, however, that the vision God had given me since the beginning of New Life was for a strong, decentralized small group system throughout New York City. We did have smaller weekly prayer meetings but not with the entire church. More of our corporate prayer was happening in smaller, less flamboyant contexts. Our focus remained on small groups and integrating the rhythms of contemplative spiritual-ity into our daily lives.

How do I hold on to myself with this woman coming on so strong to me?

I stepped back and asked myself, "God, what have you asked me to do as a leader? How do you want this church led? How do I feel about this conversation? What might you, Lord, be trying to teach me? How can I affirm her heart for more prayer and, at the same time, lovingly talk with her about the demanding way she shared it with me?"

3. Living Out the Third Dynamic: Hanging between Two Worlds

The fruit of a mature spirituality is to be an incarnational presence to another person. It was for Jesus. It is, I believe, for all his followers.

Jesus, during his incarnation on earth, was fully God, in perfect communion with his Father. He was also fully human, tasting suffer-ing and death. He hung between two worlds: heaven and earth. Life would have been much simpler for Jesus if he stayed in heaven with the Father. This world, for Jesus, was not safe. But by entering our world, he invited sorrow and pain into his life. He was misunderstood and not appreciated. He died a naked, lonely death on a cross, hanging literally between heaven and earth.

It was, in a word, messy.

Jesus said, "Students are not above their teacher, nor servants above their master" (Matt. 10:24). You and I may not die literally on a cross as Jesus did, but we will die in other ways when we incarnate. It costs time, energy, and, almost always, a disruption to our risk-free world.

When we choose to incarnate, we hang between our own world and the world of another person. We are called to remain faithful to who we are, not losing our essence, while at the same time entering into the world of another. We can be assured, however, that as Jesus' incarnation and death brought great life, so our choice to do the same will also result in resurrection life and much fruit in us and others.

> When we choose to incarnate, we hang between our own world and the world of another person.

Dead Man Walking

Allow me to illustrate from the 1995 movie *Dead Man Walking*. Sister Helen Prejean was a nun living and working in the St. Thomas housing projects in New Orleans when she received an invitation to be a pen pal with someone on death row. It turns out the condemned man, Matthew Poncelet, along with his friend, came across two beautiful teenagers, Loretta and David, in a lover's lane sugar field after a Friday night homecoming game. Loretta was raped. Both David and Loretta were left in the field, shot in the back of the head.

Sister Helen initially wonders if Poncelet's claims to innocence might be true. Matthew argues that his partner actually committed the rape and murders. He is not looking for Sister Helen to be his spiritual director initially but wants her to work on his behalf to get him off death row.

Sister Helen enters his world and finds it is not a pretty one. Matthew is not a lovable character. He is a racist, uses the "n-word," and talks of how well Hitler got the job done. He refers to women as "bitches" and talks about how he wanted to blow up government buildings. Matthew informs Sister Helen that she missed out by not being married and having sex. He evokes no sympathy.

Nonetheless, Sister Helen holds on to herself and her convictions. She invites him repeatedly to make himself right with God by confessing his sin. She tries to get him to take responsibility for what he did. Progress is slow, very slow.

At the same time, Sister Helen initiates a relationship with the grieving families. She enters their world of unfathomable loss and pain. The parents of the dead children are outraged, and pressures mount against Sister Helen to back off her involvement with Matthew. They draw a line in the sand. "You can't befriend that murderer and expect to be our friend too," says the father of one as he asks Sister Helen to leave his house. "If you really care about this family, you'll want to see justice done."

Newspapers pick up Matthew's racist, pro-Nazi views and then mention Sister Helen. Her colleagues at work also complain she is neglecting her work at the St. Thomas projects. "You care more about him than your classes," one of them says.

She hangs between heaven and earth, in the raw, brute work of the incarnation. She is hanging between her world, the condemned killer's world, the parents of the murdered teens' world, and the world of her colleagues at work.

When the male victim's father asks Sister Helen how she has the faith to do what she does, she replies, "It's not faith, it's work."

She does not give up. Over time Matthew begins to let down his defenses. Finally at 11:38 p.m., only minutes before his execution at midnight, she asks him, "Do you take responsibility for both of their deaths?"

Crying, he admits his guilt for the first time. A few minutes later, he says, "Thank you for loving me. I never had anybody really love me before."

Sister Helen recalls their walk together toward his execution. "That walk was the first time I had ever touched him. I looked down and saw his chains dragging across the gleaming tile floor. His head was shaved, and he was dressed in a clean, white T-shirt. When they took him into the execution chamber, I leaned over and kissed his back. "Matthew, pray for me."

"Sister Helen, I will."

When he is strapped to the chair to be injected with lethal solutions, she tells him to watch her face. "That way the last thing you will see before you die will be the face of someone who loves you." He does so and dies in love rather than in bitterness.

The Fruit of Choosing Incarnation

From the great theologians of church history, we learn that the incarnation is a mystery. We grasp only the smallest tip of its immensity and meaning.

As I sit, I close my eyes and reflect on the experience of asking people, "What is it like to be you? To walk in your skin?" I am aware of the truth that when we go out of ourselves and live briefly in the world of another person, we never return to our own lives the same person. God changes us into the image of his Son through the process. We learn to die to the ugly parts of ourselves. Our feet are kept on the ground.

> When we go out of ourselves and live briefly in the world of another person, we never return to our own lives the same person.

Healing and transformation take place in people's lives in ways we know not how (cf. Mark 4:26–29). God yields fruit — thirty, sixty, a hundredfold—both in us and in our churches. As Jesus promised, we will reap much more than we know.

Setting Your Priority on Loving Well

Making incarnation a priority disrupts the church's priority and definition of success. It is no longer simply doing more, "fixing" people, or arranging the world into something we consider God-glorifying. It is about loving well.

Jonathan Edwards (1703–1758), one of America's best-known theologians and preachers, reminds us that Paul says it is possible to operate in the power of the Spirit through miracles and spiritual gifts and not actually be a Christian (1 Cor. 13:1–3). You can build a great ministry for God—doing miracles through great faith, sacrificing everything you have, and moving in spiritual gifts—and not be a real follower of Jesus Christ. He reminds us that Paul calls these actions "nothing" (1 Cor. 13:2–3). Consider Judas, Balaam, Saul, and Jesus' words in the Sermon on the Mount in Matthew 7:21–23.[8]

> Making incarnation a priority disrupts the church's priority and definition of success.

Furthermore, the level of power and gifting operating through a Christian's life has little to do with spiritual maturity. Paul also makes the clear point that you can use spiritual gifts and still be very much a spiritual baby. The sign of the Spirit at work is supernatural love, not gifts or successful results. *This love requires a supernatural work of grace in the heart.*

In heaven, says Edwards in his final sermon on 1 Corinthians 13, love is the one constant that will remain forever. In heaven we will all love each other perfectly, utterly, without any limits. When we live in this radical love (defined in 13:4–7), we are living in the authentic kingdom of God. This cannot be counterfeited by either the

> The sign of the Spirit at work is supernatural love, not gifts or successful results.

devil or our human strivings. It is truly heavenly. Edwards gives one of the most beautiful descriptions of heaven outside of Scripture:

> Heaven [is] a world of love; for God is the fountain of love, as the sun is the fountain of light. And therefore the glorious presence of God in heaven fills heaven with love, as the sun, placed in the midst of the visible heavens in a clear day, fills the world with light. The apostle tells us that "God is love"; and therefore, seeing he is an infinite being, it follows that he is an infinite fountain of love ... Deity becomes, as it were, one infinite and unchangeable emotion of love proceeding from both the Father and the Son ... And there this glorious fountain forever flows forth in streams, yea, in rivers of love and delight, and these rivers swell, as it were, to an ocean of love, in which the souls of the ransomed may bathe with the sweetest enjoyment, and their hearts, as it were, be deluged with love![9]

I don't want to wait until heaven to see a church like that! We don't need to. God desires, I believe, to initiate a Copernican revolution in our discipleship in the twenty-first century, both in the United States and around the world. It is a commitment, not only to see numerical growth, but more important, a quality change in ourselves and the way we do spiritual formation.

It is the pathway to experiencing more of heaven on earth. The journey begins right now, gradually and powerfully rippling through you and then through your church to the hurting world around us. But this will require that you radically slow down your life and lead with integrity, the final principle of emotionally healthy churches.

CHAPTER 11

PRINCIPLE 7: SLOW DOWN TO LEAD WITH INTEGRITY

At the end of an Emotionally Healthy Spirituality conference, Geri and I often ask pastors and leaders to complete the following sentence: "I am beginning to realize ..." Here are a few common responses:

- If truth is not in my life, it should not be in my sermons.
- I have neglected my inner life.
- I have given away my walk with Jesus to manage my congregation; I have impoverished my marriage in the process.
- My stoicism, in reality, is a self-protective device, and it demeans who God made me to be.
- I need to have more self-awareness.
- No more "flying by the seat of my pants"; emotional health takes discipline and much hard work.
- I need to place a higher priority on time with God and trust him with the rest.
- My congregation needs emotionally healthy practices if we are going to mature as a family of faith.
- I am spiritually dry, running on empty. I need to slow down for Sabbath.
- I am more insecure and averse to conflict than I admit.
- Exploring my past is not dwelling on my past.
- I take things too personally when it is not my personal responsibility.
- The world will go on without me, but I cannot go on without Christ.

With which of these statements do you connect? How many are true of your life today? This leads us to our final, foundational principle of emotional health — slowing down to lead with integrity.

Four Conversions

My first conversion happened when I became a Christian at the age of nineteen. It was the culmination of a two-year period of soul searching in which I wondered, "Isn't there more to life than this?" Studying and seeking pleasure left me empty until I finally surrendered to an inward, downward journey to look inside. God used this time in my life to prepare me for a revelation of Jesus as Lord, that he is what life is all about. I began a spiritual journey that eventually led me to become a pastor.

Seventeen years later, my second conversion came as a result of the pain, depression, and betrayal that accompanied the Spanish church split described in chapter 1. This was preceded by two years of inner work in which it became evident that there was no profit in gaining the whole world if I were going to lose my own soul (Mark 8:36). I learned that emotional health and spiritual maturity cannot be separated, that maturity is about love and character, not gifts or knowledge. I realized, finally, the vocation of marriage as central to my spiritual formation.

> I learned that emotional health and spiritual maturity cannot be separated, that maturity is about love and character, not gifts or knowledge.

This launched me on a new journey of emotional health. I blossomed spiritually, emotionally, and relationally. Geri and I began to teach on the principles of emotional health and God transformed countless lives and marriages. After seven years of living this out, I wrote the principles down in the first edition of this book.

My third conversion occurred in 2003–2004. I realized that something was still missing. Despite our journey into emotional health, people's lives remained overloaded with activity and stress. Many people continued to live off other people's spirituality and remained scattered, fragmented, and uncentered. My central desire was for people to live with passion for Jesus and in communion with him, out of which they might love others well.

Beginning in 1996, I spent seven years exploring contemplative spirituality, especially monasticism. This culminated in a four-month sabbatical, in which Geri and I lived in the rhythms of silence, solitude, and Sabbath-keeping. We experienced a number of diverse monastic communities, from Roman Catholic, Orthodox, and Protestant traditions.

God met us in profound ways. I recognized that I was still too active and that my first work was to seek him above all else, not be a pastor/leader (cf. Ps. 27:4). The relationship of activity and contemplation in my life experienced a seismic shift. I learned about the necessity of silence and solitude for my spiritual formation, and about how much more I needed to slow down to be with God. I also came to a fresh awareness of my own stubborn heart that preferred my will over God's, especially at New Life. I realized how much of our strategic planning was coming from a wrong foundation. I stopped waiting on the Lord for a growing church and started to simply wait on the Lord for him alone.

My fourth conversion happened in 2007. Over the years, pastors of large churches asked me, "How do you apply emotional health to leading a complex organization with hiring and firing, boards, and people to manage?" I responded, "I have no idea. I haven't gotten to that one yet. I guess that's not my calling to figure out!"

> I stopped waiting on the Lord for a growing church and started to simply wait on the Lord for him alone.

For almost twenty years I, along with our board, attempted to find ways to provide executive leadership to fill this gap so I could remain the visionary, senior leader. Our church had grown large, but we repeatedly hit a wall. We had experienced only limited effectiveness in integrating emotional health and contemplative spiritual practices into the running of the church.

Because I had too many things to do (e.g., sermons, board meetings, administration, crises), I rushed through areas of my leadership. I sometimes avoided meetings I knew would be hard. I skimmed on "truth" when it was uncomfortable. I avoided discussions about people's performance when it was poor. I preferred not to ask difficult questions or speak up when something was clearly wrong. I didn't give myself the time I needed before meetings to be clear on goals and agenda, to be thoughtful and prayerful.

I didn't give myself time to remain centered and to follow through on my commitments. I didn't take the time to examine painful data that things may not be going as well as I imagined.

Finally, a number of events converged to prepare me for this fourth conversion of leadership/personal integrity. I finally admitted the truth: the greatest deterrent to New Life Fellowship Church becoming what God meant her to be was not any other person or factor, but me. The issues were inside me, not in our staff or larger church. This sent me to another painful look at unexplored areas of my iceberg.

> The greatest deterrent to New Life Fellowship Church becoming what God meant her to be was not any other person or factor, but me.

My avoidance of taking the necessary time to plan well or follow through on project details was about my character, not my gift mix. The issues of learning the skills of being a differentiated leader were not hard to learn. It was more about overcoming my fears. I learned that being misunderstood, losing friendships, and having a few people leave the church is less important than losing my integrity. I learned to seek the truth regardless of where it led. The result was a church, a leadership, and a Pete Scazzero set free in ways unimaginable to me only a few years ago.

God the Divine Archaeologist

As we progress in the Christian life, we find that it is a never-ending process. We go back, breaking some destructive power of the past. Then later, on a deeper level, God has us return to the same issue on a more profound level. I suspect more conversions will follow for me in the years to come.

Thomas Keating compares God's work in us to a Middle Eastern "tell," or archaeological site, in which one civilization is built on another in the same place. Archaeologists excavate, level by level, culture by

culture, down through history. The Holy Spirit is like a divine archae-
ologist digging through the layers of our lives.

> The Spirit intends to investigate our whole life history, layer
> by layer, throwing out the junk and preserving the values that
> were appropriate to each stage of our human development …
> Eventually, the Spirit begins to dig into the bedrock of our ear-
> liest emotional life … Hence, as we progress toward the center
> where God is actually waiting for us, we are naturally going to
> feel that we are getting worse. This warns us that the spiritual
> journey is not a success story or a career move. It is rather a
> series of humiliations of the false self.[1]

God uses disorienting events and experiences to do a profound inner
work in us.

Every spiritual journey takes us to the hardest realities in our lives,
the monsters within us, our shadows and strongholds, our willful flesh,
and our inner demons. It is essential that we understand these enemies
within us or we will inevitably project them outward on to other people.

Cultivating Integrity

Integrity with God

Most of us are in a hurry, battling to make the best use of every
spare minute we have. We end our
days exhausted from the endless needs
of our churches. Then our "free time"
becomes filled with more demands
in an already overburdened life.
We read about the need to rest and
recharge — but we can't stop.

It is like being addicted — only it is
not to drugs or alcohol but to activity
and doing. Our bodies physiologically
cannot seem to get off adrenaline to
slow down. We fear how many things
might fall apart. So we just keep going.

Like Moses, Elijah, John the
Baptist, and Jesus, each of us must

> Like Moses, Elijah,
> John the Baptist,
> and Jesus, each of
> us must somehow
> fashion a "desert"
> in the midst of our
> lives to cultivate
> our personal
> relationship with
> Jesus.

somehow fashion a "desert" in the midst of our lives to cultivate our personal relationship with Jesus. It is an illusion to imagine we can lead our people on a spiritual journey we have not taken ourselves. When we skim in our relationship with God, no program can substitute for the superficiality and self-will that inevitably follow.

Cultivating an intentional life with our Lord Jesus requires intentionally focused time—for silence, prayer, meditation on Scripture, and reading. But we are surrounded by endless distractions and voices that call us away from sitting at the feet of Jesus. Yet it is our only hope for seeing through the illusions and pretense of our world and for providing leadership to those around us.

Throughout church history, one of the seven deadly sins was described as sloth or "not caring." This referred not just to laziness, but to busyness with the wrong things. We are overly active because we cannot bear the effort demanded by a life of recollection and solitude with God. For this reason, the Desert Fathers, the first monks who lived in the desert areas of the Middle East during the fourth and fifth centuries, had no patience for activism, even godly activity, unless it was nourished by a rich interior life with God. They repeatedly warned about being engaged in activity for God before the time is ripe. They offer a timely warning to us.

Bernard of Clairvaux (1090–1153), the abbot of a Cistercian monastery in France, was perhaps the greatest Christian leader and writer of his day. When his spiritual son, Eugene III, became pope in the twelfth century, Bernard was deeply concerned that the Pope's interior life was not sufficient to cope with the level of responsibility he now carried. Bernard grieved over the demands now placed on Eugene. He counseled, "Remove yourself from the demands, lest you be distracted and get a hard heart. If you are not terrified by it, it is yours already ... You were bought at a price. Do not become slaves of men."[2]

When our life *with* God is not sufficient to sustain our work *for* God, we too will find ourselves struggling with our integrity. My training taught me to reach people for Christ, to grow the church, to engage in global missions, to use my gifts to the fullest. I also learned about quiet time and days alone with God. The emphasis, however, was outward and up toward external growth, not inward and down into my own soul.

But work *for* God that is not nourished by a deep interior life *with* God will eventually be contaminated. Our experiential sense of worth and validation gradually shifts from God's love for us in Christ to our works and performance. The joy of life with Christ slowly, almost imperceptibly, disappears.

To hold on to my integrity, I began to build monastic rhythms into my life. For example, I practiced the Daily Office as a way to structure my days. I planned my day around three to four small blocks of time to stop, center myself, read Scripture, and be still.

> Work *for* God that is not nourished by a deep interior life *with* God will eventually be contaminated.

The term *Daily Office* differs from what we label today as quiet time or devotions. The root of the Daily Office is not so much a turning to God to get something but setting aside time to *be with Someone*. It is about building a rhythm of being with God each day.

King David, the prophet Daniel, devout Jews in Jesus' day, and the disciples themselves in Acts all practiced set times of prayer three or more times a day. Jesus himself probably followed the Jewish custom of praying at set times during the day.

All these leaders realized that stepping away from the demands of the day to be with God was the key to creating a continual and easy familiarity with God's presence the rest of the day. It is the rhythm of stopping that makes the practice of the presence of God a real possibility.

The great power in setting aside small units of time for morning, midday, and evening prayer infuses the rest of my day's activities with a deep sense of the sacred, of God. All of time is his. The Daily Office, practiced consistently, actually eliminates any division of the sacred and the secular in our lives.[3]

Integrity with Yourself

Leadership in the church can do violence to your soul. The endless needs that routinely hurtle toward us can leave us exhausted and irritable. Who has time to enjoy Jesus, our

> Leadership in the church can do violence to your soul.

spouses, our children, even life itself? We assume we'll catch up on our sleep some other time. The space we need for replenishing our soul and relaxing can happen later. Few of us have time for fun and hobbies.

If we are to take time to care for ourselves, we will have to give a solid no, at times, to those around us. For years I did not give myself the gift of silence unless I had first taken care of those around me. It didn't matter if my soul was parched and my spirit depleted. I was the pastor and had to be strong.

It was inhuman. Inevitably, I became resentful. Jesus' yoke felt hard and heavy, not easy and light as he promised (Matt. 11:30).

Jesus models for us healthy self-care. With the weight of the world on his shoulders, we observe him resting and enjoying what others give to him before going to the cross (John 12:1 – 8). How many of us would allow someone to spend a year's wages on us? We don't see ourselves as that valuable.

In his great work *Loving God*, Bernard of Clairvaux describes four degrees of love:

1. Loving ourselves for our own sake.
2. Loving God for his gifts and blessings.
3. Loving God for himself alone.
4. Loving ourselves for the sake of God.

The highest degree of love, for Bernard, was simply that we love ourselves as God loves — in the same degree, in the same manner, with the very same love. We love the self that God loves, the essential image and likeness of God in us that has been damaged by sin.[4] Bernard recognized that mature love does not exist without a basis of self-love. Only in light of the love of God can we love ourselves rightly. And if we do not know what it is to care for ourselves, we cannot love others well.

This is a wonderful word for us as leaders today as so many of us often carry resentments for giving beyond what God has asked. Unrelenting duty can destroy our relationship with Jesus, the only source of long-term life and joy.

As Christian leaders, one of our greatest challenges is to manage ourselves. How can I be in communion with other people if I am not in communion with myself? How can I be in a healthy relationship with others if I am not in a healthy relationship with myself? How can I be intimate with you if I am not intimate with myself?

One key to our freedom is, I believe, a rediscovery of Sabbath-keeping as a central spiritual formation practice. Sabbath-keeping is about accepting God's invitation to stop, rest, delight, and contemplate him for a twenty-four-hour period each week. Our culture knows nothing of setting aside a whole day (twenty-four hours) to rest and delight in God. Like most, I always considered it an optional extra, not something absolutely essential to discipleship.

Jesus reminds us we were not made for the Sabbath; the Sabbath was given by God as a gift to us (Mark 2:27). I love Sabbath. In fact, the more you taste it from the inside, the more you love the gift! Geri and I often remark to one another: "How did we ever do leadership without Sabbath? No wonder pastoring a church seemed so violent to our souls!"

For me, this means stopping from Friday night at 7:00 p.m. to Saturday night at 7:00 p.m. — even if my sermon is not finished (Is it ever?). I avoid the computer, emails, and church-related work. I spend most of the day on Friday doing my other work, such as cleaning the house, repairing the car, doing laundry, and paying bills. Having these things out of the way enables me to joyfully enjoy the Sabbath.

The Sabbath calls us to build the doing of nothing into our schedules each week. Nothing measurable is accomplished. I nurture my soul. I do what gives me life. I stop all "have to's" and "shoulds." It is, by the world's standards, inefficient, unproductive, and useless. Yet it is one of the most fundamental gifts given to us by God that we might take care of ourselves.

God's ultimate intention is that our other six days of work/activity become infused with the qualities of biblical Sabbath — stopping, resting, delighting, and contemplating him. From this place of rest, our work is to flow.

Integrity in Your Marriage

Few people are willing to admit the sad state of many pastors' and leaders' marriages. It would potentially disrupt, at least in the short term, some of our fastest-growing churches.

The best leadership and denominational conferences, along with our seminaries and schools, do not train us how to have marriages that taste and point to heaven. We ignore the unique pressures and hazards of the ministry, mistakenly assuming that a great marriage will happen naturally if we work for God.

The apostle Paul understood that we minister out of who we are. He made the quality of our marriages an indispensable requirement for leadership in the church when he said: "He must manage his own family well and see that his children obey him in a manner worthy of full respect. (If anyone does not know to manage his own family, how can he take care of God's church?)" (1 Tim. 3:4–5). He knew that our ability to apply the Word into our own marriages is one of the most difficult things we do.

> We forget the biblical principle: as goes the leader's marriage, so goes the church.

We forget the biblical principle: as goes the leader's marriage, so goes the church. If we are too preoccupied to invest in our families, we're not going to be able to lead a healthy church family. If you are married, your vocation is your spouse first and then any children God has given you. This covenant takes priority over our church ministry and people. It is the only vow you will take on earth. Mike Mason captures it well:

> The problem with most troubled marriages is that both partners are trying to accomplish far too many things in the world, and in the process, like Martha in Luke 10:42, they neglect the "one thing needful." Next to the love of God, the "one thing" that is by far the most important in the life of all married people is their marriage ... For marriage involves nothing more than a lifelong commitment to love just one person — to do whatever else one does, a good, thorough job of loving one person.[5]

Geri and I made a commitment fourteen years ago that investing in our marriage was the highest priority of our lives after Christ. Our calendar began to reflect that change. We carved out exclusive, uninterrupted time each day and week to be fully present with one another. And we began a habit of regular overnights to nearby bed-and-breakfasts for getaways.

Paul refers to the one flesh union of husband and wife as a foreshadowing of Christ's union with his bride, the church (Eph. 5:31–32). Our marriages are meant to proclaim and reflect our union with Christ. Our marital union is to be a picture, an experience, of receiving and giving the love of God.

This has enormous implications for our discernment of God's will, our priorities, and our limits. For example, each time I have engaged in writing a book, Geri and I talk about it first since she will inevitably be impacted. If she says, "This is not a good time for such a commitment," I hold off. I love and feel God's call to New Life Fellowship Church. I have been here over twenty-two years. Yet if she senses God's time is up for her to leave New York, I will receive that as part of God's call for me. We are moving to a third service on Sunday evenings in a few months. I will preach and attend only once a month. One of the requirements for our church to take this step was the formation of a preaching team. Without it, we recognized the quality of our marriage and family would have suffered more than God would want.

Of course, the temptation to compromise on our integrity in our family remains. But as our theology of marriage as a vocation — as a specific call and mission from God — has deepened over the years, this temptation has weakened.

Integrity in Your Leadership

For years our church board, in their annual review of my role, asked how I enjoyed my position as senior pastor.

"I love preaching, teaching, casting vision, and discipling people," I replied, "But God just didn't give me the gift of administration or managing an organization. It's frustrating."

I continued to avoid making personnel decisions, managing staff and key volunteers, writing job descriptions, taking time to plan for meetings, or following through on project details. I saw clearly things that needed to be done, but I wanted someone else to do it. "That's not me," I told myself.

A number of events finally converged to break this twenty-year gridlock.

First, I reached a point of utter frustration. The inner workings of our staff were not reflecting the message I was preaching. I could no longer preach a way of life that our church leadership was not living.

Around this time, Geri also spoke up: "Pete, I think the issue is courage, your courage. I'm not blaming you. It's hard to make the kind of changes needed. All I know is that you are in the position to do it, but you aren't doing it. You are not enforcing our values of emotionally healthy spirituality with the staff to the degree needed. You're angry and resentful. We have a great church but ..."

She paused and then dropped the bombshell.

"I think this is about you. You may not have whatever it takes to do what needs to be done. Maybe your time is up and someone else needs to step in and lead."

I was exposed. While her words hurt, I knew there was truth in them. Truth be told, I was afraid of being misunderstood, losing friendships, having people leave the church, halting our momentum. I spent the next day alone with God and my journal.

Yes, I wanted someone else to come in and "get the house in order," to do the dirty work of hiring, firing, redirecting, and leading the church through the painful changes before us. My sin was ever before me. I saw what needed to be done. Changes in our staff leadership were needed. A few key people were not properly slotted. Others weren't doing their roles well.

I preferred doing the easy things like preaching and teaching, but my integrity was at stake. The impact on the church was becoming visible. It was time to stop trying to lead at a distance, to stop just casting vision and to take steps to implement my values on every level of our church. God finally had my attention.

Two weeks later I formally incorporated the job description of the executive pastor into mine, determined to learn the role. I cancelled speaking engagements outside New Life, said no to a potential book contract, and signed up for a round of excellent counseling to sort through my own "beneath the iceberg" blockages. I preached less, and we moved more deliberately to a teaching team.

Over the next year I discovered that the skills for doing the executive work of the church are not hard to learn. The real difficulty was making the time, thinking carefully "before the Lord," summoning the courage to have difficult conversations, and following all the way through. I was now stepping into the messy, painful truth that would set both me and New Life free.

I soon realized that I didn't like going from meeting to meeting without an awareness of God. I needed a few minutes of time for transitions between meetings and began to take them. I said my life was all about God, but I often divided my leadership into sacred/secular categories. I said all of life was holy, but I treated the executive/planning functions of pastoral leadership as less meaningful and sacred than prayer and preparing sermons.

> I often divided my leadership into sacred/secular categories.

I began to say no to new commitments without properly following through on what I was already doing. And I increasingly began meetings with two to five minutes of silence for myself to help me be still before God. I needed it!

Part of my integrity as a senior pastor related to the formation of a leadership culture that lived what we preached. So I developed for our pastoral staff team a "Rule of Life." The word "rule" comes from the Greek for "trellis." The purpose of the Rule of Life for our pastoral staff was to articulate a unique combination of spiritual practices that would provide the structure and direction we needed to pay attention to and remember God in everything we do. It is included as an appendix. I encourage you to read and ponder it.

We made our Rule of Life public to our church membership so they would know the kind of lives we seek to live. Our elders then followed in developing their own Rule of Life. Later, we moved our entire church membership to an intentional Rule of Life as well.[6]

Begin the Journey

You may be thinking, "Pete, this would require I change the entire way I do ministry. Who has this kind of time to slow down? I'll never get anything done!"

A few core issues need to be resolved in order for you to go forward.

First, you need to surrender to God in trust rather than grasp out of anxiety to make things happen. Both our flesh and culture feed striving and fear. Adam and Eve legitimately worked and enjoyed their achievements in the garden. But they were to stop and let go at the tree of the knowledge of good and evil. They were to trust in God's goodness and love. So are we. Failure to do so is the essence of sin. You and I can change. Remember the teaching of Jesus, "With humans this is impossible, but with God all things are possible" (Matt. 19:26).

Second, the most important focus is not to change your church, but to allow Christ to change you. As your inner life is transformed, your outer world will change as well. Integrity means walking in truth, beginning first with what is happening inside of you. This kind of honesty takes great courage. Christ gave his life, creating a safe environment of love for us, so that we can have a genuine, authentic relationship with him.

> The most important focus is not to change your church, but to allow Christ to change you.

Finally, recognize and embrace your limits. They are a gift. You and I are not God. We are not running the world; he is. God invites us to relax, to enjoy the fact that we are not in charge of this world, that even when we die, the world will continue on nicely without us.

Let me conclude by inviting you to this exciting journey into the seven principles of emotionally healthy churches. These principles are:

1. Look beneath the surface.
2. Break the power of the past.
3. Live in brokenness and vulnerability.
4. Receive the gift of limits.
5. Embrace grieving and loss.
6. Make incarnation your model for loving well.
7. Slow down to lead with integrity.

This is the pathway to experiencing more of heaven on earth in our work as pastors and leaders. The journey begins right now, gradually and powerfully rippling through you and then through your church to the hurting world around you.

Part 4

Where Do We Go from Here?

CHAPTER 12

NEXT STEPS INTO THE
NEW FRONTIER OF DISCIPLESHIP

I n a sense we are all lobsters. In order to grow, lobsters have to rid themselves of their old, hard, protective shell and grow a new, larger one. This process of shedding an old shell is called molting. They do this about twenty-five times in the first five years of life and once a year after they become adults.

It is an ugly, messy process. Under the pressure, the old, hard, protective shell cracks. Then the lobster lies on its side, flexes its muscles, and pulls itself from the cracked shell. For a short time—between the leaving of the old shell and the hardening of a new one—the lobster is naked, feeling vulnerable to the elements.

> In the same way, our growth into Christlikeness requires we get rid of our old, hard, protective shells and allow God to take us to a new place in him.

In the same way, our growth into Christlikeness requires we get rid of our old, hard, protective shells and allow God to take us to a new place in him. Obviously, reading a book like this does not ensure that a person or a church will do so. It calls for a commitment to do the hard work—one day at a time.

We long for everyone in our churches to grow into maturity in Christ, and this includes emotional health. Unfortunately, not everyone

217

in New Life Fellowship Church has chosen to go far beneath the surface. It is risky and scary. Preaching sets a context and an environment of safety and grace to enable people to go further, but it is not enough.

If you can work on yourself, then as you interact with others, the church will change. In short, if you do the hard work of allowing God to change you, the whole system will change. The following is our recommended path:

The Pastor/Leader Journey

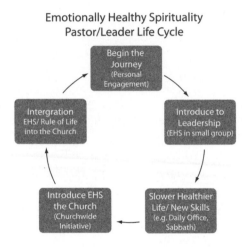

Emotionally Healthy Spirituality
Pastor/Leader Life Cycle

1. Begin the Journey

The most important thing we can do is to engage the message in our own lives and to apply personally the powerful biblical themes explored in this book. You have taken that first step. Congratulations! Consider using the accompanying *Emotionally Healthy Church Workbook, Revised and Expanded Edition* (2010) in your own times alone with God. Visit www.emotionallyhealthy.org and begin reading *Emotionally Healthy Spirituality* (Nelson, 2006). This follow-up book uniquely integrates contemplative spirituality with emotional health as an indispensable means to genuine transformation in Christ. Remember, we lead out of who we are.

2. Introduce to Leadership (EHS in Small Group)

Gather a small group of your key leaders around *The Emotionally Healthy Spirituality Workbook* (Willow Creek Publishing, 2009) and begin providing an experience for your leaders to "go beneath the tip-of-the-iceberg" in their spirituality. This serves two purposes. First, it provides time and space for you to go deeper into the material. Second, it enables you to introduce these new biblical themes to a core group before bringing it to the entire church.

3. Slower Healthier Life/New Skills

Emotionally healthy spirituality requires quitting unhealthy behaviors in order to model and to enjoy a healthier life. You will want to learn new skills and begin to do things differently as a leader, both personally and at home. Slow down to spend more time to rest, to be with God, to be with your spouse. Begin exploring and experimenting with Sabbath-keeping and the Daily Office in order to create rhythms and space in your life so that you can abide in Christ more consistently.

4. Introduce EHS to the Entire Church (Church-Wide Initiative)

This nine-week, full-church campaign introduces every leader, every small group, every Sunday school class, and every worship service to the powerful concepts of emotional health. Visit www.willowcreek. com to order the *Emotionally Spirituality Church Campaign Kit.* This will provide you with teaching notes, promotional and training materials, a kickoff DVD, a small group DVD, a workbook containing eight sessions for small groups, and an eight-week Daily Office devotional to help your people intentionally cultivate their own personal relationship with Jesus.

5. Integration: EHS/Rule of Life into the Church

As you begin to take your church into this journey, remember this is a slow process, not a quick fix. Jesus spent three years, full time with twelve people, and only eleven finished. Moreover, they needed an infusion of power from heaven to live this out!

Consider crafting a Rule of Life for your leadership, your board, or your congregation. You may want to preach a related sermon series that builds on these powerful themes or offer additional resources to your church. For a more complete listing of suggestions, visit www .emotionallyhealthy.org/resources/nextsteps.asp

The choice now is yours. Jesus asked the paralyzed man in John 5:6, "Do you want to get well?" He asks the same question to each of us. Integrating emotionally healthy spirituality into our churches will mean large changes in our lives. Ask God for revelation and the courage to take the steps he sets before you. The impact in people's lives will be profound, liberating, and transformative.

But remember, change begins with you.

NEW LIFE FELLOWSHIP CHURCH PASTORAL STAFF — RULE OF LIFE

Our Guidelines for Being Together

We believe that our ministries emerge out of a call from God to separate from the world for the purpose of prayer. It is from this place of being with Jesus that we lead others out of a heart of compassion in the fulfillment of our mission as a local church. Like David, we want to shepherd God's people "with integrity of heart" and "with skillful hands" (Ps. 78:72).

Yet we recognize that leadership brings out the best and worst in us. In many ways, the crucible of pastoral ministry "introduces us to ourselves." We affirm, as Parker Palmer has written, that "a leader is someone with the power to project either shadow or light onto some part of the world and onto the lives of the people who dwell there ... A good leader is intensely aware of the interplay of inner shadow and light, lest the act of leadership do more harm than good."[1]

In such a role, we commit ourselves to the following "rule" to keep us centered in the Lord Jesus and his call for our lives. Our purpose is, as Benedict wrote 1,500 years ago, that our "way of acting should be different than the world's way; the love of Christ must come before all else" (*Rule of Benedict* 4:20–21).

Our Being (Character)

We are essentially called to seek God above all else (Ps. 27:4), that is, to be contemplative, out of which we carry out our active ministry. At the same time, we recognize God has called us to a level of intensity to bring Jesus Christ to our city and world through serving in different roles as a pastoral staff at New Life Fellowship Church.

Freely under his grace, we determine to model the qualities of leadership laid out by the apostle Paul in 1 Timothy 3 — above reproach, self-controlled, respectable, able to teach, hospitable, gentle, not quarrelsome, free from the love of money, and managing our families well ("If anyone does not know how to manage his own family, how can he take care of God's church?" 1 Tim. 3:5). Whether single or married, we minister out of our marital status; if married, our marriage covenant takes precedence over the work of NLF.

We function as "teaching elders," while our Board of Elders serve as "ruling elders." As a result, we seek to model to the flock of God the kind of life Christ desires for his people to live: "Keep watch over yourselves and all the flock of which the Spirit has made you overseers" (Acts 20:28).

We consider the vocation of pastor to be a high calling and a trust given by God. As Gregory of Nazianus taught around AD 370: "The responsibility of pastoral office is great indeed, and no one ought to enter who has not deeply examined motive and ability, who has not struggled against call in the face of godly demands of office and the frailty of mere humanity."

Our aim, as a pastoral team, is to be a vital organism with a contented spirit. While we live in the world surrounded by unceasing needs, we desire to serve God out of a "joyful, non-anxious spirit" in a way that is peaceful and harmonious with others — not agitated, hectic, or confused. We do not claim to be perfect, by any means; we acknowledge difficult times in living out our "rule of life," but our commitment is to honesty and openness, asking for help when needed and living in brokenness and contriteness of heart (Ps. 51:17).

At the same time we want to understand who we are and who we are not, our limits and our potentials. The pastoral call involves leading out of the unique material God has given us. We desire all staff members at NLF to function in roles that are congruent with their authentic selves and families.

As shepherds, leaders, and servants of this particular flock, we must regularly ask ourselves: Which of my limits are part of my God-given nature that I need to receive as a gift? Are there limits before me that God is asking me to break through because they come out of character flaws or my "false self"?

These limits and potentials are one of the means God uses to speak to us and to reveal the particular role we are able to take in service to him at New Life. This discernment from the Holy Spirit comes, we believe, from wise counsel, self-confrontation, and those in authority over us.

Our Doing (Activity)

Using their God-given talents, our members work and serve as volunteers out of a sense of passion and mission. We too work and serve out of a sense of passion and mission; nevertheless, we function in a dual relationship with the NLF Board and congregation as "employees." In fact, we have at least three roles in the community of NLF: we are family members, leaders in this church family, and employees. These roles carry challenges in how we relate to one another and to NLF.

Each year, we are set apart by the Board of Elders to serve the body at New Life Fellowship in a unique way. Whether full- or half time, we are given a salary in order to fulfill this special calling free from the constraints of other employment. The body as a whole supports us financially so that we can devote ourselves to serving the body — praying, pastoring, and equipping the saints to do ministry (Eph. 4:11 – 12). This is our privilege and our joy.

Each person called and invited to be on staff at New Life is valued as a gift from God. We long to see each staff member growing and thriving in their respective roles.

At the same time, the elder board is responsible for the stewardship of the church's resources in our dynamic, changing environment. Our call from God to pastoral leadership may last our entire lives regardless of our employment at NLF. Yet we recognize the fit of what NLF needs and desires may change over time. Thus, our status as employees is subject to the direction God is taking the church, her resources, and our leadership effectiveness. Furthermore, we are each subject to periodic reviews regarding our job description, status, and contract.

Specific Rule of Life

The following "Rule of Life" expresses our *conscious* guidelines to keep God at the center of everything we do—to seek the "love of Christ" above all else. In a culture that does not respect God's rhythms for life, we seek to live out a balance of prayer, rest, work, and community.

This "Rule" provides guidelines for the kind of leadership we aim to embody, as well as a foundation for the relational culture we want to build and function within.

Prayer

1. **Scripture.** Our lives are built on the Word of God. It is our food and primary means of revelation from him. We spend time each day in Scripture, seeking God's face, dwelling in his presence, and praying out of his Word.
2. **Silence and Solitude.** Along with building silence and solitude into our daily routines, we spend at least one full day a month in silence with God.[2]
3. **Daily Office.** Nothing is to be preferred to the work of God (Rule of St. Benedict). We pause to be with God two to three times a day to remember him, spending time in communion with him, preferably with Scripture, silence, meditation, and prayer.
4. **Study.** We are consistently growing and taking steps to keep learning about Jesus, as well as about our unique values (emotional health, contemplative spirituality, reconciliation) and our particular area of calling in Christ.

Rest

5. **Sabbath.** Each week, we set aside a twenty-four-hour period to keep Sabbath to the Lord, structuring our time around the following four characteristics of biblical Sabbath: *Stop, Rest, Delight, and Contemplate*. We also take at least an additional half day off a week to do the "work" of life and limit our work at NLF. We trust God to build his church and respect Sabbath-keeping as an essential formation discipline in our lives.

6. **Simplicity.** We model percentage giving (using the tithe as a minimal guideline) in giving to God's work here at NLF. We manage our material resources in a manner that honors God and avoids the traps and enticements of Western culture (e.g., bad debt, gambling, etc.) as we live out the basic principles of our Good Sense Course (i.e., giving, saving, budgeting, balancing a spending plan, and planning).

7. **Play and Recreation.** We have a life outside of New Life Fellowship for balance and health. We recognize the seasons and rhythms of leadership and the church year and plan compensatory breaks accordingly. We build healthy "fun" into our discipleship and take vacations each year to allow the soil of our lives to be replenished and receive fresh "nutrients" from God as we take mini-sabbaticals along the four principles of stopping, resting, delighting, and contemplating.

Work

8. **Service and Mission.** Another critical issue for healthy service is having clear and realistic expectations. It is vital that we maintain an open discussion about expectations and allow for ongoing modifications as we adapt to the challenges of our rapidly changing environment. Together with our supervisors and the elder board, we regularly update our job descriptions and goals in order to meet these challenges. Then, in everything we do as pastoral leaders, we can continue to point others to Christ. In this way, "the whole body, joined and held together by every supporting ligament, grows and builds itself up in love, as each part does its work" (Eph. 4:16).

9. **Care for the Physical Body.** We understand the stewardship of our physical bodies is also part of our discipleship and modeling. We seek to regularly care for our physical temples through healthy eating habits, consistent exercise, and sufficient amounts of sleep, respecting our God-given limits.

Relationships

10. **Emotional Health.** We are committed to a spiritual formation model that embraces our whole person, including the emotional

component of who we are as image bearers of God. We embrace the skills and behaviors that put feet on our theology to love well (1 Cor. 13). In all our relationships we seek to speak clearly, directly, respectfully, and honestly. We aim to incarnate like Christ and to listen well. We avoid making assumptions without checking them out. We negotiate our differences and clarify expectations in all our relationships. And like Christ, we seek to be present with ourselves and others, especially in the presence of anxiety, whether it be our own or that of others.

11. **Family.** We believe in the equal value of God's call to both singleness and marriage. We affirm with Scripture the gift of singleness for leadership (1 Cor.7:25 – 40). Both Jesus and Paul were single. At the same time, we understand the limits and great potentials of the marriage covenant for our work and our personal choices. We desire high-quality marriages, out of which we are able to minister to others. If we are married, our spouses make their own choices and have their own needs and desires apart from us. We affirm this. Our expectation is for honesty and transparency regarding our marriages and family life with those whom God has placed in authority over us.

12. **Community.** Our roles as family members, leaders of our church family, and employees carry with them a unique challenge. This complex relationship requires grace, maturity, wisdom, and discernment. We encourage all staff members to be in relationships with mature people outside NLF; these relationships might be with a spiritual director, a mentor, a counselor, or a mature friend, depending on each person's unique needs and season in God.

As we embark on this journey, let us remember St. Benedict's great introduction to his Rule (Prologue 49): "Do not be daunted immediately by fear and run away from the road that leads to salvation. It is bound to be narrow at the outset. But as we progress in this way of life and in faith, we shall run on the path of God's commandments, our hearts overflowing with the inexpressible delight of love."

ENDNOTES

Introduction

1. Philip Jenkins, *The Next Christendom: The Coming of Global Christianity* (New York: Oxford Univ. Press, 2002), 3.

Chapter 1: As Go the Leaders, So Goes the Church

1. Go to www.emotionallyhealthy.org for a video of Pete and Geri's complete story.
2. "All the World Comes to Queens," *National Geographic* (September 1998).
3. Roger Sanjek, *The Future of Us All* (Ithaca, NY: Cornell Univ. Press, 1998), 1, 395 n. 1.
4. One of the many excellent resources that helped New Life Fellowship along the way is the seminal work by Edwin H. Friedman, *Generation to Generation: Family Process in Church and Synagogue* (New York: Guilford, 1985). On pages 2–3 Friedman explains that the most critical issue of changing an organization resides in who the leader is. He rightly emphasizes that healthy self-definition is more influential than expertise in leadership.

Chapter 2: Something Is Desperately Wrong

1. For further background see Ted W. Engstrom with Robert C. Larson, *Integrity* (Waco, TX: Word, 1987), 98–100.
2. Marilee Pierce Dunker, *Man of Vision, Woman of Prayer* (Nashville: Nelson, 1980).
3. Linda J. Waite and Maggie Gallagher, *The Case for Marriage: Why Married People Are Happier, Healthier, and Better Off Financially* (New York: Doubleday, 2000).
4. Blaine Harden, "Bible Belt Couples 'Put Asunder' More, Despite Concerted Efforts of Church and State," *New York Times* (May 21, 2001), A1 and A14 (National Section).
5. See www.barna.org/barna-update/article/15-familykids/42-new-marriage-and-divorce-statistics-released.
6. *Charisma News Service Update* (Jan. 16, 2002), www.strang.com.

Chapter 3:   Discipleship's Next Frontier — Emotional Health

1. Thomas Kuhn, *The Structure of Scientific Revolutions* (3rd ed.; Chicago: Univ. of Chicago Press, 1996).
2. This is a complex issue when dealing with mentally challenged or mentally ill individuals, where the measurement of emotional maturity will have to take into account neurobiological factors. For an excellent introduction to better understand the basic structure and chemistry of the brain and how it shapes our emotions and behavior, I highly recommend a book by John Ratey, *A User's Guide to the Brain: Perception, Attention and the Four Theaters of the Brain* (New York: Vintage Books of Random House, 2001).
3. Richard Foster, *Streams of Living Water: Celebrating the Great Traditions of Christian Faith* (San Francisco: HarperSanFrancisco, 1998), 406.
4. Dan B. Allender and Tremper Longman III, *The Cry of the Soul* (Dallas: Word, 1994), 24–25.
5. Helmut Koester, *History, Culture and Religion of the Hellenistic Age* (Minneapolis: Fortress, 1995), 414.
6. Henry Bettenson, ed., *Documents of the Christian Church* (2nd ed.; London: Oxford, 1963), 51.
7. Foster, *Streams of Living Water*, 277–79. For a particularly insightful commentary, see also Lutheran writer Frederick Dale Bruner, *Matthew: A Commentary*, 2 vols. (Dallas: Word, 1990), 2:983.
8. Colin Brown, ed., *New International Dictionary of New Testament Theology* (Grand Rapids: Zondervan, 1976), 2:468–70.

Chapter 4:   Inventory of Spiritual/Emotional Maturity

1. I am grateful to Lori Gordon, the founder of the PAIRS program for married couples, for the concept of emotional infants, children, adolescents, and adults; see Lori Gordon with Jon Fandson, *Passage to Intimacy* (self-published; rev. version 2000), 181–91.

Chapter 5:   Principle 1: Look beneath the Surface

1. Barbara Kingsolver, *The Poisonwood Bible* (New York: HarperFlamingo, 1999).
2. Ibid., 200.
3. Wendy Murray Zoba, "Missions Improbable," *Books & Culture* (Sept./Oct. 1999); Tim Stafford, "*Poisonwood Bible* Review," *Christianity Today* (Jan. 11, 1999), 88, 90.
4. This quote is available widely on the internet. See, for example, thinkexist. com/quotation/the_longest_journey_of_any_person_is_the_journey/157964. html.
5. C. S. Lewis, *The Voyage of the Dawn Treader*, book 3 in the Chronicles of Narnia (New York: Collier, 1970), 90–91. C. S. Lewis copyright © C. S. Lewis Pte. Ltd. 1952. Extract reprinted by permission.

6. Henry Cloud and John Townsend, *Boundaries with Kids* (Grand Rapids: Zondervan, 1998), 72.

7. Daniel Goleman, *Emotional Intelligence: Why It Can Matter More Than IQ* (New York: Bantam, 1995); idem, *Working with Emotional Intelligence* (New York: Bantam, 1998); idem, *Primal Leadership: Realizing the Power of Emotional Intelligence* (Cambridge, MA: Harvard Business School Press, 2002).

8. See another listing of Jesus' emotions in ch. 1, page 33.

9. See www.brainyquote.com/quotes/quotes/b/q133380.html.

10. Martin Luther, *Commentary on Galatians* (Grand Rapids: Revell, 1994).

11. Henry Cloud and John Townsend, *Boundaries: When to Say Yes, When to Say No, to Take Control of Your Life* (Grand Rapids: Zondervan, 1992).

12. Susan Howatch, *Glittering Images* (New York: Alfred A. Knopf, 1987); dialog is excerpted and adapted from pages 232–35.

Chapter 6:   Principle 2: Break the Power of the Past

1. For introductions to genograms see Maggie Scarf, *Intimate Worlds: Life inside the Family* (New York: Random House, 1995); John Bradshaw, *Family Secrets: What You Don't Know Can Hurt You* (New York: Bantam, 1995); Monica McGoldrich, *You Can Go Home Again: Reconnecting with Your Family* (New York: Norton, 1995).

2. See Rodney Clapp, *Families at the Crossroads: Beyond Traditional and Modern Options* (Downers Grove, IL: InterVarsity Press, 1993).

3. Ray Anderson and Dennis Guernsey, *On Being Family: A Social Theology of the Family* (Grand Rapids: Eerdmans, 1985), 158.

4. Ronald W. Richardson, *Family Ties That Bind: A Self-Help Guide to Change through Family of Origin Therapy* (Bellingham, WA: SelfCounsel Press, 1984), 35.

5. For a discussion of overfunctioning and underfunctioning applied to the church, see Ronald Richardson, *Creating a Healthier Church: Family Systems Theory, Leadership, and Congregational Life* (Minneapolis: Augsburg Fortress, 1996), 133–37; see also Friedman, *Generation to Generation*, 210–12.

6. The idea behind this illustration is adapted from Richardson, *Creating a Healthier Church*, 35–39.

Chapter 7:   Principle 3: Live in Brokenness and Vulnerability

1. Eric Larson, *Isaac's Storm: A Man, a Time, and the Deadliest Hurricane in History* (Westminster, MD: Crown, 1999). See also www.1900storm.com.

2. See Ronald Rolheiser, *The Shattered Lantern* (New York: Crossroad, 2001), 45.

3. See the comments of Gordon D. Fee, *The First Epistle to the Corinthians* (New International Commentary on the New Testament; Grand Rapids: Eerdmans, 1987), 3.

4. I owe this observation to Jack Deere, who voiced it at a conference many years ago.

5. This story is widely available on the internet. See, for example, www.lovethissite.com/crackedpot/.
6. Henri J. M. Nouwen, *The Return of the Prodigal Son: A Meditation on Fathers, Brothers, and Sons* (New York: Doubleday, 1992), 36.
7. This is the familiar Prayer of an Unknown Confederate Soldier. It is available on the internet at www.solinger.com/prayer/.

Chapter 8:   Principle 4: Receive the Gift of Limits

1. Adapted from Edwin H. Friedman, *Friedman's Fables* (New York: Guilford, 1990), 9–13. Used by permission.
2. Eugene Petersen, *Under the Unpredictable Plant: An Exploration in Vocational Holiness* (Grand Rapids: Eerdmans, 1994), 17.
3. Parker Palmer, *Let Your Life Speak: Listening for the Voice of Vocation* (San Francisco: Jossey-Bass, 2000), 44–46.
4. See Martin Buber, *Tales of the Hasidim: The Early Masters* (New York: Schocken, 1975), 251.
5. Irvin D. Yalom, *Existential Psychotherapy* (New York: Basic, 1980), 285.
6. Marc Ferro, *Nicholas II: The Last of the Tsars* (New York: Oxford, 1993), 16.
7. Dominic Lieven, *Nicholas II: Twilight of the Empire* (New York: St. Martin's, 1993), 236 (see also 261).
8. Thomas Merton, *Seeds of Contemplation* (New York: New Directions, 1987).
9. Henri J. M. Nouwen, *Can You Drink the Cup?* (Notre Dame, Ind.: Ave Maria, 1996), 28 (italics are Nouwen's).
10. Palmer, *Let Your Life Speak*, 30–31.
11. For a sampling of an eight-week Daily Office beginner, see Peter Scazzero, *Begin the Journey with the Daily Office: Remembering God's Presence throughout the Day*.
12. This concept is explored further in Edwin H. Friedman's DVD, *Reinventing Leadership* (New York: Guilford, 1996), 42 minutes.
13. Henry Cloud, *Changes That Heal: How to Understand Your Past to Ensure a Healthier Future* (Grand Rapids: Zondervan, 1990), 95.
14. Michael D. Yapko, *Breaking the Patterns of Depression* (Broadway Books: New York, 2001), 282–86.
15. For more on this concept see Wendell Berry, *Life Is a Miracle: An Essay against Modern Superstition* (Washington, D.C.: Counterpoint, 2000).

Chapter 9:   Principle 5: Embrace Grieving and Loss

1. Gerald L. Sittser, *A Grace Disguised: How the Soul Grows through Loss* (Grand Rapids: Zondervan, 1995), 18.
2. Ibid., 39, 44, 61 (cf. also p. 37).
3. Nicholas Wolterstorff, *Lament for a Son* (Grand Rapids: Eerdmans, 1987).
4. Ibid., 81.

5. Lewis Smedes, *The Art of Forgiving: When You Need to Forgive and Don't Know How* (Westminster, MD: Ballantine, 1997), 135, 137.

6. Elisabeth Kubler-Ross, *On Death and Dying* (New York: Simon & Schuster, 1997).

7. Bernhard Anderson, *Out of the Depths: The Psalms Speak for Us Today* (Philadelphia: Westminster, 1970), 47. He explains that between 30 and 70 percent of the 150 psalms are laments. He argues that at least 57 of the psalms are individual or community laments (see pp. 46–56). Eugene Peterson proposes a higher number when he writes that "70 percent of the psalms are laments" (*Leap over the Wall* [New York: HarperCollins, 1997], 115).

8. Walter Brueggemann, *The Message of the Psalms: A Theological Commentary* (Minneapolis: Augsburg, 1984), 9–11. See also his *Psalms of Life and Faith* (ed. Patrick D. Miller; Minneapolis: Fortress, 1995).

9. This famous phrase was coined by St. John of the Cross in the sixteenth century. For a good introduction to the theme, see chapter 6 of Peter Scazzero, *Emotionally Healthy Spirituality: Unleash a Revolution of Your Life in Christ* (Nashville: Nelson, 2006), chap. 6.

10. Nouwen, *Return of the Prodigal Son*, 120–21.

11. George MacDonald, *The Princess and the Goblin* (New York: Knopf, 1993).

Chapter 10: Principle 6: Make Incarnation Your Model for Loving Well

1. The full letter can be found in Ruth Miller, ed., *Black American Literature*, Part 5: *1970–Present* (Encino, CA: Glencoe, 1971), 648–49. Reprinted by arrangement with the estate of Martin Luther King Jr., c/o Writers House as agent for the proprietor, New York, NY. Copyright 1963 Dr. Martin Luther King Jr., copyright renewed 1991 Coretta Scott King.

2. Ronald Rolheiser, *The Holy Longing: The Search for a Christian Spirituality* (New York: Doubleday, 1999), 76–77.

3. See Henri J. M. Nouwen, *In the Name of Jesus: Reflections on Christian Leadership* (New York: Crossroad, 1991).

4. For an additional creative perspective on making incarnation your model for loving well, see Neil Pembroke, *The Art of Listening* (Grand Rapids: Eerdmans, 2002).

5. David W. Augsburger, *Caring Enough to Hear and Be Heard: How to Hear and How to Be Heard in Equal Communication* (Scottdale, PA: Herald, 1982), 12.

6. Henri J. M. Nouwen, *Out of Solitude: Three Meditations on the Christian Life* (New York: Ave Maria Press, 1974), 36.

7. Quoted in Brennan Manning, *Abba's Child: The Cry of the Heart for Intimate Belonging* (Colorado Springs, CO: NavPress, 1994), 29–30.

8. See www.reformedsermonarchives.com/edwardstitle.htm, sermon 12 ("Charity More Excellent Than the Extraordinary Gifts of the Spirit").

9. Ibid., Sermon 26.

Chapter 11:   Principle 7: Slow Down to Lead with Integrity

1. Thomas Keating, *Intimacy with God: An Introduction to Centering Prayer* (New York: Crossroads, 1996), 82 – 84.

2. *Bernard of Clairvaux: Selected Works, Classics of Western Spirituality*, trans. and ed. G. R. Evans (Mahwah, NJ: Paulist,1987), 173 – 205.

3. I wrote *Begin the Journey with the Daily Office* in 2008 for people to begin an eight-week journey (see comments in chap. 8). A readable and accessible three-volume series for the Daily Office is Phyllis Tickle, *The Divine Hours: Prayers for Autumn and Wintertime: A Manual for Prayer* (New York: Doubleday, 2001), *The Divine Hours: Prayers for Springtime: A Manual for Prayer* (New York: Doubleday, 2001), and *The Divine Hours: Prayers for Summertime: A Manual for Prayer* (New York: Doubleday, 2000). I know many people who also use Norman Shawchuck and Rueben P. Job, *A Guide to Prayer for All Who Seek God* (Nashville: Upper Room, 2003) and The Northumbria Community, *Celtic Daily Prayer* (San Francisco: HarperCollins, 2002). I also like to follow along the readings of the psalms as laid out in the lectionary from the Book of Common Prayer.

4. Paul Stanley and J. Robert Clinton have written an excellent book on the various types of mentoring relationships God uses. See Paul D. Stanley and J. Robert Clinton, *Connecting: The Mentoring Relationships You Need to Succeed in Life* (Colorado Springs, CO: NavPress, 1992).

5. Mike Mason, *The Mystery of Marriage: Meditations on the Miracle* (Portland, OR: Multnomah, 1985), 123.

6. For a sampling of New Life Fellowship Church's Rule of Life, go to www .newlifefellowship.org/about-us/who-we-are/rule-of-life.

Chapter 12:   Next Steps into the New Frontier of Discipleship

1. Parker J. Palmer, *Let Your Life Speak: Listening for the Voice of Vocation* (San Francisco: Jossey-Bass, 1999), 78 – 79.

2. Note: We eventually moved to choosing the third Wednesday of each month for this. Each person goes to a place outside their home, whether it is a beach, a local retreat center, or a park, to be alone with God for the day. The one requirement is not to do the work of church on that day, but to be with God.

BIBLIOGRAPHY

Allender, Dan, and Tremper Longman III. *Cry of the Soul: How Our Emotions Reveal Our Deepest Questions about God*. Dallas: Word: 1994.

Chittister, Joan. *Wisdom Distilled from the Wisdom of Saint Benedict Today*. San Francisco: Harper San Francisco, 1990.

Cloud, Henry. *Changes That Heal: How to Understand Your Past to Ensure a Healthier Future*. Grand Rapids: Zondervan, 1992.

Cloud, Henry, and John Townsend. *Boundaries: When to Say Yes, When to Say No, To Take Control of Your Life*. Grand Rapids: Zondervan, 1992.

Crabb, Larry. *Inside Out*. Tenth Anniversary Edition. Colorado Springs, CO: NavPress, 1998.

Dawn, Marva, and Eugene Peterson. *The Unnecessary Pastor: Rediscovering the Call*. Grand Rapids: Eerdmans, 2000.

Ford, Leighton. *The Attentive Life: Discerning God's Presence in All Things*. Downers Grove, IL: InterVarsity Press, 2008.

Foster, Richard. *Prayer: Finding the Heart's True Home*. San Francisco: HarperCollins, 1992.

Friedman, Edwin H. *Generation to Generation: Family Process in Church and Synagogue*. New York: Guilford, 1985.

Gire, Ken. *Windows of the Soul: Experiencing God in New Ways*. Grand Rapids: Zondervan, 1996.

Goldman, Daniel. *Emotional Intelligence: Why It Can Matter More Than IQ*. New York: Bantam, 1995.

Howatch, Susan. *Glittering Images*. New York: Alfred A. Knopf, 1987.

Lerner, Harriet. *The Dance of Anger: A Woman's Guide to Changing the Patterns of Intimate Relationships*. New York: HarperCollins, 1997.

MacDonald, Gordon. *Ordering Your Private World*. Anniversary Edition. Nashville: Oliver Nelson, 1995.

Manning, Brennan. *Abba's Child: The Cry of the Heart for Intimate Belonging*. Colorado Springs, CO: NavPress, 1994. Revised edition, 2002.

Mason, Mike. *The Mystery of Marriage*. Portland, OR: Multnomah, 1999.

McGoldrich, Monica. *You Can Go Home Again: Reconnecting with Your Family*. Scranton, PA: Norton, 1997.

Merton, Thomas. *New Seeds of Contemplation*. New York: New Directions, 1987.

Mueller, Wayne. *Sabbath: Finding Rest, Renewal, and Delight in our Busy Lives*. New York: Bantam, 1999.

Nouwen, Henri J. M. *In the Name of Jesus: Reflections on Christian Leadership*. New York: Crossroad/Herder & Herder, 1989.

————. *The Return of the Prodigal: A Meditation on Fathers, Brothers and Sons*. New York: Doubleday/Image, 1994.

Palmer, Parker. *A Hidden Wholeness: The Journey toward an Undivided Life*. San Francisco: Jossey-Bass, 2004.

————. *Let Your Life Speak: Listening for the Voice of Vocation*. San Francisco: Jossey-Bass, 2000.

Peterson, Eugene, *Under the Unpredictable Plant: An Exploration in Vocational Holiness*. Grand Rapids: Eerdmans, 1992.

Richardson, Ronald. *Creating a Healthier Church: Family Systems Theory*. Minneapolis: Augsburg, 1996.

Rolheiser, Ronald. *The Holy Longing: The Search for Christian Spirituality*. New York: Doubleday, 1999.

Scarf, Maggie. *Intimate Worlds: Life inside the Family*. New York: Random House, 1995.

Scazzero, Geri, *I Quit*. Grand Rapids: Zondervan, forthcoming.

Scazzero, Peter. *The Daily Office*. Barrington, IL.: Willow Creek Publishing, 2009.

————. *Emotionally Healthy Spirituality*. Nashville, TN: Nelson, 2006.

————. Various teachings are available at www.emotionallyhealthy.org.

Sittser, Gerald. *A Grace Disguised: How the Soul Grows through Loss*. Grand Rapids: Zondervan, 1995.

Stephens, R. Paul. *Doing God's Business: Meaning and Motivation for the Marketplace*. Grand Rapids: Eerdmans, 2006.

Swenson, Richard. *The Overload Syndrome: Learning to Live within Limits*. Colorado Springs: NavPress, 1998.

————. *Margin: How to Create the Emotional, Physical, Financial, and Time Reserves You Need*. Colorado Springs: NavPress, 1992.

Wolterstorff, Nicholas. *Lament for a Son*. Grand Rapids: Eerdmans, 1987.

ACKNOWLEDGMENTS

I have been thinking, reflecting, and struggling with the integration of emotional and spiritual health for almost over fifteen years with my best friend and wife, Geri. We learned these lessons from God together over several years. Many of the insights in this book are hers.

I have tried to work out these biblical truths in our family with our four daughters living in the midst of our multiracial, international neighborhood, church, and city. Thank you, Maria, Christy, Faith, and Eva.

This book is also the by-product of our community at New Life Fellowship Church in Queens, New York, where I have been the pastor for the last twenty-two years. We have grown up together through thick and thin. Thank you, New Life family, for your vulnerability and for entrusting the pearls of your stories to us. There are too many of you to mention here by name. I do want to express specific appreciation to the staff, elders, leaders, and family at New Life — especially those who have hung in with me from the beginning. What can I say for such patience and kindness? Thank you.

Thanks also to Ron Vogt and Recovery of Hope for launching us on this journey, and to Leighton Ford, who has been my mentor over almost two decades. I am indebted also to Peter and Carol Schrek and Manfred Brauch, professors in the Doctor of Ministry program at Palmer Theological Seminary. God used you to take this book to the next level by your outstanding example of integrating a love for Scripture with emotional health. Special thanks to Dan Shin for his assistance on the spiritual – emotional maturity inventory.

Finally, I am especially thankful to you, Warren Bird, for your hard work and gifts in administration and organization that kept this project, and me, moving from beginning to end.

I Quit!

Stop Pretending Everything is Fine and Change Your Life

Geri Scazzero with Peter Scazzero

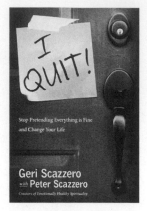

Geri Scazzero knew there was something desperately wrong with how they were doing their life and ministry. She finally told her husband, "I quit," and left the thriving church he pastored, beginning a journey that transformed her, her marriage, and her church.

Geri quit being afraid of what others think. She quit lying. She quit denying her anger and sadness. She quit living someone else's life. *I Quit!* provides you a way out of an inauthentic, superficial spirituality to genuine freedom in Christ.

I Quit! is for every person who thinks, "I can't keep pretending everything is fine!"

Biblical quitting goes hand in hand with choosing. When we quit those things that are damaging to our souls or the souls of others, we are freed up to choose other ways of being and relating that are rooted in love and lead to life.

When we quit fear of what others think, we choose freedom.

When we quit lies, we choose truth.

When we quit blaming, we choose to take responsibility.

When we quit faulty thinking, we choose to live in reality.

When we quit for the right reasons, quitting changes us. Something breaks inside of us when we finally say, "No more." But it must be done for the right reasons, at the right time, and in the right way. That's what this book is about.

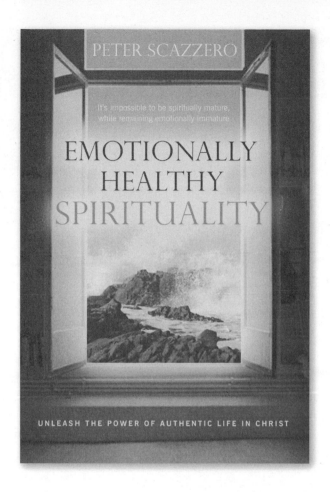

Emotionally Healthy Leadership Conference

Slowing Down to Lead with Integrity

For Pastors and Church Leaders — With Pete Scazzero

This conference is designed for men and women in leadership desiring to lead differently, from a place of emotional health and contemplative spirituality.

Biblical and Practical

In this two day intensive conference we will provide biblical background and practical experiences that will launch you on a pathway of deep transformation and equip you with tools to take emotionally healthy spirituality into your church, leadership and ministry.

What You Will Receive

- A fresh look at a biblical model for leadership
- Learn how emotional health and spiritual contemplative practices can impact your leadership and management style
- Embrace a fresh perspective for leading others without violating your personal health and walk with God and marriage
- Experience new skills for dealing with leadership and staff conflict
- Insights into the seven common leadership challenges
- How to develop a rhythm for slowing down, setting healthy, balanced priorities and limits
- Creating a "rule of life" for a leadership culture that lives the values one preaches
- 12 Tenets of Emotional Healthy Spirituality

The Experiential Difference

Unlike other conferences you may have attended, there is a strong experiential component in our conference that will guide you beyond listening to lectures into "doing" the material.

Pre-Conference Seminar

The Pastor's Marriage: The Foundation for Emotionally Healthy Churches and Ministries

This one day intensive workshop, presented by Pete and Geri Scazzero, flows out of the conviction: As goes the leader's marriage, so goes the ministry.

Few greater challenges exist for those of us serving as pastors and leaders than developing a high-quality marriage with authentic union and communion. Little training exists on how to do this, especially within the pressure of church leadership.

---

emotionally
HEALTHY SPIRITUALITY

For more information, please visit our website www.emotionallyhealthy.org

Share Your Thoughts

With the Author: Your comments will be forwarded to the author when you send them to *zauthor@zondervan.com*.

With Zondervan: Submit your review of this book by writing to *zreview@zondervan.com*.

Free Online Resources at

www.zondervan.com

Zondervan AuthorTracker: Be notified whenever your favorite authors publish new books, go on tour, or post an update about what's happening in their lives at www.zondervan.com/authortracker.

Daily Bible Verses and Devotions: Enrich your life with daily Bible verses or devotions that help you start every morning focused on God. Visit www.zondervan.com/newsletters.

Free Email Publications: Sign up for newsletters on Christian living, academic resources, church ministry, fiction, children's resources, and more. Visit www.zondervan.com/newsletters.

Zondervan Bible Search: Find and compare Bible passages in a variety of translations at www.zondervanbiblesearch.com.

Other Benefits: Register yourself to receive online benefits like coupons and special offers, or to participate in research.

ZONDERVAN

ZONDERVAN.com/
AUTHORTRACKER
follow your favorite authors